Faking It!

Donna S. Morris

Phoenix Press, Ltd.
La Verne, California

Library of Congress Cataloging in Publication Data

Morris, Donna S.
Faking It!/by/Donna S. Morris
First Printing 2001

Includes index
1. Furniture - Repairing   2. Furniture finishing
3. Furniture– United States – Collectors and collecting
4. Home Reference

Library of Congress Control Number: 2001117495

ISBN 0-9665673-9-0 $26.95 Softcover

 is a trademark under exclusive license to Donna S. Morris
in the United States and/or other countries.

Phoenix Press, Ltd.
1407 Foothill Blvd., PMB141
La Verne, California   91750

Manufactured and printed in the United States of America

This book is not intended to be a mini-course in deception. Some of the methods and techniques described in these pages might be considered by some readers to be unethical. It is the intention of this book to educate the reader so they can identify pieces of furniture that have been fraudantly repaired, properly repair a piece of furniture without decreasing the value of the piece, have a better understanding of the materials and techniques involved in the construction and repair of furniture so they are better informed and can examine furniture and work with professional refinishers with more confidence. The information is available to be used as your conscience will allow.

The instructions in this book are not intended to be used for the restoration or repair of "museum-quality" pieces. Rare or valuable furniture belongs in the hands of a qualified professional. Even a minor repair, improperly done, can have a major effect on the appraised value.

The contents of this book are intended as a guide, to be intelligently used. The restoration and repair methods have been described in detail, and precautions in handling the various chemicals that are potentially hazardous if improperly used have been explicitly pointed out. Every effort has been made to make this book as complete and accurate as possible. All instructions and precautions should be carefully followed. Because the actual use of the methods and materials described in this book are entirely in the hands of the reader, neither the author, nor the publisher, can guarantee the results of any instructions or formulas, and therefore each of them expressly disclaims any responsibility for injury to persons or property through their use.

If you do not wish to be bound by the above, you may return this book to the publisher for a full refund.

Acknowledgements

I would like to once again extend my gratitude to all of the students, clients and friends who have contributed to this book. Thanks for the use of your furniture and for all you have taught me.

Special thanks to my mother, Hazel, and to Carmen and Larry for their love, support and tolerance of the writing process. To Kevin who I can not thank enough for all of the computer doctoring, moral support and midnight crisis management. "Need I say more?" To Sharon, Jason and Buzz because they keep encouraging me and believing it's possible. To Steve Chandler for another great cover. To Paul, my Panamanian amigo, David and Carolyn Long and The College for Appraisers, and Frank Donadee and *The Collector*. Thanks also to Richard Muldawer for the incredible opportunity.

Dedicated to the memory of my father
Donald S. Betts

Table of Contents
Section One
The Real Thing

Section Two
A Brief Overview of Furniture Styles and Period
What to Look for and What to Look *Out* For

Section Three
Faking It

Faking It!

Section One
The Real Thing

When is an Antique *Not* an Antique?

Most dealers, collectors and experts seem to agree an "antique" is an item which is at least 100 years of age. An official United States government definition is stated in the Tariff Act of 1930. According to the Tariff Act an item had to be produced prior to 1830 to be considered an antique. This date was not chosen arbitrarily and was established as the cut-off date following the stock market crash of 1929. The year 1830 was chosen because it was a century prior to 1930, and also because it marked the beginning of the Industrial Revolution.

Before machines started mass-producing items it was not possible for them to be made in large enough quantities to pose a threat to the American manufacturing industry and the economy. With the Industrial Revolution, the threat became real. The U.S. government passed the Tariff Act imposing duty taxes on foreign-made items entering the United States which were made after 1830 in an effort to protect the interests of American manufacturers and to help the economy recover. Anything made prior to 1830 was considered an antique and was not subject to the duty tax.

But when is an antique *not* an antique? That can be a little more difficult to determine. Unfortunately there is no simple, glib answer to this question. There are outright fakes and frauds, marriages and modifications, copies and reproductions and pieces that have been "helped" a little bit here and there.

Antiques are considered one of the seven best investments in the world today. Antique silver, furniture and jewelry lead the list. Furniture is the fourth largest investment most families will make in their lifetime, and for many people, antique furniture may have an equal amount of sentimental and financial value. It seems human nature if something is valuable, there is a need for a reproduction or a copy of it for the majority of people who can not afford the original. Furniture styles have probably been copied and reproduced for as long as there has been furniture. There are even several popular American furniture styles based on revivals of an original style.

Old furniture which has been exposed to use and age will eventually need to be repaired or reconstructed. *Reconstructed* means putting a piece back together that has come apart. It does not include replacing missing parts. Furniture needing more repair work may need to be *restored*. Restoring is an attempt to return a piece of furniture back to what is believed to have been its original appearance. Restoring may include replacing missing parts. Restoration can increase the value of a piece of furniture if it makes it useful again. An unuseful piece of furniture will lose value. But all restorations do not necessarily increase the value and many can actually *decrease* the value. Knowing when to stop is an important part of any restoration project. An improperly restored, repaired or refinished antique can lose as much as 75% of its market value. Even if a piece has been poorly restored, it can often be redone properly without causing further damage or loss to the original piece. The same can not be said about refinishing. *Refinishing* involves removing the finish coat from the furniture and replacing it with another coat of finish. It generally reduces the value, appearance and condition of a true antique unless it is done with skill and care. Pieces of furniture that have been stripped, sanded and made to look "new again" lose virtually all of their signs of age and wear and at the same time, a majority of their market value.

The chest or coffer is the earliest form of furniture and all other pieces of furniture have evolved from it. The chest became a settle which became a chair and all of the variations of a chair (sofas, love seats, settees, etc.). The chest also evolved into the chest-of-drawers, cabinets, sideboards, dressers, etc. The earliest European coffers were made from hollowed out tree trunks. It was not until the 13th century that planks of wood were nailed together to form furniture. In some cases, bands of iron were fastened around the coffer to add strength and to help keep the boards together. In the 15th century, chests were made of paneled or jointed construction using mortise and tenon joints. Glue was not used in the construction of these chests. As chests got larger in order to hold more items, it became more and more difficult to reach the items on the bottom of the chest. To solve this problem, one or more drawers were added to the bottom of the chest. This became a "chest of drawers" or "chest over drawers". Chest of drawers became such practical pieces of furniture there was usually at least one chest of drawers in each room of the house. From the lowly coffer evolved chest-on-chests, highboys and lowboys, cupboards, cabinets, dressers and buffets.

Modifications

Furniture, like most people, isn't always what it appears to be at first glance. Time, use and the natural qualities of the furniture components will cause furniture to change. In most cases, this will not affect the value of the piece. But "fixing" furniture, replacing pieces of the furniture, and altering the furniture are quite different matters. Then of course there are copies and out-right fakes which may or may not be well made and may be passed off as older and more valuable than they really are.

Furniture is made to be used, and furniture which is used will need to be repaired. Very few pieces of furniture go through their lifetime without requiring some form of repairs. The difference between whether repairs will affect the value and often the authenticity of the piece (or not) can be determined by the extent of the repairs, the quality of the repair job and the honesty concerning the repair.

Many pieces of furniture have been altered or modified

over the years to better serve a specific use, and were not changed for dishonest reasons. Side rails on beds were lengthened to accommodate tall people, headboards and footboards may be widened, tall dressers may be cut into two pieces to make two smaller chests, larger armoires and sideboards may be shortened to fit into smaller rooms. All of these alterations can be perfectly acceptable if properly done and properly disclosed.

Other alterations may have been done with less than honorable intentions; veneer can be added or removed, carving can be done on plain wood to make it appear more decorative (furniture that is carved after its original construction is said to be "carved up"), tops, doors, legs and feet can be replaced with more decorative ones, labels can be added to furniture to make it appear more prestigious ... and that is just a partial list of the potential shenanigans.

Marriages and Divorces

A *marriage* occurs when two or more pieces of furniture, or pieces from two or more pieces of furniture are combined to make a different piece of furniture. The most common marriages involve chest-on-chests, desks and bookcases. Marriages also occur with table tops and table bases that did not start out life together. A perfectly useful base can be matched with an odd top and a new table is born, or some odd legs can be added to an top which has lost its base. Marriages are usually created to either make the furniture more serviceable or more saleable. If the furniture pieces used to create the marriage are from similar styles and periods, the work involved in creating the marriage has been properly done, and the resulting product is honestly represented as a marriage, most experts will not object. The original intent of the marriage has a lot to do with how it will be accepted. It should be noted, however, major changes like this will affect the value and result in a lower price.

Some marriages are created by combining a new/repro-duction piece of furniture and an antique piece of furniture. If the finishes are blended to match, and the styles are comparable, these marriages may pass for the real thing unless you do some further investigation. As time passes, the finishes and the woods will mellow and change with age and the mismatch will become more apparent.

Most marriages do not involve damage or major changes to the components like in *conversions* and *embellishments* and the marriage will often result in two or more unuseable furniture components becoming useful again. The marriage becomes a problem when it is passed off as being something it is not or if the potential buyer is unaware of the marriage and pays a premium price for it.

Some common points to check to determine if your piece has been married:

> * Any piece containing more than one piece is a candidate for marriage. Separate the pieces and look for an outline on the base of the upper section where it has sat on the lower section. There should be a clear outline with the same dimensions as the piece you removed.

> * Check for consistency in the grain patterns from one component of the furniture to the next. This is best checked from the sides rather than at the front of the piece. Wood tones and colors can be stained to match, but wood grain is difficult if not impossible to duplicate. Check the carcass wood or base wood to make sure it is the same on all pieces.

> * The dovetails should be similarly carved on both the top and the bottom piece. If the dovetails do not match, the two components did not start out life together. The dovetails should be of similar size and shape and there should be a similar number of

dovetails per piece.

* Old screw holes in the base which do not line up to
the top are a "dead give away" the two pieces have
been married.

* If the hardware has been replaced on one piece
check to make sure matching holes can be found on
the other pieces. Check under the hardware if necessary. If only one piece has holes which can not be
accounted for, you probably have a marriage.

* Any decorative features should be identical on the
top and bottom sections.

* Tops and bottoms from different styles or periods
which have been combined are an indication of a
marriage.

* The drawers on both pieces should be constructed
in the same manner and from the same primary and
secondary woods. The wood used for drawer bottoms,
sides and backs should all be the same.

* Most marriages are very noticeable when viewed from
the back of the furniture. Backboards on all pieces of
the furniture should match and be of similar wood.

* Furniture designed to have a top piece sit on a base
piece was usually constructed so the smaller top piece
fit within a molding on the top of the base. If the top
fits flush with the base top it may indicate a marriage.
The top of the base piece was usually not finished or
veneered since it was intended to be covered by the top
piece and never seen. A finished or veneered top on the

base piece indicates a marriage.

A *divorce* occurs when a piece of furniture is taken apart to create two or more new pieces of furniture. Divorced pieces are usually married to other pieces, but some can become a new piece of furniture on their own. As a general rule, married or divorced pieces of furniture are not a good investment and can be expensive to repair to make them functional.

Copies or Reproductions

"Reproductions" are generally considered to be pieces which are made with no intention to deceive. "Copies", on the other hand are considered to be a more intentional form of deception. Reproductions are usually done in the style of another piece of furniture and are generally constructed of new wood similar to the original wood that would have been used, and then finished to duplicate the original finish. Copies are often made from old wood and are finished with products to make it appear "aged" and to replicate the original finish.

Reproductions, while often very close to the originals, will often be produced using different dimensions than those of a period piece. The finish on a reproduction is often not the finish that would have been commonly used on a piece of furniture from the period it represents, but the finish, instead, most commonly used when it was produced. The wood used for the reproduction may be wood that was most commonly available when the furniture was produced and not the type of wood that would have been most commonly used for that particular style of furniture if it was an original.

Most period seventeenth century furniture is in a museum or a private collection. If you should stumble upon a piece in an antique store or auction the chances are pretty good that it will be a late nineteenth or twentieth century copy. The construction of the furniture, not the design style, is what authenticates a piece of furniture.

Fakes

"Fakes" are pieces of furniture constructed so that, in all respects, they appear to be what they fraudulently claim to be. Good fakes are time consuming and difficult to produce and require many difficult skills from the craftsperson. They also require special materials and tools to help pull off the fraud. The good news is because of the additional time skill and tools, fake furniture is not that common, and should be of little concern to the average antique buyer or collector. Unless the craftsperson has been extremely thorough, there are usually tell-tale signs of the fraud once you start investigating.

Old furniture was very consistent. The wood grains were matched, the colors were the same. The same finish and stain was used on all of the components of a piece of furniture, and all of the pieces of furniture in a set. All drawers were made consistently using the same techniques, the same size dovetails, the edges were all finished the same. The secondary woods should also be consistent if they are original to the piece and will remain consistent within a matched set. The drawer bottoms, sides and backs, and backboards on case pieces should all look the same. Unfinished wood may oxidize and age to a slightly different color, but the wood should still appear similar in grain and type of wood.

Start with the wood: it is the proper wood for that particular style and period of furniture? Are the decorations (if any) appropriate for the style and period of the piece? Check the backboards and drawer backs. Do they match? Are they constructed of old wood or newer wood? If the wood is old, check the sides of the backboard to make sure it hasn't been transplanted from another piece of furniture. Old furniture is often taken apart and cannibalized so the old components can be used for other furniture.

If the piece of furniture is veneered, check the thickness of the veneer. On older antique pieces, the hand-cut veneer will be considerably thicker than what is found on newer furniture. Thin veneer on an older antique is a definite indication something is amiss. Veneer can be "skinned" off small pieces of damaged furniture by steaming the veneer until the old glue lets go, and then carefully peeling it off the furniture. The "new" old wood can then be re-applied on another piece of furniture. But, while this may be done with newer veneers, it is seldom done with older hand-cut veneer because it is so scarce.

Check the inlay or marquetry. Time, humidity and temperature changes will cause the wood and other inlay materials to rise slightly above the wood surface. This unevennes is created by a natural occurrence and is very had to duplicate or simulate. Newer inlay or marquetry is usually very flat to the surface or set below the surface. Run your hand over the surface. You should be able to feel the raised grain or glue on an older piece.

Check the hardware on the furniture. Does it look as if it has been on the furniture for the life of the piece or does it not appear to have seen as much use and wear? Are the hinges, handles, escutcheons and other hardware appropriate for the style and period of the piece? Is the hardware proportionate to the piece of furniture or does it look like it belongs on a larger piece? (This would be a good indication the piece may have been "sized down".) The brass used for hardware on 18th century pieces had a much higher copper content than brass used in later periods and has a distinctive color and sheen which is difficult if not impossible to duplicate. Modern brass hardware has a thinner feel and a brighter new look. Check to confirm the color of the brass is appropriate for the age of the brass.

Are the marks around the hardware authentic looking? The wood around the handles and escutcheons will darken with age and use and accumulate dirt and grime. It is easy to attempt to duplicate this discoloration but very difficult to be convincing. Older furniture will also accumulate dirt, dust and wax in and

Faking It!

around screw heads and nails on the hinges. This is another fakery which is easy to spot. The artificial accumulation is usually applied with a heavy hand and the results will not look natural.

Metal and brass beds can be assembled from a variety of odds and ends from mismatched bed parts to create a "new" antique bed. This trickery can be made more difficult to discover if there are multiple layers of paint or accumulated blackened tarnish on the brass. A good working knowledge of the true sizes of antique beds and the amount and type of decorations on various styles of beds can help you differentiate between a "created piece" and an original.

Check for signs of wear on the wooden parts of the furniture. Stretchers will show signs of wear from feet and shoes rubbing against them. The feet on furniture will become worn from rubbing on floors. Arms will show wear from being bumped into other furniture and from human contact. Old furniture should probably have some signs of wear on every part of the furniture. Especially if it has been used and handled on a daily basis for one hundred years or more. However, wear marks can be simulated by a number of methods including rubbing the furniture with broken bones, sand paper, chains and bags of rocks. While this may distress the wood, it seldom duplicates the signs of natural wear. Simulated wear is usually too perfectly done, over-done or done in an area where that particular type of wear would not normally occur.

Check the beading and carving on the furniture to make sure it is authentically done for the period. Beading on furniture was carved from a single piece of wood during the 18th century and the grain will run true through the entire piece. The beading on Victorian furniture and furniture from later periods was often glued on and the grain pattern will not be consistent.

Carving will mellow with age. The edges will soften and dust, dirt and wax will accumulate in the indentions. If the edges of the carving appear too sharp or the exposed wood in the indentions appears too new, the carving may have been added after the piece was originally produced.

Check to see if there is stain or finish on the secondary wood. These boards would have originally been left unfinished and unstained. If they currently sport a coat of something, it is an addition made after the furniture was manufactured. The secondary wood may also show signs of previous stripping or refinishing products which have dripped or oozed on to the bare rough wood surfaces. Most refinishers do not go back and clean up these mistakes as they are too difficult to remove from the wood. They may try to sand them out which will leave a telltale light area (and usually not get rid of the stain) or they may apply stain all over the board to try to blend the mistake and make it less noticeable.

Check the furniture for holes. Are there screwholes which do not seem to have a purpose? Nail holes which do not line up to anything that has been nailed in place? These could be evidence of a piece of wood taken from one piece of furniture and added to another. Even a neatly filled hole, no matter how small, will always be evident in a piece of wood if you study the wood closely under a good strong light. Stain can be used to match the color and lacquer sticks and wax and other compounds can be used to fill in the small telltale cracks, but matching the wood grain on the outside and the inside of the wood and having it stay that way as time takes its toll on the furniture is difficult at best. A repair that was perfectly acceptable and unnoticeable today will become glaringly obvious in twenty to fifty years of exposure to light and daily use.

Old furniture should smell like old furniture. Old wood develops a very distinctive smell. If you come across a piece of furniture that smells of varnish, linseed oil or paint there is a very strong possibility something has been recently done to the furniture. Paint and most clear finishes will dry on the surface long before they completely cure and dry completely through. If you are able to make a mark in the paint or finish with your fingernail, it has been either recently applied or recently repaired.

Between the fakes and the real thing is a gray area of furniture which used to be genuine but has been rebuilt and modified into something more desirable. These pieces are known as *pastiches*. Pastiches usually appear to be genuine at first sight, but upon closer investigation new wood or veneer will often be found attached to the original framework and interior wood. Writing tables, commodes and dressing tables can be "morphed" into a more valuable, saleable style or period. Large library tables which would not fit into a modern home or lifestyle are shortened to coffee table heighth to make them more saleable or useful. Bookcases, secretary desks and other large pieces of furniture are cut up and sized down into smaller, more saleable pieces. In fact, many "antique book cases" did not start out as bookcases at all, but rather as the top part or middle part of a larger piece of furniture.

Chairs are also an easy target. A set of six or eight chairs can often be made from just a few chairs by mixing and matching the pieces. This process is known as "scrambling". When in doubt ... thoroughly check it out!

Sets of furniture can be *assembled* when the original set has been broken up. An assembled set is usually made up of pieces similar in appearance but which do not match or did not start out as being a set. In England assembled sets are called *harlequin sets.*

One last clue to the originality of a piece should be the price. If the price of an antique makes it seem "too good to be true"... it probably is.

Conversions

Furniture which is no longer useful in its original condition is sometimes converted to make it more useful as something else. An out-dated piece of furniture can be salvaged and become useful again with a little modification. Spinet pianos that have had their musical insides ravaged by time and rodents may be converted into desks or dressing tables. Butler's trays can have legs added and become coffee tables. Commodes which are no longer needed to hold a bed pan can be converted into a nightstand or small chest. These are obvious conversions and usually done with honest intentions of making an unuseful piece of furniture useful again.

A different type of conversion is done when one or more pieces of furniture are converted to make them look like rare or more valuable pieces of furniture. Chairs can be converted into double-chair-back settees, highboys and chests-on-chests can be separated and made into new chest of drawers or lowboys, toilet commodes can be converted to chest of drawers. The list goes on and on.

Another type of conversion is created from assembled pieces. Very large pieces of furniture are difficult to sell today because most modern homes can not accomodate their grandiose massive size. The large piece of furniture is broken up into smaller sections and finished off to make a number of smaller more saleable pieces. A Victorian breakfront bookcase could be cut apart and made into smaller individual bookcases with doors. Most of these conversions are built around the dimensions of modern homes and modern furniture and so their size will usually tip them off as being not quite right. The furniture will have to be finished with either new wood which has been aged to make it look old, or the old wood will have to be stripped to make it match the new. In either case, there will be evidence of refinishing and repair.

Sideboards were a standard piece of furniture in almost every home for generations, however they are often too large or too wide to fit into modern homes today. Smaller sideboards sell better than larger ones. Larger ones are often converted to make them more saleable. The case can be reduced by removing the backboards and cutting off some excess wood, then replacing the backboards. But the drawers will also need to be shortened or they will no longer fit into the case. This is easier than you would think and leaves behind less evidence than one would imagine. The faker uses a very fine saw to cut the fronts off of the drawers just behind the dovetail joints. Then, the drawer is shortened the required amount to fit into the shortened case, and the drawer fronts are carefully glued back on.

The new joint is masked by what appears to be scribe lines originally used to mark the depth of the dovetails. The best way to check to make sure this little trick has not been done is to use a bright light and follow the grain along the side of the drawer. It should run the length of the drawer and into the dovetail. If the drawer has been shortened as described above, the grain pattern will be interrupted and will not run smoothly across the drawer and will not flow into the dovetail. Also remember, if the front of the drawer has dovetails the back of the drawer should also have dovetails. Few cabinetmakers were inconsistent in their construction techniques. If a drawer has dovetails on the front and lap joints on the back, there has probably been some modification done somewhere along the line.

Another type of conversion involves making furniture from old wood, but not wood that was ever part of a piece of furniture. Old paneling and floor boards can be made into settees, chairs, tables and many other types of furniture. The wood is old, but the furniture can be new. Most conversions just don't look quite right and are fairly easy to spot. You may not be able to put your finger on it immediately, but the lines, dimensions and overall look of the furniture will often look different. When in doubt a little more checking is probably not a bad idea.

Misrepresentations

Reproduction furniture which is presented as genuine period furniture and English furniture passed off as American furniture are two of the more common misrepresentations in antique furniture. A third would be a misrepresented provenance where the furniture is presented as having once belonged to someone famous or been used by someone famous, (but that topic has been covered in another area of this book). Reproductions and copies have also been previously covered. Which leaves us with the sticky situation of English pieces being misrepresented as American ones. American furniture is generally worth more money than a similar English piece and a genuine period piece is, of course, generally worth more than a reproduction. Some basic information can help prevent a misrepresentation from costing you more money than it's worth.

Most furniture from the 17th century is either English or in a museum. Very few pieces of American furniture were made during this time period and even fewer pieces have survived. If you think you have stumbled across a genuine 17th century American piece it is more than likely an English piece from that time period, a reproduction or a fake.

English cabinetmakers used oak for drawer sides and backboards and Americans generally used pine or another local soft wood. The English also used deal wood (which comes from a type of pine tree) to produce these pieces. Deal trees are smaller than American pine trees and produce smaller logs. The wood also has more small knots in it than American pine. English cabinetmakers used beech for chair frames in much the same manner as American cabinetmakers used birch wood. Beech is a very strong wood and it takes stain well, but it has a very light natural color and very little figuring in the grain. It was often stained to imitate mahogany or painted and gilded. Beech was also used to manufacture the frame for upholstered furniture. English furniture generally appears heavier and more massive than American furniture. English chairs are often lower than their American counterparts and appear more solid.

American furnituremakers almost never made flat top desks. Partner's desks and Davenport desks were made in England and shipped over to the United States. English desks will also usually have the top drawer divided into two smaller drawers.

Split drawers are rare in early American pieces unless they were part of a highboy or chest on chest and the drawer was designed to be lifted out for use. Queen Anne and Chippendale sofas, settees, and large mirrors are also probably English products which have been shipped overseas. Very few American could afford such large pieces of furniture so there was little market for manufacturing them here.

If a chest of drawers has only three drawers it is probably English and not American. American cabinetmakers seldom made three drawer chests. The backboards on American chests and desks will generally be made up of one, possibly two, wide horizontal boards. English pieces will have the backboards made up from a number of narrow vertical boards.

The shape of the carved feet can also help to identify the origin of a piece of furniture. Hoof feet, hairy paw feet, and scroll feet were almost never used on American pieces of furniture.

Sideboards manufactured in England generally have arched center sections, bowed fronts and spade feet. American sideboards very rarely have arched center sections and seldom have spade feet (unless they were manufactured by one of a few high end cabinetmakers in New York or Philadelphia). Small sideboards were seldom produced by American cabinetmakers. American sideboards are more likely to have a central cupboard than English ones.

English Windsor chairs were made differently than American Windsors. The turnings are distinctively different on English chairs, and they have pierced central back splats and curved yoke stretchers. Some very early American Windsor chairs share a few of these qualities, but placed side by side, American Windsors are quite different in appearance from their English counterparts.

Pairs of chairs, chests or beds are usually worth more than twice the amount of a single piece. Sets of matching furniture generally are worth more than the total price of the individual pieces. Part of this is due to the fact the larger the number of pieces the smaller the chance all of the pieces will survive intact. Because sets and pairs are potentially worth more money, there is a temptation on the part of some dealers to sell furniture this way. Even if the pieces did not start out as matching pairs or sets when they were originally manufactured. Many chairs were manufactured from patterns and mass-produced in enormous quantities. But matching chairs and identical chairs are not necessarily part of a set. Carefully check the wood, the grain, the stain, the finish, the construction – and be suspicious of any variation.

Sets of chairs can also be made up by dissecting chairs and using the components of the chairs to make additional chairs. Chairs were often sold in sets. The sets were usually sold in even numbers. It is said a set of six chairs will sell for ten to twelve times the price of a single chair and a set of eight can sell for fifteen times the price of a single chair. A set would often contain two armed chairs called "carvers" or "elbow chairs" (one for the head of the household and the other for the lady of the household) and the remainder were armless side chairs. Armed chairs were always made a few inches wider than side chairs and were often proportioned differently to accommodate the arms. Arm chairs generally sell better than side chairs and consequently, fakers may modify side chairs with the addition of arms and arm supports which are not original. If you were able to remove the plugs filling the screw holes, unscrew the screws holding the arm to the chair and look underneath you would see unfinished wood if the arms were original and will see finished wood on a piece which has been modified.

"Scrambling" is another unethical method of stretching a set of chairs. Chairs are taken apart and new pieces are made to replace a few components on each chair. The removed original parts are constructed into one or more chair, depending on the number of chairs and parts. If you are interested in purchasing a set of chairs you should individually examine each chair in the set to verify the set is indeed an original set, and to look for signs of repairs and replacements

Sets of chairs can also be expanded by adding one or more reproduction chairs. If the seller and buyer are both aware the set is not completely original and there are reproductions which have been added to the mix, then there is no fraud or faking involved in the transaction. The problem occurs when one or more of the parties involved is unaware of the mixed age and history of the furniture.

Shifting or adjusting the period

Inexpensive furniture from one period can often be quickly "adjusted" to make it appear to be a more valuable piece of furniture from a different period. This is easiest to do with case furniture, especially if the drawers are all still intact and have the old handcut dovetails. Victorian mahogany pulls or Federal brass rosette knobs can be removed and replaced with Chippendale reproduction hardware with solid back plates which will camoflauge the characteristic single holes from the original pulls. The top of the chest can be given a molded edge and the feet can be reshaped or replaced with bracket feet. The top drawer can be removed to make the chest more closely match 18th century dimensions and after some refinishing and color adjusting you can pass off the chest for a Federal or Georgian chest which is worth much more than when it started out as just another piece of Victorian furniture.

A careful examination of the insides and backsides of a piece of furniture will usually help you to identify this type of conversion. You should be able to see evidence of cut or replaced backboards and drawer sides and backs, and the stain and finish on the piece will generally not match closely enough when examined carefully under good light. The dimensions of the furniture are also a red flag that something may be amiss. As mentioned previously, most furniture is very consistent and dimensions varied very little. Unless the piece was custom-made for a specific purpose it will generally have been made to very strict dimensions. Also, if the drawer was removed to shorten the piece of furniture down to the proper dimensions for the period it was trying to represent, it would usually be left with only three drawers, which would not raise an eyebrow if it was English, but would be unusual if it was an American piece since American cabinetmakers seldom made three drawer chests.

Enhancement by statement

The value of a piece of furniture, whether it is an old piece or a newer piece, can often be enhanced by attributing it to a particular designer, craftsman, or shop. The mere suggestion the furniture was associated with such greatness is often enough to warrant a noticeable increase in price. When you look at the vast amount of furniture which has been produced, a very small percentage of it has actually been signed, labeled or otherwise definatively identified. This leaves the field wide open for anyone who wants to suggest a famous cabinetmaker may have contributed to its construction. Of course, the more famous the craftsperson, the greater the value of the furniture! Like provenance, statements made about the manufacturer of the furniture should be well documented in order to have any creedence.

Furniture styles and designs were copied and used by craftsmen on both sides of the Atlantic ocean. Famous craftsmen and the apprentices and journeymen who worked under them all used the same tools and techniques. There were a limited number of suppliers for the materials necessary to construct furniture and all of the crafts people within a certain geographical area would have probably purchased their materials from the same sources. Most statements of enhancement or unwarranted attributions are simple guesses or wishful thinking on the part of the owner or the dealer.

In order to validate the statement you should have some proof. There should be a legitimate label or signature. (Check even this carefully as labels and signatures can be easily faked.) There should be documented evidence, in writing, to connect that particular piece of furniture to the famous name. A receipt or bill of sale, for example, with a clear and concise description of the specific piece of furniture (not simply a receipt that says "one chest of drawers and a price"). Word of mouth or word of mouth which has been written down on a piece of paper is not sufficient evidence if it is going to affect the value of the piece or the price. The piece of furniture should have a truly unique design or feature which can be directly attributed to only one craftsperson or shop in a particular region. There were few shops and fewer carvers who can be classified in this catagory. As a last resort, the piece should be identical to or nearly identical to a well documented piece of furniture in its entirety, not just a few isolated details. This can be a weak argument, but can help to identify a piece when there is no other evidence available. Most unwarranted attributions are difficult at best to prove and the buyer or collector should beware and not believe everything they hear.

Enhancement by modification

Some furniture has been embellished after it was manu-factured to make it blend in with other furniture that someone may have had in their home, or to make a plain piece just look a little nicer. Other pieces are modified by a less than scrupulous dealer who wants to increase the value and the price of the piece of furniture. Incised carving can be added to a plain, uncarved piece of furniture, relief carved pieces can be tacked on along with molding and banding. New carving on an old piece of furniture will usually reveal a lighter color of wood because the patinaed wood will be removed during the carving process. Most fakers will make an effort to camoflauge this with stain, but the carving will usually have more rigid edges than one would expect to find on a piece of furniture that has been in use for a hundred years or more. Inlay can be added to a piece in an attempt to add value. Old inlay can often be identified because of the way it sits slightly above the surface of the wood. This is a result of the wood shrinking and forcing the inlay to rise. New inlay generally sits too low into the wood, often below the wood surface.

Fake labels can be added to a piece of furniture to enhance, not its appearance, but its value. Fake labels can be made from old advertisements from period newspapers or magazines, or from an old bill of sale. Most genuine labels (and the operative word here is "most" because there are variations) will have a decorative border around all four edges and will usually have some space between the border and the edge of the label. A bill of sale will often have a border on three sides (the top and the two sides, but not on the bottom section). You should be able to research a famous cabinetmaker's label to see what a genuine one should look like. Do not accept part of a label, or a badly damaged label as indesputable evidence and proof of who the manufacturer was.

If there is a label on a piece of furniture, and it was applied when the furniture was originally manufactured, the surface under the label should have been protected from oxidation and exposure to light for many years. The wood underneath the label should be considerably lighter than the surrounding area, and the area around the label should be rather uniformly darkened up to the edges of the label. If the label is loosened at the edges you should be able to peek underneath and see the lighter protected wood. If the wood underneath is not lighter, then the label has probably not been on the furniture for very long.

* Mirrors and clocks are among the two most commonly labeled pieces of period furniture.

Missing pieces

The older a piece of furniture and the more components it is comprised of, the greater the chance it will lose some of its parts over the years. Some may be intentionally removed and some may just get broken or lost. Regardless of why they are gone, the missing pieces can affect the price and the value of the furniture. Crests and attached relief carving are usually attached with glue or small tacks. These pieces can easily be lost in transit, but are also removed in order to shorten a piece of furniture. If you look closely, you should be able to see evidence of the small tack holes or marks from a previous glue line.

Old sideboards often had a brass gallery rail across the back and sides. It is believed napkins were draped over the railing to prevent wine from splattering the walls or wallpaper. These railings are quite often missing today, but the holes will still remain if you look for them. The holes may be carefully plugged and filled or may occassionally be hidden under a piece of molding or banding.

Cornices were made as a separate component of the furniture and were often removed in an effort to reduce the overall size of the piece. Some cornices were then converted into another piece of furniture others were eventually lost or destroyed. Original cornices were big and wide – often wider than the feet on the base of the furniture. A replacement cornice will often be smaller in size than the original and will look out of proportion when the piece is viewed as a whole.

Secretary desks and highboys can lose their top sections and then be passed off as smaller desks or lowboys. The giveaway here is the top board. Since the board between the secretary desk and its bookcase or the highboy and its base was never intended to be seen, it usually consisted of a piece of secondary wood, not primary wood. The wood may be stained to match the color of the rest of the piece of furniture, but the grain will be different even if the color is close. Highboys and secretary desks both usually had a piece of molding which went around the base unit to help contain and define the top section. If the top section is missing, the small nail holes will probably still be visible in the wood. Secretary desks which have lost their bookcases will also generally look too wide and out of proportion.

Small chest of drawers and wash-stands often had splashboards across the back. Dressers may also have had attached mirrors or small sets of drawers. Dresser or washstands will have a series of holes across the back and sides where the pegs for the splashboard would have been inserted into the wood. The top of the dresser may show a series of small tack holes where drawers or a mirror were attached to the top. Mirrors which have been removed from dressers can go on to have a new life of their own. But if you examine the sides of the mirror carefully you should be able to see the small holes that indicate where it was previously attached to a swivel holder or where it was attached to the dresser at the base.

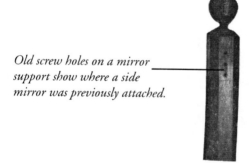

Old screw holes on a mirror support show where a side mirror was previously attached.

Major restorations

A major restoration, if it has been properly done, can be harder to detect than a small repair. Furniture has been undergoing restorations for as long as there have been cabinetmakers and craftsmen to make furniture. A review of old work records indicate a large percentage of the work done by the average cabinetmaker a century ago was repair and restoration work. Without their skills, there would be far fewer antiques available for us today. Some old repairs will age with the furniture and begin to blend into the original structure, other repairs will become more obvious over time because the materials used for the repair will age at a different rate than the original materials. As a general rule, the higher the quality of the antique, and the older the piece, the greater the chance it has undergone some sort of repair or restoration during its lifetime. The amount of restoration is often due to the age of the piece and to the amount of use the piece has been subjected to. Restoration is often justified because of the rarity of the piece. Dealers obviously want to sell a piece of furniture for as much as possible and are usually willing to pay a talented restorer to make the necessary repairs as unobtrusive as possible. Restorations become a problem when they are not disclosed to a potential buyer who may believe they are paying a premium price for an unaltered piece of furniture.

When considering a major purchase, carefully look at the furniture to determine where the weaknesses in the furniture design would be or where natural signs of wear would normally be found. If you see no obvious evidence of wear or repair you may need to take a closer look.

As we've discussed in other sections, drawers are usually a good place to start looking if you are trying to determine whether a piece of furniture has been restored. Check the drawer fronts to make sure they are original, they all match and they have not been altered. Check for hardware holes on the inside of the drawer which do not match up to holes on the front of the drawers, or do not consistently match from one drawer to the next.

Pieces of furniture which have been moved around a lot during use, like old tables and chairs, will eventually show wear on on their feet. In some cases the wear becomes so great that new feet are added to the furniture. If the repair is properly done, it should be very difficult to determine where the repair has been made. If the legs are turned, the splice can be added at one of the turning lines and if properly aligned will be almost impossible to detect. If the furniture has a clear finish, you should be able to follow the grain down the length of the leg. If you come to an area where the grain becomes inconsistent, you may have found a patched area.

If the furniture has a painted finish, you can often see the spliced area by shining a bright light on the area at an angle to the leg. If the repair has been more recently done, you may need to look no further than the bottom of the feet where a modern lathe chuck will have left its dinstinctive "X" mark

Remember furniture construction follows a very consistent set of rules. If you find one leg made of a different type of wood, or one spindle turned from a different type of wood it has probably been replaced. There should be consistency within the piece of furniture. All spindles will be of the same type of wood. All legs will be carved from the same type of wood and attached in the same manner.

If a major restoration is undertaken, the biggest problem is usually how to get the repaired areas to blend in with the rest of the piece so the repairs are not glaringly obvious. Unfortunately, the most simple and most effective way to blend a major repair on a piece of furniture is to do even more repairs. A repaired area which has been stripped, stained and refinished can duplicate the color, finish and sheen of the rest of the furniture. However, the replaced wood may look too "new" and "aging" and signs of wear may need to be added to blend the new additions with the older components. An old piece of furniture which appears to be in "perfect condition" should be suspect. Few things survive for a hundred years or more without showing some signs of age or wear. There are a few pristine examples of fine old furniture out there, but most of them are in museums or private collections. If a piece of furniture appears to be in perfect condition it has probably either been impeccably cared for or it has been restored. If it has been restored you should wonder why.

Genuine Antique Facts

Drawers
• Drawer linings are usually made from oak or pine. The linings on older furniture were usually made much thicker than linings on modern furniture. The sides of a 17th century drawer could be up to 3/4" thick. Drawer linings became thinner during the 18th and 19th centuries and 1/4" became the standard width.

• Drawers on furniture made during the 18th century may appear today as if they do not fit properly in the spaces they were designed to sit in. The furniture was originally intended to have extra space around the drawers so the contents could have ventilation. Moisture loss and wood shrinkage may also have contributed to the size of the gap over the years.

• Machine made dovetails indicate the furniture was made after 1880.

Chests
• Chests without locks on the drawers were manufactured during the 19th century or later.

• The 19th century produced an increase in the production of chests and an increase in their size, but a general decrease in the quality.

• If the chest-of-drawers has lipped drawers you should see an outline on the carcass when the drawer is pulled out showing where the drawer overlaps.

Tables
• Victorian refectory tables or farmhouse style tables

were long rectangular oak tables mounted on four legs which were held together with pegged tenons. Later tables were held together with screws which were countersunk and then camoflauged by false pegs. The wooden pegs were handmade and will vary accordingly. They should also shrink with age and not fit in the sockets uniformly. Very long tables had two extra legs in the middle to support the extra length of the table. The legs were joined together by stretchers on refectory tables.

On farmhouse tables the legs were usually square and were not joined with stretchers. The table tops on both refectory tables and farmhouse tables were made up of two or three large planks of wood with cleated or wedge-shaped ends. The top was rarely fastened in place and just sat on the base. If the top is lifted, there should be marks where the heavy planks of wood have rested on the legs and a shadowy image of the top of the legs on the underside of the top where they meet.

• Gateleg tables were almost always oval in shape. Some European tables (Dutch in particular) were square or rectangular. These tables were available in a variety of sizes from small tables with small leaves needing one "gate" to support them to very large tables which needed two gates to support each leaf. Most English gateleg tables were made from oak, with the occassional table made from walnut or a fruitwood.

American gateleg tables were made from maple, pine, oak and walnut. There should be evidence of wear under the top of the table from where the gate has rubbed back and forth on the wood during use. The top of the gate should also show wear. Larger gateleg tables are rare today because many of them were sized down during the 20th century when smaller tables were more popular.

The gateleg table was replaced in popularity in the 18th century by the drop-leaf table. The gate, stretchers and legs took up space and made it difficult to pull chairs close to the table. The drop-leaf table allowed more space for chairs, the overhang of the tabletop was greater and it provided more comfortable seating. These tables were constructed from very high quality wood, usually walnut or mahogany, and finished in a dark rich color. The most common repair or replacement on a drop-leaf table is the ear-piece which is joined to the top of the leg.

• Side tables were intended to be placed against a wall, not to be free standing in the middle of a room, and the backs were always left unfinished and undecorated. The backboards were made from rough sawn secondary woods like pine or oak. Side tables have been made in just about every furniture style throughout the history of furnituremaking and from just about every type of wood. In upperclass homes there were two forms of side tables: the *console table* which originated in France and was a table which was attached to the wall at the back and supported by legs at the front, and the *pier table* which was designed to stand in the space between two windows. Mirrors were often hung above the pier table to reflect the light in the room for better illumination and these mirrors were called *pier mirrors.*

• Tripod tables which were used to serve tea and as dumb waiters in the dining room, evolved from the small round candlestands used to hold candlesticks or lanterns. They have a tripod base and a round top and all but the very smallest tables have a top piece which can be tilted to a vertical position so the table could be stored flat against a wall and not take up extra space. The legs on a tripod table were attached to the base with dove-tail tenons. Pie-crust tops were particulary popular in the United States during the 18th century but other than the fancy edging, tripod tables were usually uncarved. Tripod tables were originally 27" to 29" tall which is much higher than most modern reproductions. The extra heighth would have been needed if the table was to be used to hold a reading light and would have had to be at least shoulder heighth for it to be used for proper illumination when reading.

• Small tilt-top tables and stands became popular in Colonial America and have remained popular ever since because of their compact size and versatility. The "bird cage" mechanism was an expensive addition to the table and added about half to the price, so this device is not found on all tables.

• Drum table tops are made separately from the bases and are sometimes mismatched with pedestal bases from other tables. The table top of a drum table sits on the base and a peg on the top of the column slots into a hole in a block which is fixed to the underside of the table top. This holds the table top securely in place but allows the table top to turn. Check the block on the underside of the table. There should be no evidence of plugged holes or excess holes. The holeon the block should show no excessive wear or markings from the top being removed.

Chairs
• The older a chair is, the more times it has probably been reupholstered so more tack holes should be evident

in the framework. Antique furniture should have horse-hair padding and tacks not foam rubber and staples from staple guns.

• Sets of chairs are almost always worth more than a single chair. Most sets will include one or two *carvers* (a chair with arms). Carvers will always be at least two inches wider than the other chairs in the set. The more original pieces in the set the greater the value. A pair of chairs can be worth three times the price of a single chair. A set of four chairs can be worth six to seven times the price of a single chair. A set of six can be worth ten to twelve times the price of a single one, and a set of eight could be worth fifteen times the price of a single chair. The more original pieces in the set the greater the value.

• Early Hepplewhite and Chippendale chairs were made of mahogany wood that was oiled and rubbed smooth, not varnished.

Sideboards
• Early English sideboards often had *cellarets* or deep drawers attached to the sideboard to hold bottles of wine (often lined with lead to hold water to keep wine cold). They were usually on the lower righthand side of the case, unless the sideboard had two drawers, one on each side. Cellaret sideboards were not made in America until the early American Federal period (almost twenty years after they became popular in England).

• The top of the sideboard should be made of one timber on earlier sideboards. Victorian tops were constructed from two or three pieces.

Commodes

• The Victorians were very prudish and called any piece of furniture designed to conceal a chamber pot a "commode". Commodes were also called "night tables" because the chamber pot stored inside was used at night in lieu of a trip to the out house. The small bedside variety was produced in great quantities and were the most common style. But chest of drawers and other pieces of furniture were also designed with cabinets to conceal a chamber pot. Commodes were occassionally sold in pairs, but these are very rare. Commodes often had marble tops. White Carrara marble was most commonly used on 18th century pieces. Colored marble was more commonly used on commodes from the 19th century.

Beds

• American beds were often made bigger than English beds.

• The four poster bed with a full canopy over it and rails for bed curtains (called a *tester)* or a bed with the canopy over the head area only (called a *half tester*) were the most common form of beds until the 19th century. Very few of these beds have survived in their original state. The beds were often taken apart and rebuilt because room sizes got smaller and people got taller. The drapes were an integral part of these beds and of the bedroom decor. Very few beds still have their original drapes and those which do are quite valuable.

• In the 16th and 17th century oak tester beds had chunky, turned or carved posts. Starting in the 18th century the posts at the foot of the bed were usually made from polished mahogany and were slender and elegant. Headboards and back posts were often made from secondary woods because they were intended to be covered by bed draperies, pillows and bolsters and not intended to be seen. Tester beds were held together with bolts which went through the posts and into the siderails. Brass swinging covers concealed the bolt holes.

Bolt hole covers were used to cover bedpost bolts. They attached to the bed with a single screw at the top which allowed the cover to swing from side to side to provide access to the bedbolts.

Bookcases
• The earliest bookcases with adjustable shelves had rabbets cut into the sides of the cabinet case for the shelves to slide into. The next evolution of the shelf holder was a toothed ladder on each side of the case with removable shelf rests. By the end of the 18th century, movable pegs which fit into holes drilled into the side of the case were used. The pegs were often made of brass or gilt coated metal.

• Furniture made during the 18th century was exceptionally well proportioned. If a bookcase has a groove for the first shelf that is six inches from the bottom of the case, then the groove for the top shelf will be six inches from the top of the case.

Hinges and hardware
• Brass hinges on furniture from the 18th century were not attached to the furniture with brass screws. Cabinetmakers did not feel these were strong enough to do

the job and used steel screws instead. Old steel screws were not made like modern screws and had the thread running right up to the screwhead.

Miscellaneous

• If two pieces of furniture have been married it is often necessary to add some molding or inlay to make the marriage less noticeable. Woods which are not similar look even more so when placed next to each other. Inlay or molding placed between the two pieces tricks the eye. If inlay was added to veneer, you can often feel the roughness where the old veneer was cut to make room for the inlay. Once the veneer has been glued it will need to be chipped away from the glue backing leaving rough edges behind as evidence .

• Caning on English furniture generally had smaller holes and was woven with finer cane than American pieces.

• Many "country antiques" are not genuine antiques. They are reproductions constructed from antique wood.

An Examination to Determine the Real Thing

Experience is the best teacher in determining "the real thing" from a fake, a copy or a reproduction. The more furniture you examine, the easier it will be to determine its authenticity by its looks, feel and smell.

Start by looking at the piece of furniture. *Really* looking at the furniture. Try to look at it from all angles. Walk around it if possible. Does any part of the furniture "not look right"? Are all of the parts of the furniture proportionate? Do the legs fit the style of the furniture? Are the decorations or trim consistent with the style of furniture? In most cases, if the piece doesn't "look right" it probably isn't.

Different styles of furniture may have qualities unique to that particular style, but most furniture is produced to set proportions. Chair seats are usually about 17 to 18" above the floor. Low chests of drawers have three to four drawers and are 34" to 40" high. Antique candlestands will usually be much higher than modern stands or reproductions. They are often 26" to 29" from the floor to the top of the table. This extra heighth was necessary so the illumination from the candle would be at the proper over-the-shoulder heighth even when the candle was burned down to a stub. Hepplewhite and Sheraton sideboards are usually 3" to 4" taller and deeper than their more modern counterparts. Empire sideboards will be even higher than Hepplewhite and Sheraton ones.

Rectangular tray-top tea tables were generally much larger than modern reproductions. They were often 26" tall, 32" long and 20 " deep. Larger pieces of furniture are proportioned for balance as well as aesthetics. Any piece which differs radically from the norm should be suspect as a reproduction or modification.

Queen Anne and Chippendale chests of drawers are usually the same heighth as modern ones, but Federal and Regency chests of drawers are normally 40" high, which is approximately as high as they are wide. Early wing chairs had thick down cushions. If the original cushion has been replaced, the chair will seem too low. Early wing chairs were also bigger and wider than their modern counterparts. Interestingly enough, wing chairs were originally used more in bedrooms than in living rooms or parlors, and the seat often had a hole in it that would contain a chamber pot.

The width and depth of Windsor chairs varies widely. Early low-back and comb-back chairs from Philadelphia have very wide seats which can be as much as 6" wider than modern Windsor chairs. Many old Windsor chairs have very shallow seats compared to modern chairs, possibly because people were not as tall then as they are today.

Examine the finish on the furniture. Is it original? Can you see evidence of repair or restoration when you look at the corners or crevices? An antique finish should feel smooth and worn in the areas which would have received normal use and may be bumpy and crinkled in other areas. *Patina* is a mellowed, aged look caused by environmental factors and is acquired over time. Almost everything acquires a patina: wood, wood finishes, cloth, paper and metal. It is one of those things that is difficult to describe with words but is easily identified with your eyes and your hands. It is very important not to damage the patina on an old or potentially valuable piece of furniture.

Wooden furniture with a protective coating will acquire a patina on two levels: in the finish and in the wood itself. The finish will lose its gloss from dusting, normal use and exposure and will often darken with age. The wood will expand and contract with exposure to heat and humidity and the grain may become more obvious over time. Many woods will darken in color. Unfinished wood on the bottom of the drawers or the back of a case piece will gain patina too, but it will patina differently than finished wood.

Chemical removers will destroy the patina of a finish on contact, but most will not destroy the patina of the wood. However, sandpaper, coarse steel wool, metal scrapers or electric heat guns can remove 100 years of patina in a matter of seconds. Once it is gone – it is gone forever! It is possible to duplicate the patina of a finish if it is damaged or removed, but it is virtually impossible to duplicate the patina in the wood.

Patina can vary greatly on different types of wood but will remain fairly consistent on the same wood except where it has been exposed to sunlight or strong fluorescent lights. Light will bleach the color from wood and affect the grain and the finish.

Heavy coats of wax on a piece of furniture can be a warning sign they may be concealing replaced or repaired areas on the furniture. Over the years, antique counterfeiters have tried to duplicate the aging process with a variety of methods: exposing furniture to weather, applying various chemical combinations, even going to the extreme of burying furniture under piles of horse manure or soaking it in lakes or rivers. Painted pieces can be "aged" by dousing the surface with lighter fluid and then igniting it. The fluid will flash and burn off, leaving behind a honey-colored, crackled finish. While this may help to accelerate the mellowing process and give the furniture an "aged look", the results are never the same as those acquired naturally over time.

> * It was a common practice during the 18th century to apply a base coat of oil varnish to walnut furniture, then apply coats of wax polish. This combination resulted in an off-yellow, soft-sheened finish which is almost impossible to duplicate or fake today.

No matter how well manufactured and finished a piece of furniture may be, new furniture will never have the look of an antique. A new piece of furniture, even a quality reproduction, will lack the patina of an old piece. Many collectors look for patina on a piece of furniture and consider it to be *the* most important element of the piece. Lack of patina not only makes a piece of furniture appear "new" but it also strips the furniture of the character associated with older pieces and quality workmanship.

Consider the original use intended for the furniture and check for wear marks which would be consistent with what would have been considered normal wear for that particular piece of furniture. Plant stands and fern tables will bear water marks from the plants that sat on them. Desks will often have ink marks and the indentions of handwriting. Chair stretchers will show wear from years of feet being placed where they shouldn't have been. Signs of wear are one of the easiest things to fake. Unfortunately, many fakers do not take the time to make the placement of the wear realistic.

Look at the drawer pulls, escutcheons and hinges. Do they match the age of the piece? Have they been replaced or are they reproductions? Have they been refinished? Original hardware should show signs of age and there should also be signs of age around drawer pulls and handles. The wood around the hardware is often a darker color from exposure to body oils, dirt and grime.

Check the back of the furniture to see if the backboard is original or if it has been replaced. Backboards may dry out and crack and may fall off or need to be replaced. Check the fasteners holding the backboard to the furniture. Are they original or do they look too "new"? Backboards on antiques were almost always attached with nails. If you discover screws or staples you will have evidence the piece has been tampered with. Take a look at the nails. Are they the appropriate type of nails for the time period when the piece was supposedly made?

A replaced backboard on a mirror which has been spray painted in a poor attempt to camoflauge the new wood.

If possible check underneath the furniture. The bottom of the feet should look worn. If the wood looks new, it is possible thin pieces of wood have been applied to the feet. Checking the bottom of the feet is also a good way to see if they have been broken in the past. Most repairers are concerned with how the repair looks from the angle from which the furniture will be used. Not from angles which are normally not visible.

Check the bottom boards under the furniture. They should have an even aged look. The wood should be naturally darkened, as no cabinetmaker would have applied stain or finish to this area. The bottom boards are usually a great source of information as to whether the piece has been stripped or refinished. Most refinishers do not think to remove traces of paint, stain or finish from these rough, unfinished areas. Very light wood on the bottom of a piece of furniture would indicate the wood has either been recently replaced or, perhaps, the bottom of the furniture did not start out being the bottom of that piece of furniture. It may have been removed from another piece and "married" to the one it is on. Check around the legs. Is the wood aged the same up to where the legs join? Are there lighter areas surrounding the legs or are there marks left from different shaped legs?

After you have thoroughly examined the outside of the piece of furniture it is time to examine the inside. Are the hinges original? Do they fit into the area carved for them or do they sit too far into the groove or too high above the edges? Does the hardware fit the time period of the piece?

Drawers can be very helpful in determining age or authenticity. Remove one of the drawers. Check to see if the runners or the drawer bottom has been replaced. If you do not see evidence of repair, the wear on the sides and bottom of the drawer should match the wear on the runners. If the wear doesn't match, the drawer may be in the wrong place or may be a replacement. Does the wood look evenly aged? Or is it a light color which would indicate the bottom has been replaced?

The sides and bottom of most drawers were made from softwood which ages and wears quickly. Constant use will wear down the wood. Uneven wear can be an indication the piece has been placed on an uneven surface or is no longer square. The top of the piece should be level and the sides should be perfectly plumb for drawers to work properly. You can check for this by using a carpenter's level.

Check the inside of the drawer front to see if the drawer pulls or other hardware are original. If the hardware has been replaced you will often find plugged holes or open holes on the inside of the drawer front. These holes can be plugged with wood or with a variety of patching compounds. If you find plugged holes on the inside, check to see if the holes go through to the front of the drawer. If they do not, this is evidence the drawer front has been re-veneered. If the drawer front is veneered, look for signs to see if the veneer is original. Some pieces of furniture have had veneer applied to them in an attempt to enhance the value. If the wood on the inside of the drawer front is solid oak, and the outside of the drawer front is veneered with another type of wood, this is usually a good indication the piece has been re-veneered. Commercial furniture makers would not have applied veneer over a piece of solid oak. This would have been a waste of wood. New veneer can also be used to camouflage a drawer which has been reduced in width and added to a piece of furniture.

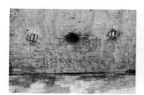 

The inside of two drawer fronts showing evidence of replaced hardware. The drawer on the right has mismatched modern screws.

While the drawer is out, smell it. Old wood should smell like old wood. New wood or replaced wood will have a distinct odor. Refinishing or restoring will leave behind tell-tale odors. Odors can be camoflauged or covered up, but that old wood smell is as difficult to reproduce as a new car smell.

Provenance is a term that comes up when discussing a true antique. Provenance is simply the history and documentation of what is known about the piece of furniture. It can greatly increase or decrease the value, but often is difficult to prove and should be "taken with a grain of salt". Very rarely will a piece of furniture have its original bill of sale from the cabinetmaker or shop that originally sold it and a continuous written history of every family who has owned it since. Most furniture will have, at best, an original label, a previous bill of sale, or some written family history. Although limited, these do contribute to provenance and are important to the furniture and its market value. However, not all furniture owned by someone's grandparents is old or valuable. It may have been owned by them for a week or for seventy five years and just being owned by grandparents does not grant it antique status. Some pieces add to their provenance by being auctioned or sold by a particular dealer or auction house or by being previously owned or used by a famous person. In these cases, documentation is critical to verify the information.

The furniture brand aboves states the furniture is "authentic furniture" made by a company in El Segundo, California. But the circular brand below it says "made in Japan". The label on the right shows the manufacturer's name and the address of the sales room where the music box was purchased.

Stamps, brands and labels are generally found in accessible places such the top of a drawer front, on the swing legs of a card table or tea table, on the inside of a cupboard door or beneath a chair seat or chair rail. Signatures are more rare and are usually found in less obvious places such as backboards, the bottoms of drawers and underneath table tops.

A stencilled manufacturer's label on the inside of a slave cradle giving the manufacturer's name, city and the patent date.

In attempting to document the provenance of a piece of furniture you should try to get at least the following information: the accepted name for the type of furniture, the manufacturer's name if it is known, an approximate date when the furniture was manufactured, the type (or types) of wood used in the construction of the piece, prominent features of the piece of furniture, the price paid for the furniture and the date.

Spider, Bugs and Other Creepy Crawlies
When you are investigating a piece of furniture, be on the lookout for spiders and bugs that may have moved in and decided to call the piece home. Some of the inhabitants can pose a threat to the furniture and wreck havoc – eating it away

from the inside out leaving nothing behind but a thin shell of the former piece. Others can provide a threat to you.

Spiders like to live in out of the way places, especially in corners and other angled areas. They set up home and can happily feed on passer-bys without distraction. Unfortunately some spiders have dangerous bites. There are only six kinds of spiders in North America whose bites are harmful to humans: the brown recluse spider, the sac spider, the female black widow, the brown widow, and the varied widow. Learn to recognize the dangerous spiders indigenous to your area and be on the lookout for them when investigating a piece of furniture that has been kept in a crowded antique store, barn, garage, or other storage facility.

Other furniture bugs will not cause direct physical harm to you. But they can cause considerable financial harm. The woodworm, is not a worm at all, but rather a type of dry-rot caused by a wood-boring beetle. It is the larvae or grubs, not the beetle itself which causes the wood damage. Depending on the type of beetle, the larvae state may last up to two years. When the larvae are full grown, they change to pupae and remain dormant for a few weeks, then develop into adult beetles. The mature beetles, which usually measure less than 1/8 inch, gnaw their way out of the wood, usually following the grain of the wood. They bore a round exit hole and then fly off to mate. The female lays her eggs in the wood and the cycle begins again. The holes we see in the furniture are the exit holes. A maze of tunnels is hidden under the surface of the wood and can structurally ruin a piece of furniture.

You will usually see the first signs of an infestation in spring and early summer. Tiny, light-colored piles of powder will appear on the floor underneath infested pieces of furniture. This is *frass*, a combination of fine wood particles from the furniture and deposits from the larvae. Furniture should be thoroughly inspected several times a year if you have any reason to suspect an infestation. Wood-boring insects can travel from one piece of furniture to another, and damage a whole roomful of furniture if left undetected. Check all of the wooden areas on the furniture, top to bottom to make sure no small holes appear. Dark holes are evidence wood-borers have been there but are presently inactive in that spot. Light colored holes contrasting with the surrounding wood, or holes with fine powder in or around them indicate a current infestation.

The pinhead-sized holes on the surface of the wood are only the tip of the iceberg as far as wood damage is concerned. Tunnels under the surface can weaken wood to the point where the furniture becomes unstable and unusable. The flight holes can usually be found around joints or dusty cracks in the furniture. If the insects are left untreated, future generations of larvae will travel further and further into the furniture and the deterioration of the furniture will spread. The majority of the infestation, however, will remain in the area of the original attack.

Wood-boring insects seem to prefer walnut, chestnut, maple, oak and fruitwoods, but will also attack softwoods like pine and poplar. They are also fond of wickerwork, and because of the small diameter of the spokes, can do substantial damage to a piece of wicker furniture in a very short amount of time. Some woods such as mahogany, cedar and teak are rarely attacked and the beetles do not seem to like the heart wood of oak.

Woodworm damage is very common in European antiques but not as common in American antiques unless they have been exposed to damp, dirty floors or European antiques. Moisture, stagnant air and dirt create the perfect growing conditions for wood-boring insects. American furniture is most often attacked by the Chestnut borer (Agrillus bilineatus) which can leave a larger tunnel than most other wood boring insects. The tunnels can be as wide as 3/32" diameter. The Chestnut borer has a voracious appetite and singlehandedly almost caused the American Chestnut trees to become extinct during the early 20th century.

Woodworm infestations can be very persistent and are

rarely completely eradicated. If possible, the furniture should be treated several times during the first few months after the infestation is discovered. The treatments should be repeated for at least two years. Furniture should be thoroughly inspected at least twice a year to check the progress of the treatments. Furniture in the immediate vacinity of the infested piece should also be routinely checked to prevent the infestation from spreading. If the infested furniture is rare, valuable or a true antique consult a professional instead of trying to solve the problem yourself.

There are two basic methods of extermination: fumigation or the use of liquid insecticide such as Cuprinol or Stop-Rot. Both products are available at boat yards and hardware stores that sell marine supplies. Fumigation exposes the entire piece of furniture to toxic gases, not just the infested areas, and is a very effective treatment. But, because fumigating gases are extremely hazardous and require the use of a fumigation chamber, it must be done by a professional.

Liquid insecticide or fungicide can be used by nonprofessionals but to be most effective, it will need to be dropped into each and every hole in sufficient quantities to penetrate the entire depth of the hole. A small oil can be useful in squeezing the liquid into the holes and keeping it off the surrounding wood. Aerosol insecticide for wood-boring insects is available in some areas. Check your local hardware store or marine supply store. Common fluids such as kerosene, benzene and turpentine can also be successfully used in some cases to kill wood-boring insects.

Take care to protect your eyes and skin when applying any insecticide. The holes tunnel through the wood and create uneven channels and liquid can squirt back out from another hole when you least expect it. Wear rubber gloves and goggles and work in a well ventilated room. Insecticides and fungicides may contain solvents of varnish, so take care to protect the floor and any nearby furniture with plastic drop cloths. Wipe off any spilled fluid immediately to prevent damage to floors or furniture finishes. Use a paint brush to apply the solution to all unfinished areas (i.e.: interiors, backboards and undersides).

When the insects have finally been killed it is very important to eliminate all possible grounds for future egg laying. Thoroughly clean and vacuum the furniture and fill all cracks in the woodwork with wax. Relocate the furniture to an area with good ventilation that is free from moisture or dampness, if possible, and keep it clean.

If you are working on a true antique, every effort should be made to save the wood. If the furniture has been structurally damaged by the infestation, wooden braces may have to be applied to the interior of the furniture to provide additional support. If woodworms have honeycombed the wood it may be impregnated with synthetic resins and bonding agents to help hold it together. The repair of severe structural damage is a job best left to a professional restoration expert.

To repair minor damage, carefully scrape away the damaged wood and remove any dirt and loose particles. Fill the damaged area with wood putty, wood dough or a homemade putty consisting of sawdust and wood glue. When the patched area is dry, sand the repair to smooth it, and then stain it to match the surrounding wood. Finish by applying several coats of shellac or varnish.

The feet of furniture can be severely weakened by woodworm infestations. You can reinforce damaged areas by drilling a hole through the affected area and up into the unaffected area of the wood. Apply woodworker's glue to the inside of the hole and then insert a piece of wooden dowel the same diameter as the hole. Use a hammer to lightly tap the dowel into the hole. Glue applied to the inside of the hole will create less of an oozing problem on the surface of the wood than if the dowel is coated with glue and then inserted into the hole.

Woodworm holes seem to be a particular favorite of

many furniture fakers. As mentioned previously, wood-boring beetles create the damage known as "wormholes" not wood worms. It is also a common misbelief that wormholes are an indication of age and prove the furniture is old. "Woodworms" are not a thing of the past and continue to destroy furniture even today. What the holes can prove is whether or not the furniture is structurally sound.

Fakers and improvers can combine wood dust and pumice with a small amount of paste wax and blow it or brush it into the holes. This concoction resembles frass and can help make fake wormholes appear more real. It is possible to duplicate the frass powder in the wormholes, but it is difficult for a faker to accurately duplicate the hole itself. Fake holes are tunneled into the wood with ice picks, drill bits or nails and brads which have been sharpened to needle-like points. All of these tools create holes which go straight into the wood and are perfectly round. Most fakers do not take the time to place the holes in a believable, natural pattern like beetles would have created and tend to leave rounded holes with clean sharp edges, unlike a natural hole. Fake holes will go straight into the wood and are generally not very deep.

Natural holes twist and turn and are not really holes at all, but rather tunnels under the surface. To help determine whether wormholes are legitimate or have been improvised, take a small piece of wire or a thin needle and probe the holes. If the holes are uniformly symmetrical and appear to penetrate straight into the wood, they were probably done with human hands.

Fakers also tend to use wood that exposes the worm tunnels. Genuine craftsmen would never have used a piece of wood with an obvious flaw like a worm tunnel on a period piece of furniture, and would have filled the tunnel with wax if they had to use the board at all. Real wood-boring beetles *never* work along an exposed surface they always tunnel *under* the surface. If the tunnels are exposed, it is because someone has brought the tunnel to the surface or broken the thin piece of wood surface.

Use and Wear Marks

Furniture gets worn and dirty from normal use. Areas exposed to constant use should be worn smooth and be darkened from contact with body oils and dirt. Grease, dirt and wear marks are commonly found around drawer handles, key holes, pulls and latches, on the arms of chairs and along the edges of desks or tables. Dust, dirt and grime will also accumulate in cracks, crevices and carving as a result of use and exposure. A piece of wood made from soft woods will generally look older and more aged than a comparable piece made from harder wood. A piece of furniture in pristine condition, with no wear or hidden dust or grime has usually either been repaired, restored or is a fake. Generally speaking, the older the piece of furniture the more likely the signs of wear.

Exposed wood on furniture will darken with age and often becomes quite dry, especially if it has not been properly treated with regular applications of lemon oil. Unexposed wood will also darken, but not to the same degree as the exposed wood. The unexposed wood is often unfinished and will usually be dry and rough. The feet on furniture, especially on frequently moved and used pieces like chairs, should show wear marks on the bottom from the constant contact with the floor. Sharp edges and corners should start to lose their crisp sharp lines with age and develop rounded or chipped edges from use. Painted surfaces usually become darker and more subdued with age. A brightly painted finish is usually an indication of a recently restored piece. Painted surfaces will also craze and crack as they age because the wood dries out and shrinks and the paint does not shrink to the same degree as the wood. If the painted areas are smooth, be suspicious.

Wood will lose moisture as it ages and moisture loss will cause the wood to shrink. Wood will shrink across the grain. This can cause tabletops to warp and chest of drawers can shrink to the point where their drawers are too long to fit into their compartments. Shrinking cabinet wood can also cause backboards to break loose or crack.

Veneer was applied to the basewood of furniture with animal based glues. These glues were not water soluble nor were they extremely durable. As the basewood dries out and shrinks, these old glues will deteriorate and crumble and the veneer will be left with nothing to hold it to the basewood. Pieces of veneer will then start to loosen and fall off the furniture.

Shrinkage

Wood contains a large amount of moisture. When it is cut and trimmed into logs it begins to lose its moisture. The moisture content continues to be reduced as the logs are trimmed into boards and billets. As the moisture evaporates, the wood dries out, the wood cells contract and the wood begins to shrink. The moisture loss is very great at first but tapers off over time. However, the moisture loss never really stops during the lifetime of the piece of wood. As a general rule, the harder and more dense the wood the less it will shrink. Modern furniture is made from kiln dried wood, but it too will eventually shrink, just not as noticeably as antique furniture.

The amount of shrinkage depends on the type of wood, the run of the grain and how the cells were aligned in the tree. It also depends on the moisture content of the wood when the piece of furniture was first made and how quickly it dried out. Furniture made from unseasoned wood will often show considerable shrinkage and distortion. Cracks in a log will generally be in the direction of the grain and go from the bark in towards the heart of the tree. Radial shrinkage is always less than tangential and longitudinal shrinkage is the least likely of all. Cabinetmakers preferred logs cut into quarters (known as "quarter sawn wood") because it helped eliminate the risks of shrinkage, warping and moisture loss.

Shrinkage can be very obvious on some pieces of antique furniture and not as easy to spot on others. Legs, stretchers and stiles were often turned while the wood was still green because unseasoned wood was easier to turn and carve and less likely to split. Green wood would also tighten as it dried making a better joint which did not require the addition of glue or nails. Because, as previously mentioned, tangential shrinkage is usually greater than radial shrinkage, these once round components will now be slightly out of round. Round table tops will become out of round with age, sometimes by as much as an inch or more. A circular table top made many years ago will no longer be perfectly round. Check the diameter of the grain across the grain and then with the grain. If the measurements are the same, the table has been probably been modified. The measurement across the grain should be 1/8" or more shorter per foot of diameter than along the grain.

Square table tops or square legs will often dry out and become out of square. They will shrink and become narrower across the grain on a table top or in a tangential direction on a leg. Chair splats which once sat tight in their grooves will often shrink by 1/4" or more and begin to float loosely in their sockets. Wooden pegs and pins will not shrink if they were carved lengthwise of the grain of the wood. Otherwise they will begin to pop above the surface or "stand proud" as the wood dries. Pegs were cut to the exact size needed to hold two pieces of wood together. As the wood dries the pegs may fall out and the wood being held together will fall apart.

Wood containing mortise and tenon and dovetail joints can also shrink and dry out and the wooden components they join will break apart. In some instances, people will attempt to use nails to fasten the joints back together. This usually results in the dry wood being split by the nails and the joints being broken apart creating permanent damage.

Veneered surface can be strangely affected by shrinkage if the grain of the secondary wood used as the base wood runs in a different direction than the grain on the veneer. Veneers can be pulled from the base wood and break free from the glue holding them in place. Base wood can bend or curl in a concave or convex direction as it dries which can change the shape of furniture components. Mitered corners on old frames will often separate leaving a gap in the inside corners due to shrinkage across the grain.

Wide panels of secondary wood used for drawer bottoms and backboards will often shrink and break because they have been fastened at the edges prohibiting the wood from contracting. Door panels and side panels made from the primary wood will also shrink, especially during warm weather or if the furniture is kept in an over-heated room or too near a heat source (like a fireplace or a radiator). Shrinkage can create gaps between the wooden panel's edge and the door frame or side panel frame. Wide boards will often shrink and begin to twist if they have not been secured properly along the edges. This is most evident on the leaves of card tables or dining tables. Wide table tops secured to table rails tend to split lengthwise along the middle of the panel, with the grain.

Wood will shrink, but metal, mother of pearl, ivory and other types of material used for inlay do not. When the wood loses its moisture and begins to shrink and dry out the inlay begins to push above the surface of the wood. Smaller pieces may become completely loosened and fall out and get misplaced. Brass strapping used on trunks or cellarettes can become loosened and slip off if the wood shrinks sufficiently enough because of moisture loss.

Furniture Construction

You may find a label or a stencil on the back or other unexposed part on some pieces of furniture that states the furniture is "made from selected hardwoods". This is not a guarantee the furniture is durable or of high quality. Good furniture is made of *hard woods* not *hardwoods.* "Hardwood" comes from any tree that bears flowers during the growing season and has broad leaves which it loses each year. "Softwood" comes from cone-bearing trees in the evergreen family that retain their greenery year-round.

The label or stencil may also tell the species of wood used in the construction. If it says "genuine" preceding the name of the wood (i.e.: "genuine mahogany" or "genuine oak") it means all of the exposed parts of the furniture are made of that particular wood. In furniture terminology, the "exposed parts" of the furniture (the top, sides, etc.) are made from the *primary wood.* The structural woods that are usually unexposed are made from *secondary wood.*

Before furniture was mass-produced by machines the primary woods used in construction were usually the hardwoods and softwoods native to the particular region where the furniture was made. The secondary woods were also local woods which were inexpensive or easily attained. Transporting wood was difficult and expensive, and roads were primitive, so there were few furniture makers who did not use local woods. One interesting exception were the cabinetmakers in Baltimore in the early 19th century. They used imported mahogany as a secondary wood because it was less expensive to ship mahogany from the West Indies than to transport "local" wood by wagon. As furniture-making became more mechanized other woods were more commonly imported and used.

Certain styles of furniture are commonly identified by a specific type of wood. Mission style furniture is associated with oak. Primitive furniture is associated with softwoods like pine and cedar. Chippendale style furniture was predominately made from mahogany wood (although walnut, maple and cherry wood were also used on less expensive pieces). Knowing the style of the furniture, and what species of wood was most commonly used in its construction can help to identify the age of a piece of furniture.

A genuine antique should have consistency in construction. Overall, the style of the piece should remain consistent. Furniture styles may vary over time and often vary in different areas of the country or different parts of the world. But the style should be consistent within the piece of furniture. The feet should all be carved the same. The drawers should all be constructed in the same manner. The type of board used on the backside of the furniture should be consistent throughout the piece. All of the finished parts of the furniture should feel the same, and all of the comparable interior parts of the furniture should feel the same.

Cabinetmakers have always had to deal with the characteristics and idiosyncracies of wood. It expands and contracts with heat, cold and humidity and dries out and shrinks with age. Because of these tendencies, furniture had to be constructed with the grain running the same direction to avoid uneven shrinkage. Drawer slides, side panels and moldings attached at right angles would split or push out over time if they were attached too securely. To remedy this, side panels were not glued in place and were allowed to "float" in their frames. Drawer slides were locked into half dovetail slots without glue. Molding and drawer slides were also occassionally attached with a minimum number of small nails. Early veneered drawer fronts were usually bordered with a cross-band or herringbone pattern of contrasting wood to minimize the effects of wood shrinkage and to frame the drawer. Later drawers were *lipped.* The lip framed the drawer and allowed the wood to shrink without showing a gap and allowing dust to get into the drawer. The trouble with lipped drawers is the lip tends to break at the corners. This was most often caused by the lip sticking out after the drawer was closed, but also by people trying to pry open a stuck drawer.

Wood will lose moisture as it ages causing it to shrink. Hardwoods (like mahogany, cherry, rosewood, maple, oak and walnut) will shrink considerably less than softwoods (like pine, spruce, poplar and cedar). Shrinkage will usually occur across the grain of the wood. Very little shrinkage occurs with the grain. Shrinking wood can result in cracked panels on chests and sideboards, drawers which do not slide properly, uneven tops and backboards and drawer bottoms that crack or pull away from their fasteners.

Some furniture can shrink to such an extreme it will change shape. Old round pine or other softwood tables can lose their symmetry and become slightly oval in shape. Furniture can also lose its shape if it is manufactured from wood which has not been properly seasoned. Furniture made from unseasoned wood or wood which would normally be considered too "green" to be used is likely to show considerable shrinkage. I personally saw an oak tablemanufactured during the "reproduction oak boom" of the early 1980s which was so warped, the top looked like a vinyl record that had been left out in the sun. The table was manufactured from unseasoned wood, and after it was purchased the owners placed it in a bright, sunny breakfast nook. The condensed heat of the sun dried out the wood and warped and cracked the top from the base.

Dust panels or *dust dividers* are found more frequently on English antiques than on antiques manufactured in America. We generally consider them to be a sign of a quality piece of furniture today, but, even cheap, poorly made English antiques often had them. If they are found on an antique manufactured in the United States it is generally a sign of quality work because they are not as common.

Drawer bottoms had to be thin and lightweight, but not so thin or lightweight that they would sag or bind up the drawer. Wood was seasoned and carefully chosen so it would not split the bottom panel when the wood started to dry out and shrink. But early drawers had the bottoms nailed to the sides, and in spite of good intentions, when the wood dried it would shrink and often split because it was fastened in too well and had nowhere to go.

The shrinkage problem was partly solved by running the grain of the wood sidewise rather than front to back which reduced the shrinkage by minimizing the width across the grain. (It is important to note block-front furniture and furniture made in Philadelphia continued to be made with the grain running from front to back.) The drawer bottom was also fitted into a groove or *dado* in the bottom of the drawer which allowed it to expand and contract without splitting the wood.

Drawer bottoms on English furniture were often divided into two sections with a *muntin* across the middle of the drawer to supply support and prevent sagging. Drawer bottoms on American furniture were usually made from pine and were often cut thicker than English drawer bottoms so they seldom needed a center support. Later drawers were not nailed at the front and the back but were fastened only at the back of the drawer to hold the bottom panel in the groove. The panel could float in the groove and the expansion and contraction of the wood was not restricted.

Occassionally you will come across a piece of furniture which has been "fixed" by a well-meaning but misguided restorer and the drawer bottom will be glued in place. If you are lucky enough to get to the bottom panel before it splits, you can release it by dissolving the glue holding it in place and it will once again be free to float in the groove. If the board is already broken, you will have a more difficult repair on your hands.

Quality furniture can be identified by looking at the top edges of the drawer sides. If they are curved or molded rather than flat or square, it is generally a sign of a higher quality piece because more time was spent finishing the wood, and time, even back then, cost money.

Cabinetmakers used patterns made of paper or thin sheets of wood to save time, wood and money. Patterns were used to cut out seats, legs, rails, stiles and other furniture components. Calipers were often used to help maintain a consistency in the diameter of stiles, legs and other rounded pieces, but many were cut "by eye" without the aid of calipers and it is not unusual to find asymmetrical old turnings.

The methods and techniques of furniture construction have changed radically over the years as new tools and new materials were introduced. Even a brief knowledge of which construction techniques were used at which specific time can help date a piece of furniture or determine if a piece is a fake or a reproduction. The simplest construction methods are generally the ones used by the earliest furniture manufacturers. However, country furnituremakers continued to use these methods long after their urban contemporaries had begun using more advanced forms. Because of this, it is important not to use the method of construction as the only information or the most important piece of information when dating a piece of furniture.

The four most common types of construction are: *six-board, paneled, mortise-and-tenon,* and *dovetail.*

Six-board construction - Probably the most basic form of furniture construction is "six-board construction". It consists of fastening six boards together to form a chest: one board for the top, two for the sides, one for the front and one for the back. The boards were often just nailed together on simpler pieces. Pieces of a higher quality may have dovetail joints to hold the pieces together. The top on a six-board chest was usually held on with hinges so it could be lifted easily. Six-board construction was extremely popular during the Colonial years and remained popular in rural areas into the 19th century. The basic six-board method created simple sturdy furniture and is still often used by craftsmen today.

Paneled construction - Paneled construction was common in the late 17th, early 18th and late 19th centuries. It consists of horizontal boards (called *rails*) which are fastened to vertical elements (called *stiles*). The stiles and rails are grooved so the panels can be inserted into the grooves. The panels were often recessed and some were elaborately carved. Paneled construction was often used for doors or sides of a piece of furniture, but seldom used to construct an entire piece of furniture. Paneled construction is still used in furniture construction today.

The panels were not glued into place but were left to "float" in the socket to accommodate for the expansion and contraction of the wood. Unfortunately, finishes can build up in the grooves binding the panel or well-meaning repairmen glue the panels in place. When the wood can no longer float it will begin to crack, resulting in the cracked panels one often finds on antique furniture.

Mortise-and-tenon construction - The mortise-and-tenon joint was brought over to America with the first settlers. It is the primary method for constructing tables and chairs and is often used in the construction of case pieces. Like paneled construction, it uses horizontal rails and vertical stiles. The end of one piece is cut into a rectangular projection (or *tenon*) which fits into a corresponding hole (or *mortise*) chiseled into the other piece.

In the Colonial period, the mortise-and-tenon joints were further strengthened by the addition of a "pin" or small wooden peg. The *pinned mortise-and-tenon joints* were often used when constructing tables and chairs. The mortise-and-tenon joint was similar to the joints found on modern furniture with the exception of the added pin which was used for additional reinforcement. Both the mortise and tenon had holes drilled in them, then the pin was inserted into the hole, locking the two pieces together. There were two methods used to pin the joint: the *draw-bored tenon* and the *locked joint*. The *draw-bored tenon*, (which was used on 16th and 17th century furniture and reproductions of this furniture) had a hole bored in the tenon and through the rail or leg into which it went. The two holes were slightly offset, and when the pin was driven into the furniture it would pull the tenon tightly against the rail or leg, creating a very strong joint which did not require glue. Nails and glue did not come into common use as a means to reinforce furniture joints until the 19th and 20th century.

The heads of the wooden pins are visible on most pieces of furniture although some may be camouflaged by a thick finish coat. The pins were carved by hand and were not perfectly cylindrical, and each pin was carved for a specific spot on the furniture. If you should need to remove the pins, mark them so you know where they came from and they can be properly repositioned. The pins normally penetrated the entire thickness and came out the other side. To remove them, use a small dowel of a similar size to the pin, place it against the pin and use a hammer to gently tap them through.

The *locked joint* is often found on the frames of uphol-stered arm chairs and settees where the seat rails are joined to the back legs. This joint is commonly broken by people who tilt the chair backwards while sitting in it. The excessive pressure put on the joint will usually snap the pins leaving broken pieces in the holes.

The back seat rail usually contains the dowels, and they penetrate the tenons on the side seat rails. Locked joints were always held together with glue. A true antique would have had some type of animal glue used as the adhesive. If remnants of synthetic glue are in evidence, then the joint has been recently made or previously repaired.

Dovetail construction - Dovetails are another method used to interlock furniture components. They are triangular projections on one piece of wood which fit into similarly shaped slots on another piece of wood. Dovetails are predominately found on drawers, but were also used to join tops and sides of chests, chest of drawers and other case pieces.

The dovetail joint came into common usage during the late 1600s and early 1700s (during the William and Mary period) and for the first time allowed construction of furniture with reliable functional drawers. Prior to this time, most furniture consisted of simple box shapes (called *coffers*) or some type of open shelving arrangement or cabinets with shelves behind doors like the old court cupboards.

Early dovetails were hard to make because they had to be crafted entirely by hand, and they were usually quite a bit larger than modern ones. Generally speaking, the older the piece of furniture, the fewer and larger the dovetails. Some drawers from the 17th century contain only one dovetail. Early cabinetmakers carved the wedges by hand using very fine saws and this resulted in uneven, sometimes crude wedges which were often of differing widths, even on a quality piece of furniture. By the middle of the 17th century, the dovetails were carved considerably smaller and several dovetails would be found on each drawer. In the middle of the 19th century dovetails were cut with jigs that were used to help guide hand powered saws, and then finally evolved to being cut by machine. Dovetails were the last holdout of hand work in a machine era. Machine produced dovetails were smaller (1/2" to 3/4"), more similar in width and had a less sharply angled shape than hand-made ones.

Some machine-made dovetails manufactured during the Victorian period were rounded instead of the familiar wedge-shape and look like a series of half moons with a dot in the center. The dot was the tip of a peg which secured the joint and gave it additional strength. There are several names for these odd looking joints: *scallop and dowel joint, pin and scallop joint, half moon joint* and *Knapp joint.* These unique joints were cut on a special machine invented by Charles B. Knapp of Waterloo, Wisconsin. His first joint machine was patented in 1867. Three years later he sold the rights to an improved version of the machine to a group of investors who formed the Knapp Dovetailing Company in Northhampton, Massachusetts. After refining the machine, they put it into production in 1871.

By the mid 1870s, furniture manufacturers were mass

producing Renaissance Revival and Eastlake furniture and most of the Eastern and mid-Western companies (with the exception of those in Grand Rapids) were using the Knapp machine to create dovetail joints. A machine could produce two hundred or more drawers a day. By comparison, a skilled cabinetmaker could only make fifteen or twenty drawers per day by hand.

By 1880, almost all mass-produced furniture had machine-made dovetail joints. Machines which could simulate handmade dovetail joints were perfected in the late 1800s, and by 1900 American furniture manufacturers had stopped using the Knapp joints entirely and replaced them with the more traditional looking wedge-shaped dovetail joints. If you see a piece of furniture with Knapp joints you will know, without a doubt, that it was manufactured between 1871 and 1900.

As a general rule, early dove-tails were larger, uneven and hand cut, and later ones are smaller, evenly shaped and machine-cut. If you find machine-made dovetails on a piece of furniture supposedly manufactured before 1880, you either have a reproduction, a fake or a repaired piece of furniture.

There are three types of dovetail joints: *single lapped, double-lapped,* and *mitered.* Single-lapped dovetails are used in the construction of drawers. Double-lapped dove-tails and mitered dovetails are usually used in the construction of other components of a piece of furniture.

Check the dovetails on all of the drawers. All dove-tails on all drawers should match. If they don't, this is an indication the piece has been repaired or the drawers may have been replaced. Check the dovetails at the back of the drawer. If you find altered dove-tails at the back of the drawer, the drawer may have been reduced in depth and may be from another piece of furniture.

If you should have to dismantle a dovetail joint which has loosened and needs to be reglued, hold a block of wood against the joint and use a rubber mallet. It is a good idea to use a sharp knife to trace the outlines of the dovetails prior to dismantling. This will help to dislodge any remaining glue or finish and will help the wood release more easily with less danger of breakage. Applying white vinegar to the area can also help to loosenthe grip of old glue.

Hand cut dovetail joints.

Wooden pegs - Wooden pegs (also called *treenails*) were often used in early furniture construction as a means of holding furniture together because hardwood dowels create a very strong joint. Early pieces had hand-carved pegs, later pieces had machine-made pegs. Hand-carved pegs were not perfectly round and were not of a uniform length. They were slightly rounded and had tapered ends. Machine-made pegs are more uniform in size and width.

Any piece of furniture held together with irregularly shaped hand-carved pegs of wood can almost certainly be dated to before 1840. After that time, machine made dowels were used. The machine made dowels were almost perfectly cylindrical and identical to one another.

Wooden dowels were originally sized to have a tight fit so glue was unnecessary and the furniture was held together with the pegs alone. But wood will shrink and lose moisture as it ages and many of these pegs on a true antique will now be loose in their sockets or protruding a fraction of an inch above the surface of the wood. Furniture collectors and repairers will often say these pegs have "popped" or are "standing proud of the surface". Pegs were carved lengthwise of the grain of hard wood and the peg will generally not shrink but the wood surrounding it will.

A wooden peg or "treenail".

When studying the construction of an antique it is important to keep in mind that at the time the piece was created time and materials were quite valuable. Shortcuts were taken to produce more quality furniture with less production time, but a cabinetmaker still had to produce a large enough quantity of furniture to make a profit. Only surfaces which showed were given a finish coat. Backboards were usually rough and unfinished with the wood often being used as it came from the mill. The undersides of tables may have been smoothed with a wood plane, but they too were left unfinished. The high tops of chest and other large pieces were never finished. The insides and sides of drawers were left bare.

Desks, chests and tables with carved feet will almost always have more simple rear feet with less carving than the front ones. Even tables with claw and ball feet will often have two feet carved only on the front half and not the back half as they would have gone against a wall and would not have shown. Headboards were often of a similar shape as footboards, but were less decoratively carved or inlaid where it would be covered by the pillows and bolsters during use.

Lapped dovetails were never used where simple dovetails could be used. Mitred dovetails were never used where lapped dovetails could be used. Any variation from this is an indication the piece has been reworked since it was originally made.

The Wood

Wood is the most basic component of most furniture and can reveal quite a bit about the age of the furniture and the techniques used in its construction. Wood is a natural product and will go through natural changes from exposure to heat, cold, and moisture and from use and time itself. Heat and humidity will cause the wood fibers to expand and contract and cause the grain to become more apparent. But wood will only show the affects of age on the surface. The wood under the surface is protected from the aging elements and if cut, scraped or otherwise exposed, it will once again appear to be new wood.

There are two categories of wood used in furniture construction: *primary wood* and *secondary wood*. Primary woods are those used in the construction of the main body or carcass of the furniture. Primary woods are almost always used for exposed areas on the furniture. These woods are chosen for their color and grain pattern. Common examples of primary woods are mahogany, walnut, rosewood, and maple. Secondary woods are used for concealed areas of the furniture. They are usually inexpensive woods that are locally and readily available, and are usually lighter in weight than primary woods which helps to reduce the overall weight of the furniture. Secondary woods are often used for the backs and undersides of chests and other case pieces, and for the bottoms, sides and backs of drawers.

Wooden furniture with a protective finish will acquire a patina at two levels: in the finish and in the wood itself. The finish will become thin and dull from use and may darken with age. Even unused wood will show its age. The surface will mellow and darken and develop a patina all its own from exposure to air and all of the impurities in it. Different types of woods will mellow and darken to different degrees. Dark walnut may take on a reddish hue, oak will develop into a rich golden brown, maple will evolve from white to tan.

Wood will show varying degrees of aging even within the same piece of furniture depending on the amount of air, light, moisture and use each particular piece of wood was exposed to. The unfinished wood on the backboard of a chest of drawers will darken due to exposure to air and other elements. The backboard of a drawer inside the chest will darken to a much lesser degree because of the protection it has had from those same elements. Natural discoloring of wood will only be uniform where the exposure to air and other elements has been uniform. Artificial colorants intended to "age" the wood will generally be applied uniformly throughout the piece. Ammonia will darken wood and give it an "aged" look and stains (including coffee and tea) can be used to darken wood, but they will usually produce a noticeably uniform look which is obviously fake.

Wooden surfaces with a protective coating will age differently from unfinished wood. Most protective finishes will lessen the wood's ability to darken. Shellac or lacquer which was accidentally dripped on unfinished wood during construction should have noticeably lighter wood showing from beneath it. If the wood under the finish is the same color as the surrounding wood, then, more than likely, the finish has been applied after the wood has aged.

Occassionally furniture represented as being a particular type of wood turns out instead to be a composite of several types of wood. For example, not all old oak furniture is made of oak. Hickory, elm, ash and chestnut were often used in combination with oak wood. Oak is a very strong wood, but it does not bend well. If the piece of furniture was designed to have a rounded back or frame those pieces were often formed from elm or hickory. Oak has a tendency to splinter when it is turned on a lathe, so one of its substitutes may have been used for the turnings. Many "oak" ice boxes are really made of ash or elm wood. So how can you tell the difference between oak and its substitutes? By learning to recognize some of the basic qualities of each of the different woods. Let's take a quick look at the woods listed alphabetically below.

Ash wood has a very prominent grain that resembles oak's grain. It is a very heavy, light-colored, dense wood. Many upholstery frames are made from ash because of its strength and durability.

Chestnut wood is a grayish brown and has a very coarse open grain. It is softer than oak, not as structurally tough, and does not have large rays in the grain pattern like oak. A fungus disease attacked a subtantial number of chestnut trees in the United States during the early 20th century and almost caused the species to become extinct. Some furniture companies used wood from these damaged trees and called it "wormy chestnut".

Elm wood bends easily and is often used to make curved furniture parts. It is frequently used for chair seats. Elm is porous and similar to oak in both color and texture. It is often cut into veneers because of the nice figuring in its grain pattern. When used as a whole board, however, it has a tendency to warp.

Hickory wood is strong and hard, and difficult to work with, but bears a very close resemblance to the color and texture of oak. It was often used for bow backs on chairs and other bent parts which require similar thinness and flexibility to assume various shapes.

Oak is a light colored, hard, durable wood with a very distinctive coarse open grain. It was the most popular wood used for furniture manufacturing from the late 1800s through the early 1900s. Different methods of cutting oak produce a variety of distinctive grain patterns. For example, quartersawn oak produces a flake pattern and plain-sawn oak produces a curved pattern.

There are about sixty types of oak trees in the United States, but only about fourteen of them can be used for commercial furniture manufacturing. Most of the wood used for furniture manufacturing is grown east of the Great Plains.

Cabinetmakers used dense, close-grained woods whenever possible because it was very strong and did not shrink as much as other woods. As a general rule quality furniture was made with quality wood and other quality materials. Wood and labor have always been expensive. Cabinetmakers did not waste wood, nor did they waste time finishing wood or carving wood where it would not show. Nothing unessential was done to a piece of furniture, even on the most expensive pieces. Extra time and money spent on production reduced the craftman's income. Figured wood was used where it would be the most visible and less expensive secondary wood was used elsewhere. Some pieces of furniture were made up of two or more different types of wood so the cabinetmaker could take advantage of the characteristics of each wood. A single Windsor chair may have been made from as many as five different kinds of wood. The result was a quality piece of furniture which is still sturdy and useful after several hundred years of service.

Artificial graining (also called *false graining*) is also a common substitute for oak wood. Inexpensive wood with little or no grain was often stained and then painted to mimic the grain patterns of oak. Hotels and other public buildings which needed large quantities of dressers, washstands or other pieces of furniture could buy artificially grained furniture at a much cheaper price than real oak. Artificially grained oak furniture allowed middle class and lower-middle class families to have the look of oak without the price of oak. The 1897 Sears, Roebuck catalogue advertised "elm or ash furniture in an 'antique oak' finish". Sometimes the base wood on the furniture was not identified and was described as "the best selected material finished in 'antique oak' ".

Oak was not the only wood to be false grained. Pine or poplar could be made to look like maple or cherry. Birch could be made to look like mahogany or rosewood, bird's eye maple was often duplicated, and the only real limitation was the talent and workmanship of the craftsmen.

False graining is done by applying a base coat to duplicate the color of the desired "wood to be". Then, using an artist's brush, feathers or various other tools, colorants are applied to duplicate the wood grain. The finished product is then carefully sealed in under a coat of shellac or lacquer to prevent the false graining from wearing off.

On the left is a false grained panel which was accidentally stripped. On the right is the same panel after the false graining was repaired.

To detect false graining, look at the inside of a solid wood (not a veneered) drawer front and notice whether the pattern has similar characteristics on both the outside and the inside of the drawer. On a table, nightstand or desk you can look under the top piece and compare the grain on the outside of the top and on the inside. Check around the drawer knobs and other frequently touched areas of the finish. "False graining" is just a coating and will eventually show signs of wear. Lastly, take care if you plan to use a stripper, remover or solvent on the finish or you may accidentally dissolve the "wood grain".

New wood and "new" looking stains and finishes are the easiest way to detect restored, repaired or faked furniture. Wood stains can be as simple as a homemade concoction of tea or coffee or a complex formula containing ammonia, lye or other dangerous chemicals. Unfortunately, no matter how well the stained area may match the older wood at the time of application, it will eventually age differently than the surrounding wood and the color of the stain and wood will change over time.

All wooden furniture exposed to daily use will eventually show some signs of natural wear. Scratches or stains in the finish, wear marks around the hardware, on the arms and legs, even scuffs and dents in the wood are almost unavoidable during daily use. However, artificial wear is one of the most commonly used faking techniques. New wood is often subjected to scratches, burns, stains and even insect infestations in an effort to prematurely "age" the wood.

It is not necessary to learn to identify every type of wood used for furniture construction by sight alone. There are over 100,000 different species of wood. Books containing color pictures or actual wood samples of the most common furniture woods are available from woodworking supply stores. Acquaint yourself with the most commonly used woods so you can recognize them on sight and then use reference books and tools to confirm any others in question.

If you need to confirm a particular piece of wood, you can send a small sample of it with a letter asking for it to be microscopically analyzed to: United States Department of Agriculture, Forest Products Laboratory, One Gifford Pinchot, Madison, Wisconsin 53705.

It is difficult if not impossible to determine where a piece of furniture was made simply based upon the type of wood used for its construction. Similar types of trees grow in both the United

States and Europe, and wood was imported from the United States to be used by European furnituremakers and imported from Europe to be used by American furniture manufacturers. However, there are a few guidelines which can be used:

• Oak was seldom used for furniture manufacturing in the United States from the late 17th century until the late 19th century, but it was widely used in Europe during that time period. Around 1880 the supply of walnut was becoming depleted in the United States and furniture manufacturers needed something to replace it. Oak was their wood of choice and remained the most popular wood from the late 1800s until the 1930s when veneered walnut and mahogany furniture came in vogue.

• Pine was commonly used as a secondary wood in American furniture manufacturing but seldom used as a secondary wood for English furniture. Deal wood (which is a type of pine) was used in England.

• Poplar is another wood characteristically used as an American secondary wood but not by Europeans.

• European furniture was more likely to be composed of one type of wood. American furniture was more likely to be composed of several types of wood.

• Fruitwoods (i.e.: apple, cherry) were more commonly used in the United States than in Europe.

• English Queen Anne furniture was usually made from mahogany wood, but mahogany was not used for fine furniture in the United States until about 1750, and didn't became commonly used until the Chippendale period (between 1750 and 1780).

Furniture styles varied greatly over the years, and different styles are often associated with a particular type of wood. Consequently, knowing the basic style of the furniture and the wood commonly used for that particular style can help identify a piece of furniture and date when it was manufactured. The following list identifies the basic American furniture styles and the woods most commonly associated with them.

Pilgrim - 1630-1690
Primary woods: oak (occassionally maple, hickory).
Secondary woods: maple or hickory

William and Mary - 1690-1725
Primary woods: walnut or maple
Secondary woods: pine or poplar

Queen Anne - 1725-1750
Primary woods: Maple, cherry, mahogany and some birch
Secondary woods: pine, poplar, maple, cherry, ash

Chippendale - 1750-1780
Primary woods: Mahogany, walnut, cherry, maple
Secondary woods: pine, cedar, beech, poplar

Federal - 1780-1820
Primary woods: Mahogany, maple, cherry, with inlay and veneer using figured maple, birch or satinwood
Secondary woods: pine, cedar, poplar

Empire - 1815-1840
Primary woods: walnut, cherry, mahogany, rosewood, grained maple
Secondary woods: pine, birch and local woods

Victorian - 1840-1900
Primary woods: mahogany, rosewood. Later Victorian pieces used walnut oak, ash, cherry, pine. Bentwood furniture was also popular.
Secondary woods: pine, oak

Modern - 1900-present
Primary woods: mahogany, maple, fruitwoods, pine, ash, exotic woods, laminated wood, pressed wood, composition board
Secondary woods: pine, ash, plywood

American forests were literally brimming with an abundance of large healthy trees when Colonial craftsmen first started making furniture. Twenty to thirty inch wide boards were common place, and cabinetmakers used wide boards to make furniture whenever possible instead of gluing narrow boards together. Time was money, and why waste time gluing the wood together when wide single boards were already available? As the forests became depleted, trees were harvested at a younger age and the resulting boards became narrower. Older furniture was made using a smaller number of wider boards. Generally, the older the furniture, the wider the boards it is made from.

Early cabinetmakers had the luxury of an abundance of quality hardwoods available to them. They seldom used wood with obvious defects like knots or damaged areas such as wood worm. Restorers and fakers will often use a piece of old wood to make a repair and are more likely to use a piece of wood damaged by woodworm or with a knot or other type of natural disfiguration.

Saw marks and tool marks

Early furniture manufacturers had to do all of the construction by hand and each piece was very time intensive. Time was money and craftsmen did not waste time or energy to smooth or finish the backs, undersides or other unexposed parts of furniture where they thought no one would look or where they believed the marks would not show and detract from the piece. Time and materials were spent on areas where it would show. These unexposed areas often have visible hand tool marks and saw marks. This is especially evident in furniture made prior to 1900. Early craftsmen had no reason to try to cover their tool marks. Evidence left from woodworking tools is usually found in out of the way places where the craftsman didn't think anyone would look, where they originally felt it didn't detract from the piece of furniture, or where they were overlooked by someone who forgot to remove them. Fakers trying to duplicate furniture today will often try to remove their tool marks so they can not be identified.

Furniture made prior to 1830 was constructed of wood sawn and cut by hand. Hand saws leave very distinctive marks which are straight but very irregular in appearance. Power-driven saws were not used in furniture construction until around 1830. The early power saws (some of them powered by water) still used straight sawblades and left straight, smooth, parallel marks in the wood. Circular buzz saws came into use in the saw mills around 1840 to 1850 and are still used by furniture manufacturers today. The circular saws left distinctive circular marks in the wood. As a general rule, furniture with archlike semicircular scratches dates from after the Empire period (1840-1850). If you are looking at a Federal style piece, and the backboards have distinctive semicircular scratch marks on them either the backboard has been replaced or the piece is a reproduction or a fake.

Saw marks (technically called *kerf marks*) can be used to help determine the age of a piece of furniture. Shine a bright

81

light at an angle across the rough unexposed wood on the furniture. Bright lights will help to highlight saw marks and you should be able to identify whether the piece was sawn by hand, by straight blade machinery, or by a circular saw.

Furniture makers use a small pointed tool called a *scribing awl* to mark outlines for mortises and dovetails, and to mark the placement of hardware. The indentions left by the tool are called *scribe marks.* These marks are often visible on the softwood of the sides of drawers or on rough unfinished backboards. Scribe marks around a dovetail joint can help to authenticate the age of the joint and help determine whether it was hand-made or machine-made. Scribe marks would be absent on machine made dove-tails.

Power-driven belt sanders and other mechanical equipment was not used in furniture production until after the 1900s. Furniture made prior to that time should show plane marks and marks from other tools used to smooth and shape the wood. The absence of tool marks on a piece supposedly made prior to that time is an indication the piece has been repaired, had pieces replaced, or it is a reproduction or a fake.

It is interesting to note that furniture manufacturers in the United States started using machinery on a commercial basis at an earlier date than furniture manufacturers in England and most other countries in Europe. Handsawn lumber was common in small lumberyards there well into the 20th century.

The circular saw and the steam engine were used in some larger cities during the late 18th century and started to change the woodworking techniques used in Great Britain. However, it was not until the middle of the 19th century that the quality of steel and the manufacturing methods for blades improved to the point where the circular saw could be reliably used for manufacturing furniture. The machinery was only used in larger industrial areas and country craftsmen in smaller areas continued to use manual methods.

The invention of the bandsaw did not come until the

early 19th century and it was not until the middle of the century before a reliable machine was developed because of the inferior quality of the metal used for the blades. The bandsaw did not come into common usage until the end of the 19th century.

Saw blades are not the only tools which will leave their marks on furniture. Planes were used to smooth wood and will leave lines parallel to the grain of the wood. Scribing tools, compasses, gauges and other cabinetmaker tools all leave telltale marks behind.

When a cabinetmaker needed to smooth a piece of wood he would plane it as carefully as possible with a sharp wood plane adjusted to a very fine setting. Any remaining ridges were taken down with a steel scraper. Wood that required further smoothing was rubbed with a piece of *shagreen,* the dried abrasive thick skin from a shark. Shagreen was so abrasive it could be used to smooth even the hardest woods. Sandpaper as we know it today was not invented until the turn of the 18th century. Before that time it was made in the cabinetmaker's shop by coating heavy paper with glue and sand.

Width of boards and width of the wood

Few large components on a piece of furniture (i.e.: tops and sides) are made from one solid piece of wood. If you look closely at the top of an oak table, for example, you will see it consists of multiple pieces of wood glued together. Older furniture was often constructed of wider boards. Some boards used on older fruniture were 20 to 30 inches wide. It was easier and faster to make a piece of furniture out of one wide board rather than joining multiple thinner boards together, and the forests were filled with mature trees which produced wide boards.

Antique furniture was also constructed using boards of varying widths assembled in a random pattern. Most furniture today is constructed of boards of similar width. The wood on older furniture is also generally thicker than wood used on modern furniture. Part of the reason for the thicker boards was the crudeness of the tools used in the construction process. It was difficult to achieve an even thin cut of wood with hand tools. Another reason could be that craftsmen took pride in their work and created furniture was made to last and be handed down from generation to generation.

The cut of the wood

There are five principle methods of cutting lumber into wood for furniture manufacturing: *quarter slicing, rotary cutting, half-round slicing, flat slicing,* and *rift-cutting.* Different styles of furniture are typically constructed of wood cut in a specific way. For example, much of the 19th century oak furniture found in antique stores today was constructed of *quarter sliced* or *quarter sawn* wood.

Quarter slicing is the most expensive process because it wastes a lot of wood. It produces a distinctive grain pattern which varies with the species of wood being cut. The log is cut into four pieces and then cuts are made at roughly 90° angles to the growth rings in the wood.

Rotary cutting produces exceptionally wide boards with a bold, zig-zag grain. The log is mounted in a lathe and turned against a cutting blade, much like unwinding a roll of paper or peeling an apple.

Half-round slicing is a variation of *rotary cutting* and is also done on a lathe. The log is cut in half and then fastened to the lathe. It is then revolved against the cutting blade producing boards which are slightly rounded. Half-round cutting produces a grain with some of the characteristics of rotary cutting and some of the characteristics of *flat sliced* wood.

Flat slicing produces a prominent and variegated grain pattern. The log is cut in half and then mounted with the flat side (the *heart* of the wood) against the guide plate of the slicer. The slicing is done parallel to a line through the center of the log.

Rift cutting is unique to the various species of oak wood.

Oak has *medullary ray cells* which radiate from the center of the log like spokes on a wheel. The log is quartered, then cuts are made at 90° angles to the rays of the grain using either a lathe or a slicer. This produces a rift or "comb" grain effect.

Unfinished or unexposed wood

Antique furniture was seldom painted or stained on the undersides or backs of the piece. This was a waste of time, labor and materials for the cabinetmaker and served no purpose. The tops of large chests and secretary desks were never finished. The backboards were seldom smoothed let alone stained or finished and the wood was often used just as it came from the mill. Likewise, components on the furniture which did not need to be smoothed or sanded were left rough or unfinished. Drawers sides and interiors were left bare. The underside of tables were smoothed with a plane and left unfinished. Dust panels and the bottom boards on furniture were left unstained and unfinished. If a piece of furniture has a coat of finish or wax applied to these areas it has probably been altered after production.

Veneer

Veneer is a very thin layer of wood, usually cut from a more expensive hardwood species and chosen for the beauty of its grain or wood pattern. The technique of veneering has been around for about 3,500 years – probably longer. Murals in Egyptian tombs show veneer makers working at their trade. Veneering was used by the ancient Egyptians, Greeks, Romans and Chinese, but reached its peak in the 18th century when cabinetmakers such as Sheraton, Hepplewhite, and Chippendale used veneers to great decorative advantage. Veneer making declined during the Middle Ages, but with this exception, it has flourished and been improved over the years and become an important part of furniture making.

During the early 1900s, veneered furniture was considered by many people to be a cheap imitation of good solid wood furniture. They assumed furniture manufacturers were trying to save money by using cheap wood and covering it with thin sheets of good wood. They did not realize veneering requires considerable skill and is a very time intensive technique. It can produce a whole new kind of wood grain beauty which can not be duplicated in nature, and make the piece more valuable than if it was made with "the real thing". Veneering isn't a form of deception – it is instead, a very old form of furniture decoration.

Veneer's bad reputation still lingers today. Many people believe veneer is applied to cover defects in the base wood; and in some cases this may be true. Other people base their negative view of old veneer upon the veneering techniques used for today's furniture. It is not uncommon today to find plywood or composition board covered with a sheet of veneer. This results in inexpensive and inferior furniture. Fortunately, antique furniture was made to a much higher standard.

Veneering allows the cabinetmaker to use wood from sections of a tree which have a particularly pronounced and beautiful natural grain pattern. If not sliced into veneers, these sections might only produce a few solid pieces of useable wood or be discarded altogether. Veneers can be made from parts of the tree which would normally be considered waste wood because they are too unstable for wood construction. The veneer-making process uses wood so efficiently that just about every part of the tree can be used. The *crotch* of the tree (the point where the branches fan out from the trunk) produces beautiful grain patterns which are often used for veneer by furniture manufacturers but would produce little usable wood if it was not sliced into veneer. The section of the log closest to the root will often show a flamelike pattern. Veneer cut from *burls* (tumorlike growths on the tree) have textured patterns with intricate spirals.

Veneer woods were originally shaved by hand so the

process of making a piece of veneer large enough to cover a table, for example, was a long and tedious task and required great skill. It was extremely difficult to maintain a consistent thickness of the wood while trying to get an optimum thinness. The earliest veneers were more of a facing of wood than the micro-thin sheets of wood we purchase today. Very early hand-cut veneers can be 1/8" thick or more. Some can vary in thickness between 1/16" and 3/16" on the same piece of veneer. By comparison, today's veneers are of a consistent thickness and average between 1/28" and 1/40" (the latter being equal in thickness to four average sheets of paper).Veneer sheets are glued to a thicker base board of a less expensive type of wood. Old veneers were often applied to the rough finished base wood and then finish sanded after application. This can help to explain some of the discrepancies in the thicknesses.

Today veneers are peeled from turning logs in continuous sheets using huge veneer knives. They can turn a log into veneer at a rate of 400 feet per minute. A single log 8 foot long by 2 foot square can produce 30,720 square feet of veneer.

Veneer was very labor intensive and expensive, so it was only applied to the principal surfaces of antique furniture and the pattern of the veneer was commensurate with the importance of the surface. Loosely translated this means a beautiful flamelike veneer would be put on a table top, or the front of a desk, where it would show and be appreciated – it would not be placed on the top part of a cabinet or inside the piece of furniture. If you discover intricate veneer in an out of the way place on a piece of furniture it is a dead giveaway the piece has been modified in some way.

There is almost always an exposed edge on a piece of furniture where you can check to determine if the furniture has been veneered or if it is a solid wood piece. Use a small flashlight to help expose the thin line that should clearly show on the edge of veneered furniture. Veneer was applied to flat surfaces and on curved areas as well. Check the furniture carefully for the telltale seam. Some veneers have the edges covered with a thin strip of wooden beading to protect the edge of the veneer from chipping and to prevent it from lifting.

Thicker veneers will indicate the veneer was applied to the furniture during the 18th century. Towards the end of the 18th century, machinery was developed which allowed veneer to be cut thinner and with more uniformity. Veneers of at least 1/16" can be found on furniture made up to the first half of the 19th century, after which thinner veneers resembling what we use today became more commonly used.

If the veneer on an older piece is considerably thinner than 1/16th it has either received extremely hard usage, been sanded with a power tool, or the veneer has been replaced. Check the veneer from drawer to drawer or panel to panel. You should see consistent veneer thickness on the same piece of furniture. You should also see consistency in the grain pattern of the veneer. A section of plain veneer on an otherwise decorative piece could indicate replacement. At the very least, it is an indication of poor craftsmanship. Check also to make sure veneered panels have not been combined with solid wood pieces. Fakers who combine pieces of antiques to create new ones will often intermix veneered and solid wood pieces on the assumption their deception will go unnoticed.

You may find pieces of 18th century oak furniture which have had walnut veneer applied to them in the hopes of increasing the popularity and price of the piece. Check the inside of the drawer fronts. If the inside of the drawer front is solid oak it is usually a good indication the furniture was originally a solid oak piece and veneer was applied over the original cabinet. If an antique piece of furniture has been re-veneered during its life, for any reason, it can significantly reduce the value of the piece.

Veneered furniture is more apt to be damaged by hard usage, age and dampness than solid wood furniture. This abuse can loosen the glue bonding the veneer to the base wood, resulting in raised edges, cracks, blisters or waves. Most veneer damage appears on the top of a piece of furniture. Fortunately, this makes it easier to repair. Unfortunately, a repair which was done incorrectly in the past can cause irreparable damage.

Veneer was applied to an inexpensive local base wood which was quite often pine because it was commonly available and held glue well. The base wood had to be absolutely smooth before the veneer was applied or the dents in the wood would show through the veneered surface. The veneer was dampened to make it pliable, then hot hide glue was spread on the surface before the veneer was applied. Excess glue was forced out with rollers before it had a chance to set and removed from the wood surface so that it did not leave a stain.

Old furniture glues were made from hides, horns and hooves of animals which were boiled down to a jelly, then allowed to harden. The dried mass was broken up into flakes or a coarse powder then mixed with water and heated in an iron glue pot to between 140°-150° before use. It is important to maintain this temperature during use to keep the glue in a liquid and workable state. Hide glue was hard, brittle, brown in color, was not water-proof and often left a stain on the wood. The base wood and the veneer often did not expand and contract similarly, and the glue bonding the two together would eventually break. If it let go in the middle of the veneer sheet a bubble would result. If it let go on the edges, the edge would curl up and lift from the base wood.

Hide glue is still the best glue to use for veneer repairs and furniture repairs in general because it is flexible and will expand and contract with the wood unlike newer synthetic glues. Synthetic glue will form a bond which is stronger than the wood surrounding it. When the wood goes through its natural expansion and contractions it will break around the glued area. Hide glue is also reversible and can be removed if necessary without causing further damage to the furniture.

Hide glue is available as *pearl hide glue* and *ground hide glue*. Pearl hide glue is stronger than ground hide glue, but both of them create a stronger bond than the liquid hide glue which is now commercially available in a squeeze bottle. Bottled glue has the advantage of not needing to be heated prior to use. But it is important to note "hot glue", the stick form of craft glue which is melted in an electric glue gun before use, is not the same thing as hot hide glue, and it is not recommended for furniture repairs. "Woodworker's glue" is a special glue formulated for repairing wood. It is the best glue to use for repairs if you can not find, or do not wish to use, hide glue.

A bubble or blister in the veneer can actually be a benefit and can help you date a piece of furniture. If the bubble can be easily punched down with your finger it usually indicates the veneer was machine cut not hand cut (because hand cut wood would generally be too thick to push down) or the piece has been subjected to unusually harsh treatment or been heavily sanded (possibly to remove damage to the wood).

If the bubble can be pushed down you can repair the damage by using a sharp razor blade to cut a slit in the wood (along the grain line if possible) and then inject some hide glue into the bubble area. If you do not have a glue injector you can use toothpicks to carefully push glue inside the bubble. Do not lift the veneer or force the opening too wide or you may break the veneer and cause a bigger problem. Press the veneer down, wipe off any excess glue, and apply a weight to the area until the glue dries.

Glue was seldom used by early furniture manufacturers for anything except adhering veneer. Pegs, and dove-tails and mortise-and-tenons were used to hold furniture together and glue was seldom needed. If you see evidence of glue used to hold the structure of the furniture together, it should be a "red flag" someone has repaired the furniture.

Repairing dents in veneer – Dents can be safely removed from veneer by pricking a few small holes into the grain of the wood in the dented area, then placing a small piece of damp lint-free fabric over the dent. Apply a clothes iron (set to the "nylon/silk" setting) to the material to produce steam. Remove the iron after a few seconds to check your progress. Do not keep the iron in contact with the wood too long as the heat and steam may damage the finish or soften old glue. Allow the repaired area to dry thoroughly, then apply a coat of wax or lemon oil.

Repairing lifting edges on veneer – Lifting edges can be repaired by carefully lifting the edge with a thin knife blade and scraping the broken old glue out from under the veneer and off of the base wood. Be careful not to punch the blade through the veneer surface. Take your time and remove as much glue as possible. Brush the crumbled glue forward and out to remove it from the pocket so it will not get trapped under the veneer and create small bumps in the surface when it is reglued.

When the glue is completely removed apply a thin, even coat of hide glue under the veneer by either injecting it with a glue injector or using toothpicks or a flat thin blade to distribute the glue. Do not use ordinary household glue as it will eventually lose its grip and cause the veneer to buckle and break. Apply clamps or weights to the edges to hold the veneer in place until the glue dries. Do not over-tighten clamps if you use them or you may bruise the wood or force out the glue leaving an insufficient amount to bond the wood.

Repairing veneer blisters or bubbles – Veneer blisters are generally caused by moisture penetrating between the veneer and the basewood. Moisture causes glue to soften and deteriorate. If the glue holding the veneer is the original hide glue it is often possible to repair the blister by applying heat. If the veneer has been previously repaired with a synthetic glue or contact cement it will be necessary to cut the veneer to make the repair.

To repair the blister with heat: cover the blister with a piece of wax paper, then apply several layers of lint-free cloth. Heat a clothes iron to the "silk/nylon" setting and touch the tip of the iron on the cloth. Remove the iron every couple of seconds to check on your progress. Some old glues are softened by heat and will once again grip the wood. If the glue appears to bond, apply pressure to the repaired area until the glue has completely set.

If the heat method does not work, cut the blister with a new single edge razor blade or X-Acto knife, down the full length of the blister. Cut along the grain line of the wood whenever possible to make the repair less noticeable. Apply white vinegar to the inside of the blister with a small artist's brush to remove as much old glue and dirt as possible. Allow sufficient time for the veneer and base wood to dry before proceeding.

Inject hide glue into the blistered area with a *glue injector* or syringe, or apply with the edge of a knife blade or toothpicks. Roll the area with a *veneer roller* or wallpaper seam roller to apply pressure and force out excess glue. Clamp the repair if possible or apply weights to the area for at least 3 or 4 areas. A glass of water can often supply sufficient weight to hold down a repaired veneer blister. Allow the glue to dry overnight.

Inlay and marquetry

Veneering opened up a plethora of possibilities for furniture manufacturers. Different types of veneers could be combined to make borders, highlights and patterns to decorate furniture. This technique came to be called *inlay* in American furnituremaking terminology but is actually called *marquetry.* Purists would say that "inlay" is the name for the technique where the core wood is cut into and a contrasting wood is laid in.

Inlay or marquetry usually adds to the value of furniture and, because of that, some furniture has been inlaid after production in an attempt to increase the value or the collectability of the piece. Original inlay will have raised edges of glue or wood grain and can easily be felt if you run your fingers over the top of the inlay. Replaced marquetry, or marquetry added after the original production, usually appears lower than the surrounding wood.

Marquetry is not limited to wood veneer and can also include mother-of-pearl, bone, ivory, etc. Metal (especially strips of brass) were often inlaid into solid wood in European furniture, but the technique was seldom used on American pieces. Marquetry on walnut pieces generally is considered more valuable than marquetry on mahogany pieces, and mahogany generally more so than oak. Flowers are the most common subject for marquetry. Birds and insects are considered more rare and thus more collectible.

Repairing inlay or marquetry - Old glue attaching small pieces of inlay or marquetry to its base wood will dry out as it ages and quite often crumble away from age leaving the pieces unsecured. If the inlay is in good condition, and is just unglued, it is a very simple repair.

Before attempting the repair, use your finger to lightly push the loose pieces back into the channel where they belong. If they do not settle in to the same depth as the surrounding pieces, you may need to clean broken glue, dust or dirt out of the channel. Use tweezers if necessary to remove the loose pieces, and then use a small paint brush to clean the channel of any obstructions. When the channel is clean replace the pieces to check for fit. If they still do not line up correctly repeat the cleaning procedure. If crumbled glue remains in the channel and is a problem, use a small artist's brush dipped in white vinegar to dissolve the glue. Do not use too much vinegar – you do not want to dissolve the glue on the surrounding pieces! Dab the area with paper towels or cotton swabs to absorb the excess vinegar. Allow the area to dry completely before proceeding with the repair. When the channel is dry, squirt a small amount of wood worker's glue or hide glue into the channel and replace the pieces. Tap them into place with your finger. Wipe the surface with a slightly dampened paper towel to remove any excess glue from the surface. Place a piece of wax paper on top of the repaired area and apply weight to hold the wood in place until the glue bonds.

Turnings and Decorative Carving

Turned wood is carved on a *lathe*, which is a device used to rotate a piece of wood while various cutting tools are applied to it. Early lathes were powered by hand but later ones were powered by machinery. The hand-turned lathes produced simple lines and slight variations were expected from one piece of wood to the next. No two pieces were exactly alike. Machine powered lathes produced uniform pieces and were capable of reproducing much crisper and more defined lines.

Not all carved furniture is actually carved by hand. Many pieces of furniture made at the end of the 1800s had the design forced into the wood with a metal die. This technique was commonly used on chairs and the resulting "carved chairs" were called *pressed backs*. The seats on these chairs were either solid plank, or hand-woven or machine-made cane.

"Carving" on a pressed back high chair.

Furniture was also decorated with precarved pieces of wood which were attached to the furniture during the manufacturing process. Many oak drop lid desks, bookcases and dressers from the late 1800s and early 1900s had applied carving decorating their drawer fronts.

Carving is also added long after the piece of furniture is manufactured in an attempt to add value or make a plain piece of furniture more desirable. It is helpful to have a basic understanding as to the type of decorative carving which should be found on particular styles of furniture. For example, furniture from the 17th and 18th century generally had deep carving with thick cuts since thick wood was used in the construction of the furniture. Carving added after the manufacturing date is generally either too simplified or too complex for the piece of furniture if you stand back and view the furniture objectively. Applied pieces of carved wood such as *moldings, reeding* and *fluting* can also be added to furniture in an effort to improve its value. Moldings, reeding and fluting can be hand-carved or machine-carved before they are applied. Hand-carved examples will be more uneven than their machine-made counterparts. Machine-made pieces will be smooth and very regular and even in their appearance.

Added-on carving can be easy to spot if you look for a few tell-tale signs. Does the carved wood trim appear to be the same age as the other wood on the piece? Has it aged similarly? Check the edges of the trim at a joining. Do you see a build up of dirt, varnish or wax at the joining? If the trim is loose, gently lift the trim and look underneath. If the color of the wood and the patina of the wood are the same under the trim as they are around the trim, then you have a dead giveaway the trim was applied after the piece left the factory. When you look underneath you should see an outline of the trim on the wood and the wood should be a different color. Old wood will darken with age and exposure to air and light. The wood protected under the trim will not have been similarly exposed and so it should not be a similar color.

Carving can also help to determine the origin of a piece of furniture. The carving on American claw-and-ball feet is more simplified and abstract, the claw-and-ball feet on English furniture are carved more realistically.

Not all "carved wood" is carved, or wood for that matter. "Carving" on some pieces of furniture may actually be *gesso* (a hard, plaster-like substance) or plaster imposed on to the wood instead of being carved into it. Gesso or plaster could be colored with paints or stains to match the surrounding wood. Gesso is easily dented and chipped, and develops fine hairline cracks as it ages. If you want do a simple test to determine whether the carving is wood or gesso, take a small needle and lightly pierce the carving in an inconspicuous area. The needle will not penetrate wood but will penetrate gesso.

Desks and chests with carved feet will often have more simple carving or even less carving on the rear feet. Even claw and ball feet may be more simply carved on the backside of two of the feet where the table was intended to sit against the wall. Carved fluting was seldom applied to the rear of Sheraton sofa legs where it would not show. Headboards on early beds were often minimally decorated or carved because they were intended to be covered by draperies or bed pillows and bolsters.

Glue

In the early days of furniture construction, glue was used to fasten veneer to base wood and was not used to hold furniture together. Most furniture joints were fastened with nails, screws, or with wooden dowels, pegs or wedges.

Early glue was made from the hides, horns and hooves of animals. They were boiled until a jelly formed and the resulting jelly was then allowed to harden. The dried mass was then broken up into flakes or ground up into a coarse powder. When the glue was needed, it was mixed with water and heated in an iron pot before it was applied to the furniture.

This smelly brown glue was hard and brittle, was not water-proof, and often left a brown stain on wood. You can use some of these idiosyncrasies of the old glues to help identify the age of a piece of furniture. Old glue is often broken or crumbled out from where it belonged, leaving the wooden components loose. If you separate them further, you may see the brownish stain left behind from the glue or see crumbling flakes of glue. If you moisten a Q-Tip swab and rub on the formerly glued area you can often restore some of the smell and stickiness.

Animal glue is still available today in two forms: the old fashioned flake form (sometimes called *Scotch glue*) and ready to use liquid form. It is still the preferred glue of craftsmen and professional restorers for making furniture repairs. The newer formulas do not create stains on wood like their earlier counterparts and the smell is not as strong.

Another type of animal glue used by early furniture manufacturers on some delicate or expensive pieces of furniture was *fish glue*. It was made by boiling heads, skins, bones and swimming bladders of fish until a foul-smelling jelly-like liquid formed. The resulting jelly was then used like hide glue. Fish glue was comparable to hide glue in adhesive ability, but it was expensive and the high price prevented it from being more widely used. It is still available today in a liquid form from a limited number of woodworking supply stores and is still used by some restoration purists.

By the 1920s, most furniture manufacturers, especially those who manufactured veneered furniture, were using a glue made from the milk by-product casein. *Casein glue* is a pow-dered glue made from skim milk, hydrated lime and other chemicals. It has to be stored dry and sealed against carbon dioxide in the air. But it does not require heating, it worked well in low temperatures, could be spread by machine and was low in cost. All of these qualities were conducive to mass producing furniture. Unfortunately, it had a tendency to develop a fungus which caused the glue to deteriorate over time. Remnants of casein glue can often be found in the sockets of chair rungs and in the crevices of other furniture produced during the '20s.

Applications of glue can change the way wood ages. Glue will seal the wood pores and change the porosity of the wood. Glue applied at the time of construction would form a protective coating over lighter wood. A repair done years later would seal in a darker color of wood. Because of the changed porosity of the wood, glue can affect the saturation of stain or the penetration of finish coats.

Nails and Screws

Specific types of nails and screws were manufactured during different furniture periods. You can use what is holding the furniture together as an aid in dating the age of the furniture. As a general rule, a piece of furniture is roughly the same age as its earliest nail. Furniture fakers, however, have been known to use old nails to construct and "age" a "new antique". Almost all case pieces of furniture have some form of nail or screw holding them together. Check the backboards, bottom boards, drawer sides, bottoms, etc. If you can find a loose nail remove it and check the hole. If the nail is rusty, there should be rust in and around the hole. If the nail has darkened, the wood around the hole should be darkened. If the nail is discolored and the wood is not or vice versa there is a good possibility someone has altered the piece of furniture. Furniture fakers know most people will not remove screws from an antique until they have purchased it and taken it home. If the screwhead can be made to look authentic a piece of furniture can be aged enough to pass a cursory inspection.

When the time comes to remove an old screw, *always* use a screwdriver that is the correct size for the slot. File down a screwdriver for a better fit if necessary. Take your time and do not force the screw. You do not want to snap the head off the screw or damage the slot or the wood surrounding the screw.

Thoroughly clean the slot on the top of the screw before starting so you can get the best grip possible on the screw. Start by trying to turn the screw a fraction clockwise, as if you were tightening it. Then try to turn the screw counterclockwise. If that does not help to loosen the screw, hold the blade of the screwdriver into the slot and tap on the end of the screwdriver handle with a mallet or small hammer. If the screw still will not budge, use the tip of an electric soldering iron to apply heat to the screwhead for a few minutes. Allow the screw to cool and then try to remove it again. Heating and cooling the screw will often loosen the grip of rust and oxidation on the screw. Be careful when removing old screws. They may break off while you are trying to remove them and create a real problem.

Nails -There are three major types of nails used in the construction of American furniture: *wrought-iron nails, machine-cut nails,* and *wire nails.*

Wrought-iron nails are the earliest type of nail and were used from the time the settlers started making furniture until around 1815. They have round or rectangular heads and are sharply pointed. The blacksmith or nailmaker made nails in various sizes, but all nails, regardless of size, were made the same way. A piece of iron called *nailer's rod* was heated and then hammered on all four sides to make it longer and thinner and to bring it to a point. A piece was then broken off of the length of the rod and was dropped, point first, into a hole or clamp leaving a bit of the thick stump of iron protruding. The blacksmith would then use about five strokes to hammer the end to form a head. These nails are sometimes called "roseheads" or "five clout nails" because of the unusual shape of the head. If you use a magnifying glass, you should be able to see marks on the head of the nail from the blows of the hammer. Some nails were made without heads or have small heads that form an "L" or a "T" shape. These nails were used where the larger headed nails would have been obtrusive.

The rosehead or five clout nail is the most commonly faked fastener today. Fakers will use rusted mis-shapened upholstery tacks and they are almost indistinguishable from the real thing without removal and close examination. Reproduction nails are also available from most major woodworking supply stores and catalogs. These nails can be "aged" to make them look even more like originals.

Machine-cut nails (or *square nails*) came into use around 1815 and continued to be widely used for about 75 years. They quickly replaced hand-wrought nails because of the savings in time and money needed to produce them. Machines cut off pieces of metal plate (one piece tapering to the left and the other to the right, alternately across the plate). If you look carefully with a magnifying glass you may still see burr marks left from the cutters. The heads on these nails were L shaped or had no head at all, and the body of the nail tapers to a blunt end.

The *wire nail,* similar to what we use today, came into use around 1890. These nails were manufactured from round not square stock, and have round heads, round bodies and pointed ends. Wire nails are easily recognized because they are the only nails to have perfectly round heads.

The part of the nail just below the head can help to identify the various types of nails because the three types of nails have three distinctly different shapes – square, rectangular and perfectly round – based upon their origins as square rod, a flat sheet, or round rod. It is this part of the nail which will leave the hole in the wood. When examining a piece of furniture, check the nail holes. What shape is the hole? If it is square the hole was made by a nail from the 17th or 18th century. If the hole is rectangular the nail which made the hole was made between the early 1800s and about 1880. If the holes are round they were either caused by a modern nail, a wood beetle, or a drill or other tool.

Screws - Drawer pulls and hinges are almost always attached to furniture with screws. Screws are easier to remove from furniture than nails and can often help you identify the age or authenticity of the furniture. Very early screws were hand forged, the slot was cut with a hand saw and the thread was filed to a point by hand. They had a tapered shape and a pointed end. These old screws were very labor intensive and were not made in large quantities. Screws have been recorded in furnituremaking since about 1700, but they did not become commonly used until mechanical methods were improved.

From the middle 1700s to the early 1800s, screw blanks were still hand-forged. The core of the screw would occasionally have a slight tapering – but not the threads. Mechanical devices were used to cut the slot and threads on these screws, but there was not a high degree of accuracy and you can often see marks left from the dies used to hold the blanks, varying degrees of precision in the cutting of the threads, off-center slots and file marks on the screwhead. The length may also vary from screw to screw. It is interesting to note the earliest hand-made screws had a slight taper to their shape but it would take a hundred years before machine-made screws would be tapered.

Between 1820 and 1850 screw blanks were formed from drawn wire instead of being hand forged. The threads on these screws were more accurately cut and the screwheads were trimmed cleaner, but there is little tapering to their shape, the end is blunt not pointed which made them difficult to drive into wood and there is often evidence of the drawing process left on the shank of the screw.

The machine which created the pointed-end screw was an American invention and made its appearance in 1847. The manufacturing rights were purchased by an American named John Sutton Nettlefold and he started commercial production of "the new screw" in 1854. These screws were an improvement over their predecessors but had one major design flaw – they still did not have any taper in the area where the thread meets the shank.

A patent was applied for in 1858 which put an end to the tapering problem. By 1860 commercially manufactured screws had a thread core tapering into the shank of the screw, round heads (which often had lathe marks left from the manufacturing process), a consistent length and a pointed end resembling the screws we use today. Screws were once again tapered and pointed like they had started out 100 years before. From that point on, factory made screws were commonly used in furniture manufacturing.

Early furniture manufacturers usually tried to camouflage screws that were in high visiblity areas. In the 18th century screws and often nails were concealed by colored beeswax. In the 19th century the screws were countersunk and the screwhead was concealed with a wooden plug stained and finished to match the furniture.

If modern looking screws are found on a piece of furniture supposedly made before 1860, it may indicate the parts they affix have been repaired, or they are replacement parts, or the piece of furniture is a fake or a reproduction. Screws resembling those made before 1840 have not been copied and manufactured, and reproduction hardware, no matter how authentic-looking, is almost always attached with modern screws.

New screws will usually not be the same size as the old screws and the holes will have to either be lengthened (which can not always be done without having the screw penetrate through the wood) or widened (which can not always be done because of restraints like the size of the holes on a hinge or lock). In the case of the former new screws are often cut to make them shorter and in the case of the latter the holes are either widened on the hinge or lock or the piece of hardware is replaced.

A piece of antique furniture may contain newer nails or screws if it was repaired during its years of use. But as stated before, a piece of furniture should be about the same age as its earliest nail or screw. Some unethical repairers will use old nails or screws on a piece of furniture to help "age" the piece. Or they may become creative and "make" an "antique fastener". Old wrought iron nails will corrode leaving a black mark in the wood where they have been (especially in oak wood which contains a large amount of tannic acid). The acids in the wood react with the iron's ferrous oxide which creates black bleeding around the nail site. Careful checking can confirm that any nails and screws you find are of similar age to the piece.

Nails and screws obviously have to be removed from a piece of furniture before the age can be verified. Nailheads and screwheads are easier to fake than the complete item. If you suspect the furniture is an antique, use great care removing the nails or screws. Always use the correct size screwdriver for the screwhead. A screwdriver which is too small or too large will ruin the edges on the slot. Also make sure the slot is cleaned of dirt, accumulated wax or other grime before attempting to remove the screw. Mark the screw and the location of where it belongs on the piece of furniture as you remove them. Stick them into a piece of cardboard and write the information next to the screw or use a piece of masking tape and attach it to the screw. Old screws are not of similar size, and putting a screw back into the wrong place can alter the stability of a piece of furniture or could drive a "too long" screw through a piece of old wood.

When replacing nails and screws, make sure you are putting the correct one back in the corresponding hole. As you start to tap in the nail or turn the screw put your hand on the wood directly opposite the hole. You will be able to feel the fastener as it approaches the wood surface and can stop in time should it get dangerously close to the surface and before it damages the wood or the finish.

Nails are harder to remove from furniture without damaging the surrounding wood. If the point of a nail is exposed you can tap on it and drive the nail back out of the wood. Rusted or stubborn nails can be coaxed out of the wood using the soldering iron trick described on page 99.

If a stubborn nail keeps slipping through the claw of your hammer, and you can't approach it from a different angle without marring the surrounding wood, clamp locking pliers over the nail shank, then slide the claw of the hammer under the jaws of the pliers. You will be able to remove the nail with ease.

Pro Tip: Screws are used more on tables than on any other type of furniture. Even if some of the screws have been replaced over the years it should not be difficult to find a few original screws simply because of the large number of screws used. If no originals exist, it should be cause for suspicion.

Hardware

The type of hardware used on a piece of furniture is to a large extent determined by the period and style of the furniture. Reference books are available to help you become familiar with the types of hinges, pulls and escutcheons used for different furniture styles or periods. This knowledge will aide you in dating a piece of furniture. Not all furniture was intended to have drawer pulls, but that does not mean it may not have acquired some over years of use. Drawers not intended to have pulls will have special finger grooves under the drawers to be used when opening the drawers.

The earliest hardware was cast or hand-wrought using either iron or brass. By the mid-19th century, hardware was usually made by hand stamping. In the 20th century the stamping was done by machine presses. Cast or wrought hardware is much heavier than stamped hardware.

Primitive antiques often have crude hand-made hinges made from uneven sheets of iron. The screwholes on the hinges may be irregularly spaced unlike modern hinges where the holes are evenly spaced and symmetrical.

Most old hinges are *butt hinges* and look very much like modern ones. They have two rectangular plates with two or three holes on each plate for the screws which fasten the hinge to the furniture. Cast brass butt hinges were imported from England in the mid-18th century to be used for bookcase doors. Iron and brass butt hinges were the standard hardware used on table leaves and desk lids from the beginning of the century and many are still in place. Some were recessed into the wood so they would sit flush with the surface. Occasionally you will find a smaller hinge set into the recess carved for a larger previous hinge. Also be on the look out for wood used to fill in the area left behind when a hinge was replaced.

Cotter pins were used to fasten wooden lids and early brass handles. Two interlocked cotter pins could make a very serviceable hinge. As a matter of fact, it was the primary hinge of the 17th century. Most 17th century cotter pins have broken from use and wear, but their marks may be left behind on the wood. You should see an irregularly shaped hole large enough for the two branches of the pin to go through, and then, radiating out from the hole in opposite directions, there should be two indentions formed where the two splayed branches of the pin were hammered into the wood to be flush with the surface. But cotter pins can be made by fakers too.

Cotter pins were used on primitive furniture throughout the 18th century, but iron or brass hinges were used on most furniture from the earliest part of the 18th century on. The big iron hinges that people mistakenly associate with "Colonial" furniture were originally used more for architectural purposes than for furniture. It was not until the late 19th century and early part of the 20th century that restorers and manufacturers of reproduction furniture started using these hinges and they then started working their way into the fakes and frauds because that is what people expected to see.

Few cotter pin hinges are left in existence, but even fewer original cotter pins exist that are still holding a drop drawer pull in place. Original drawer hardware can be hard to find still intact. Drawers are one of the most commonly used component on a piece of furniture. Handles and pulls break and fall off, and tastes change. Some people change the hardware on a newly acquired piece of furniture just because they don't like it.

Wooden knobs were the standard for drawers and doors on 17th century furniture and continued to be the most commonly used pulls on primitive furniture and simple styles of furniture like Shaker furniture for many years. The back of the knob had a dowel attached which went through the drawer or door to attach it. There was often a hole in the dowel and a pin would be placed through the dowel on the inside of the drawer to hold the knob in place. At the end of the 17th century and the beginning of the 18th century, cotter pins were used to hold the pull in place. There is usually evidence left on the wood on the inside of the drawer or door from the spread of the cotter pins.

The wooden knob on the left has a dowel which penetrates through the drawer front and is then secured on the inside of the drawer. The knob on the right has a screw which is inserted from the inside of the drawer and then screwed into the knob to secure it.

During the first part of the 18th century, the plate between the handle and the wood of the drawer front changed from a small piece which served little purpose except for covering the hole for the drop handle, to a large plate covering two holes and extending down to protect the wood from damage from hanging bail handles and drop handles. The plates were often decorated with hammered punchwork for an engraved appearance. A genuine antique with its original hardware will often have scars on the wood where the bail or drop has rubbed the wood and left an arc-like indention in the wood by the pull. If the damage and the pull line up, you know you have an original match. If you do not see scars by the pull on an old piece of furniture with drop pulls, check the inside of the drawer or door to see if the hardware is original or if it has been replaced. There should be a single hole, centrally located, and there should be a cotter pin mark if the drop pull was original.

Drawer pulls like the one on the left can damage the wood or the finish on a piece of furniture. The Hepplewhite style handle on the right has a back plate which provides protection from damage from the bail.

The brass on older plates should be thicker than what is found on more modern plates. Old brass hardware was often hand-finished and the edges were hand filed. You should still be able to see evidence of the filing if you check the edges with a magnifying glass. Check the back of the plate to see if it has a grainy texture or if it is smooth. A grainy texture on the back will tell you the piece was cast in sand. Reproduction brass hardware is cut from sheet brass so it will have a smooth back. Sometimes you will find the backplates are original but the bails have been replaced. Modern bails are rounded on the ends whereas handmade bails had sharp ends and are rough to the touch. Earlier bails turned inward towards themselves forming a "C" shape and the holes were not spaced very far apart. On later bails the ends spread further apart and turned outward.

Some furniture from the Federal era had brass pulls with two small round or oval plates covering the two side holes, but did not have a back plate or anything to prevent the bail from hitting the wood. These drawers will often have sustained damage from the oval plates digging into the wood and from the bail wearing a groove into the wood. Most brass pulls from the Federal era had an oval or round back plate which protected the wood from the bail. These plates were stamped from thin metal and usually had edges turned back towards the wood. The edges would, over time, dig into the wood behind them creating a permanent scar. As the Federal period progressed the holes for the bails on the drawer pulls returned to being closer and closer together, and by 1830 the pull was once again a single knob with one hole.

19th century knob handles were made of a variety of materials – brass, glass, or wood were all common. Regardless of the material, the knob screwed on to a threaded shaft which penetrated the drawer, and a nut was screwed on to the inside to fasten it in place. All types of hardware in an assortment of sizes and shapes could be found during this time period. Then, hardware changed to resemble the knobs we are familiar with today – where the head of a bolt was placed flush with the inside of the drawer and the knob would be screwed onto it on the front of the drawer acting as a "nut" to hold the knob in place.

The early 1900s introduce a new popular type of hardware made from *pot metal*. Pot metal was inexpensive to produce and could be finished to duplicate more expensive hardware. But once broken it is irreparable.

If you discover a multitude of holes inside one drawer, carefully check the other drawers around it to make sure they have similar holes. If they do not match up, you may have a piece of furniture made up from pieces of other furniture. There should be consistency within the piece of furniture.

Many furniture repairers do not take the time to conceal holes when replacing old hardware with new. A quick look inside the drawers will often show a collection of holes of various sizes and spacings. Quite often, if the holes do not show on the front of the piece the inside is left well enough alone. When earlier hardware was replaced by larger hardware or hardware which had a back plate covering the holes, it was often thought unnecessary to bother filling the unused holes. Sometimes one of the original holes would be used for the new hardware and one new hole would be drilled to accommodate a new wider pull. These new holes were made to accommodate bolts not cotterpins. Quite often the soft wood on the inside of the drawer front was damaged by the bolt and nut being over-tightened until it dug into the wood in an effort to countersink it so it would not snag the contents of the drawer.

Early nuts and bolts were more primitive than their modern counterparts and were irregular in shape. Early bolts like early screws were often square at the top of the shank. Modern ones, of course, are round. Modern nuts are usually square, or at least flat-sided. Old nuts tend to be round. Nuts and bolts were often made to fit each other, and it is important to mark them if they are removed so they can be rematched properly before being reattached.

It is probably safe to say the older a piece of furniture the greater the chance the furniture will *not* still have its original set of hardware intact. Handles and hinges were subjected to constant use, and will eventually break or wear out and need to be replaced. If the hardware is replaced with hardware from the correct period, and it matches up to the existing holes in the furniture it is almost impossible to determine whether it is original to the furniture or if it is a replacement.

Modern technology has created reproduction hardware which can duplicate 18th and 19th century so closely identification of the reproduction from the original can be difficult. Many of these pieces are perfect in replicating details and can even duplicate the content of the brass to the point where a metallurgical laboratory might not be able to differentiate between the newer piece and the older one. This can come in handy if you are trying to replace missing hardware on an antique piece. But can also be used to a disadvantage by someone who is unscrupulous. Older hardware should have wear marks and the metal should be aged and have a patina.

Some people feel confident they can identify brass hardware as antique based on its color, but this can be difficult even for a well-trained expert eye. Older brass used to have a higher copper content than modern brass (about 75% copper to 25% zinc versus the 60% copper 40% zinc used today) but the "modern" brass has been around since the 1920s and will often be so aged and patinaed it is all but impossible to differentiate between an older piece and a newer one. Older brass can be polished to shine like new, and newer brass can be artificially "patinaed" to look old. One of the only definitive ways to identify a newer brass piece is to remove it from the furniture and examine it with a magnifying glass. A newer piece should show traces the piece has been cast or stamped instead of cut from the metal. Handle posts will often show a very fine seam on the shank, just above the threads.

Older brass escutcheons, handle plates and other small brass decorative pieces can often be distinguished between their more modern counterparts by examining them with a magnifying glass. The detailing on the older handles is more crisp and defined, the modern versions are noticeably less so.

A carved wooden drawer pull with fruit and leaves.

Some drawer pulls are not made of metal but are instead carved from wood. This is especially true on Victorian furniture made from oak or walnut. Wooden drawer pulls were often ornately carved in the shape of fruit, flowers and leaves. Some other antique furniture has glass or porcelain handles or pulls. Reproductions are available and can be "aged" to make them look more like the originals.

Pro Tip: Some pieces of furniture did not originally have brass hardware when they were manufactured and the hardware on it today was added later. Turned wooden knobs cost very little to produce, and furniture buyers could purchase some furniture with plain knobs and then save up their money to buy more expensive brass hardware at a later date when they could afford it.

Locks - While most hardware can not verify the age of a piece of furniture, there is one piece that can – the lock. Eighteenth century furniture manufactured up until about 1780 will usually have a thin-gauge steel case with a steel bolt inside the lock. These older locks were simple *back-spring locks*. As technology improved the back-spring locks were fitted with *wards* to provide more security. Wards are thin curved lengths of metal fitted to the inside of the case and cap, centered on the pin, which made an extra barrier that had to be matched by slotted wards in the key bit before the key would move the bolt and open the lock.

Some locks were secured with four screws and the lock case will have four holes drilled in it to allow the screws to be countersunk. Other locks had two countersunk holes for screws at the top of the lock case and two small holes at the bottom of the case for nails. Screws were expensive and difficult to make and this rationing of screws helped to defray the expenses of manufacturing.

Brass lock cases came into common usage in the late 18th century and locks became more sophisticated and more secure. Steel back-spring bolt and wards locks were still manufactured, but *tumbler locks* were becoming more widely used and locking mechanisms quickly became more complex. Smaller tumbler locks used on little doors or drawers commonly had one or two parts on the steel bolt. Larger doors would have locks with three or four parts on the bolt. Tumbler locks and back-spring locks were both used through the Victorian period and it is sometimes difficult to differentiate between the two without opening the lock to see the internal components.

The *lever lock* came into production during the middle of the 19th century. The early ones had brass cases with a steel bolt, and often had the words "secure" and/or "lever" stamped on the bolt face of the case. "Patent" was also frequently stamped on many bolt faces, but this was no gurantee the lock was truly patented. As a general rule, the more lettering you find stamped on a bolt face, the less likely the lock is an early made one.

The Victorian *Chubb "detector" lever locks* usually had a serial number stamped on the bolt face which can help date the lock and the furniture. The Chubb lever locks were unique in that they were designed to jam if the wrong key was used or any attempt was made to pick the lock. If a key was used that did not precisely operate each of the seven levers the lock would jam and would only be able to be freed by the correct key.

You can check to see if the lock currently on the furniture is the original lock by removing it and looking at the wood around the lock area. If there are screw holes that do not line up with the screws used to hold the current lock, then you will have evidence the lock has been changed. If there are no other screw holes it is a safe assumption the lock is original. Some locks can be determined not to be original even before they are removed. If the lock does not fit completely into the area carved for it, then it is probably not the original. If the lock is too small there will be a gap around it or there may be small pieces of wood fitted around the lock to fill the gap. If the lock is too large you can often see evidence that wood around the lock has been chiseled away to accommodate the new, larger lock.

If you remove a lock from a piece of furniture for any

reason, carefully mark the screws so you can return them to their original location. Do not overtighten the screws when replacing them. Check to make sure the lock works properly *before* you close the drawer or door. A lock may decide to freeze-up and refuse to unlock because of pressure on the cap caused by over-tightened screws.

This sounds almost too obvious to even mention, but a lock will also suddenly refuse to open because you are using the wrong key. Check to make sure you have the correct key, and *never* try to force an old lock. Spray some WD-40 or graphite into the lock to lubricate the mechanism and then use gentle pressure and wiggle the key slightly clockwise and then counterclockwise to try to loosen the stuck lock. As mentioned previously, some locks were originally manufactured with an added security feature to prevent them from being picked, and any effort to open the lock with any key but the correct key will cause the lock to jam.

If a lock is missing, it generally will not devalue a piece of furniture. If the lock is replaced it will also usually not devalue the piece as long as you do not have to cut away wood to make the replacement lock fit.

Some pieces of furniture need to be kept locked to keep the doors from swinging open. However, I have found from personal experience (expensive personal experience at that!) it is not a good idea to lock an old lock unless it *needs* to be locked. Old locks can decide to break when you least expect them to, and locksmiths who make housecalls can be very expensive. If you should decide to experiment with an old lock do so with the drawer removed or the door open. *Do not* experiment with an old lock under any other conditions.

Keys - Since we are on the subject of locks, we should briefly mention keys. Many antique dealers and proud owners will boast about having the original key to a piece of furniture.

Antique dealers and auction houses may even charge extra for the keys. While it is often the case the key is original, odd keys can frequently be purchased at garage sales and flea markets and a collection of keys will often contain one that is the perfect match for a lock.

New keys can also be "aged" to look like original keys. After the key is cut to fit the lock, the ring at the top of the key can be widened and narrowed with files or dremmel tools, and the key can then be rubbed down with emery cloth to remove the tell-tale "new look". The metal can also be aged by soaking it in ammonia or a mild acid.

Old keys can often be found at garage sales and thrift stores and your collection can come in handy when working with antique furniture. New keys can be "aged" to make them appear old.

Escutcheons - Until the 19th century, most furniture containing doors or drawers was equipped with locks. All furniture except the most primitive or plain had *escutcheons* around the key holes, and of all of the old hardware you may encounter, original escutcheons are the most likely to have survived because they are difficult to remove without causing damage to the surrounding wood. Escutcheons surrounded the key hole and protected the furniture from potential damage from the rough edges of a key. Some small drawers which did not have locks had escutcheons applied for decorative affect. Escutcheons varied in geometric shapes and decorative designs, but the majority were cut from pieces of sheet brass and had their designs and decorations pressed into them. Escutcheons from the late 18th century had much sharper detailing than their 20th century counterparts.

Escutcheons can be made from wood or metal and be simple metal inserts or decorative shapes applied to the wood surface.

Wooden escutcheons could be elegantly carved or simple raised-edged buttons. These thin wooden carvings took a lot of abuse from keys and use and it is not uncommon to find the escutcheons broken or missing.

Replacements are easy to find at woodworking supply stores, and the repair job is quite simple to do. Use a knife blade or a chisel to carefully pry off any broken pieces. Use white vinegar applied to a soft rag to remove old glue from the area. Use hide glue or woodworking glue to secure the replacement escutcheon in place. Allow the glue to dry completely. Then touch up the color of the escutcheon to match the rest of the furniture if necessary.

Casters - *Casters* (or *castors*) are small wheels which are applied to the legs or feet of furniture to make it easier to move without lifting. Our ancestors frequently moved tables and chairs about the house on a daily basis. Furniture was pushed against the wall when not in use to save space and brought into the middle of the room when needed.

Swiveling castors were invented in the early 1700s. The material used for the wheels evolved from wood, to leather, to brass which came into use around 1770. Early casters were mounted to a brass pad fastened to the bottom of a furniture leg with small screws. During the late 1700s, casters began to be mounted on brass sockets which were fastened to the thin tapering furniture legs in vogue at the time. The rollers on these casters were made of iron or brass. Modern casters are principally made of rubber and synthetic materials.

Casters were rarely used on American furniture prior to the American Revolution, but afterwards became commonplace on furniture which needed to be moved around for use. The Federal era brought with it brass-wheeled casters to decorate the furniture and raise it off the floor. Most of these casters fit into holes drilled into the feet, but some surround the foot with a decorative brass cuff.

The caster as we know it today, which fits inside a hole drilled inside the leg of the furniture, first appeared about 1820. The white ceramic caster commonly found on Victorian antiques did not come in to common usage until around the middle of the 19th century. Nineteenth century furniture was often manufactured with casters, but not all 19th century pieces had them. During this time period, many people added casters to their furniture. Holes were drilled into furniture feet, and legs and feet were cut off to accommodate the addition of a caster. Even ball and claw feet were not safe and were sawn in half so the furniture could accept a caster. All of this drilling and sawing devalued the furniture and left many pieces with unstable feet or legs.

A quick look at the size of the screws or tacks used to attach the caster to the furniture and the thickness of the feet or legs should give you an idea of the original intent of the casters.

Old casters can be made inefficient by age and wear and can snag on carpet or an uneven floor. Because of the potential damage, most old furniture should be lifted, when feasible, instead of pushed or pulled. Old casters and modern wall to wall carpet can be a bad combination for an old dry furniture leg, and the pressure caused on the leg if furniture is pushed across carpet may cause the wood to break.

Furniture casters consist of a wheel, a stem or shaft that goes up into the leg or foot of the furniture and a tube-shaped socket which holds the stem in place and prevents the metal from wearing out the wood. Some casters have an optional hood over the wheel. The base plate of the socket has sharp teeth which secure the socket to the foot or leg. If the wood shrinks, or the teeth lose their grip, the socket and the caster can become wobbly and fall out.

The caster on the left has a metal shaft which fits into the leg of the furniture. The caster on the right has a cuff which encloses the bottom of the leg. It is held in place with a small tack or a screw.

Some casters are part of the original design and construction of the furniture and removing them can ruin both the lines and the functuality of the piece. Other casters were added after the furniture was manufactured and can potentially damage the structure of the feet or legs.

The design of the leg and the feet, and the age and style of the furniture will usually provide clues as to whether casters were an original part of the furniture. If the feet currently have no casters, look at the underside of the feet for evidence of previous casters. An open hole or a filled hole is usually evidence a caster used to be there. If the caster had been of the cuff variety, you should see evidence on the back of the leg or foot of the small nail which would have held the cuff in place. Furniture with its casters removed will generally lose anywhere from one to two inches in height resulting in chairs which are too short to reach their matching table, or tables of an unusual height. The empty sockets can snag carpets and scratch floors.

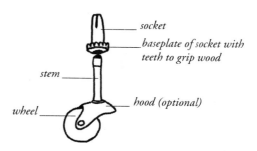

Repairing loose caster sockets - Remove the caster socket from the leg and coat the outside of it with epoxy putty. Be careful not to get any epoxy on the top end of the socket; it may interfere with the tip of the shaft. Tap the socket back into the hole, then lightly grease the shaft, especially the tip, and drive it into the socket. The grease will make the insertion easier and will help to prevent epoxy from accidentally adhering to the shaft. As the epoxy cures turn the shaft from time to time to make sure it is not being held by the epoxy.

Repairing loose casters - A temporary caster repair can be made by winding a small piece of steel wool or plastic tape around the stem to make it fit more tightly in the socket.

Labels, Stencils, Brands and Cabinetmaker's Marks

Many furniture manufacturers applied paper labels to the back of furniture or on the side of the drawers. Tables often have a label on the underside of the table top, or on top of the base on a table which pulls open to add leaves. Desks may have

119

a label on the side of a drawer or on the back of the small door separating the cubbyholes. Chair labels can be found on the underside of the seat.

Many of these labels have been damaged or completely destroyed from age and use unless they were in a protected area of the furniture. Paper labels will become brittle, yellowed and darkened with age, and the glue holding the label to the furniture will often have deteriorated. The edges on the label should show wear and the corners will often become rounded. Wood will darken as it ages from exposure to light, dirt and other contaminates. The wood under a label will have been protected from exposure since the label was applied and should be a lighter color than the wood surrounding the label. Dark wood under a label or wood lacking this pale color in a protected area is a dead give-away the label is not original to the piece or the label has been removed and re-applied.

Some furniture repair books recommend covering an old paper label with a coat or two of semi-gloss polyurethane varnish to protect it from deterioration. This is *not* a good idea. Polyurethane can irreversibly and permanently damage labels and cause old ink to smear and bleed making them illegible. Once the varnish is applied it can not be removed without causing further damage to the label. If you feel the label needs protection, a piece of plastic wrap cut larger than the label can be placed over it and then held in place with tape. *Do not* allow the tape to come in contact with the label.

If the glue on a label has worn away and part (or all) of the label is coming loose, you can use toothpicks to help work a little bit of "all purpose glue" under the label. Use glue sparingly – do not saturate the label. Gently tap the label in place with your fingertips. Carefully wipe off any excess glue.

Some furniture manufacturers stenciled their company name or other information (item numbers or stock numbers) on the furniture in an inconspicuous spot. Others used a hot branding iron and branded the furniture with this information.

Some manufacturers used pencil or chalk to record this information.

Branded labels showing the company name, stock number and an inspector's approval stamp.

Cabinetmaker's marks identified not only the company but often the particular craftsman. Most cabinetmakers did not mark their furniture, and many older pieces found today containing marks are not authentic. It is believed 1% of all pre-Civil War furniture has an original manufacturer's mark and possibly as much as 60% of 20th century furniture has been marked.

An authentic mark or brand can help to confirm the age of a piece of furniture and add to its value. However, fake brands and marks can be easily applied to furniture. Advertisements can be cut out of old magazines and newspapers and "labels" can be created and glued on to the furniture to try to prove its age. Since so few early pieces of furniture were originally marked, anyone who thinks they have an original mark on a potentially valuable piece of furniture should have its authenticity confirmed by an expert.

Before the invention of shelf lining paper, old newspapers were used to line drawers. Many drawers were coated with a thin coat of shellac to help seal the wood and prevent it from absorbing odors or moisture. The shellac would soften during warm weather and some of the newspapers would occassionally get stuck in the finish. Today you may find pages of newspapers still stuck inside the drawers and the articles can help date a piece of furniture. But remember, some newspapers may have been kept for sentimental reasons and some may have been recently stuck in the finish in an attempt to "age" the piece of furniture. Newspapers should not be used as the only piece of evidence when trying to prove the age of a piece of furniture.

Part of a newspaper clipping found stuck in the finish on the bottom of a drawer describing a memorial service after the death of Chief Seattle.

Glass

You will only encounter panels of glass used for two purposes on antique furniture: as an insert to a cabinet door or as a mirror. Glass table tops were not found on antique furniture.

Old glass, truly old glass, is very easy to identify. It was made by hand and was either blown or cast. It has a characteristic tint, an uneven thickness and usually contains imperfections. Clear, perfectly smooth glass was not produced until the late 19th century. If you hold a white piece of paper behind a pane of old glass it will no longer appear clear and will have a yellow or blue tint caused by the metallic impurities in the glass. The glass is also seldom flat and will usually curve in one direction or the other. Unfortunately, only a few pieces of very old furniture still have their original glass panes – and most of them are in museums or private collections. The good news is that because old glass is extremely brittle it is almost never found reworked into a piece of furniture "created" by a faker.

Glass panes are held in place with thin strips of wood called *muntins* and with glazier's putty. Unlike window glass, furniture glass is puttied on the inside not the outside of the pane. The strips of wood holding the glass panes on the furniture may well be original on many pieces of furniture, but on a very old piece, the glass may not. Glass panes can be found in a variety of pieces of furniture including secretary desks, hutches, sideboards and china closetss.

Mirrors are commonplace in homes today, and are often taken for granted. But this was not always the case. Before the invention of mirror plating, mirrors were made from burnished plates of gold or silver. Less expensive mirrors could also be made from pewter or other base metals. Early plate glass mirrors were handmade using a long difficult process. Glass was blown into cylinders which were slit open, flattened and then silvered on the back with a coating of mercury. The resulting mirrors were small because of the limitations of the process involved in creating them. These early mirrors were a very high priced luxury item which could only be afforded by the very rich and powerful. At one time mirrors were one of the most sought after luxury items in Europe. Catherine de Medici created an extravagant room in her home paneled with 109 Venetian mirrors. Louis XIV's minister of finance is said to have owned a mirror which was valued at more than the price of one of his Raphael paintings. These were the exceptions rather than the rule.

The original process for creating *looking glasses* (as they were originally called, and remained named until about 1875) was discovered around 1480 in Venice. The process was a closely guarded secret and divulging the information was a crime punishable by death. Glassmakers were forbidden to travel beyond their local area, but the knowledge of the process eventually made its way across Europe and beyond. Even so, mirror making remained an expensive and exclusive process. A mirror manufactory was built in Paris in 1665 allowing Charles Le Brun and Jules Hardouin-Mansart to complete the Hall of Mirrors at Versailles for Louis XIV. During the 1680s, a 3 foot by 4 foot mirror may have been worth as much as $40,000 in today's currency. Because of the expense and time involved in creating a new mirror, old ones were frequently reframed to keep up with the latest changes in furniture fashions.

The mirror production process became more techno-logically advanced in the early part of the 1800s. This allowed mirrors to became more affordable and commonplace and by 1820, they could be found in most working class homes. By the 1870s, working class families may have had as many as twelve or more mirrors of various sizes in their homes.

Large mirrors were manufactured to be placed between doors or windows (these mirrors were called *pier glass* or *pier mirrors*), and small mirrors were available in almost every size and shape. Nearly every type of cabinet wood was used as a mirror frame, but, by the end of the 19th century, oak framed mirrors were the most popular and remained so for almost half a century. The oak wood used on mirror frames was not usually used in its natural light color. It was often fumed or artificially darkened or painted white, green or black. Small and medium-sized mirrors in a variety of shapes from square and rectangular to oblong, had double hooks attached and were placed on the wall in entryways to hold small articles of clothing and hats since most houses did not have entry closets at the turn of the century. The hooks could be plain or fancy shapes resembling plant or animal forms.

Oak framed mirrors continue to be reproduced today because the style has remained so popular. Check to make sure the age of the hardware matches the age of the frame. Beware of mirrors with tin backs or pieces of oak joined together with modern angle irons. Check the mirror using the tests described on page 127 to help determine the age of the glass.

Pier glass mirrors were manufactured to hang on walls and flank doors and windows of Victorian parlors and drawing rooms. Long mirrors attached to dressing tables and bureaus were usually smaller than pier glass mirrors (usually 36" to 44" in height) and have screw holes at the base of the mirror frame, or metal supports or other evidence of where they were attached to a piece of furniture rather than hung on a wall. Some large Victorian mirrors were made to hang over fireplace mantles. These can be differentiated from pier glass mirrors by their width. Mantle mirrors were wider than pier glass mirrors.

Cheval mirrors were portable mirrors which could be placed on top of dressers or dry sinks and used while shaving, grooming or dressing. During the Queen Anne period, a similar mirror was called a *dressing glass* or *dressing mirror*. During other periods they were known as *shaving glasses* or *toilet glasses*. These mirrors were usually mounted on adjustable swivels in a frame (usually made of wood), and often had one or two drawers underneath the mirror. During the last decade of the 18th century, the mirror making process had advanced so that single pane mirrors could be successfully cast in larger sizes, often in excess of ten feet in heighth. These larger standing Cheval mirrors were called *horse dressing glasses* because of their four-legged frame. Some frames had adjustable candleholders attached which is usually an indication of a quality mirror, and will generally increase the value of the mirror.

During the Victorian periods cheval mirrors were also made from cast iron. Cast iron was typically painted white, but other colors were available. Few pieces probably remain with their original paint intact. Cast iron pieces were durable but occasionally sustained damage which was subsequently repaired by soldering. A coat of paint was often applied over the repaired area to help camouflage the spot. Examine the backs and underside of any cast iron cheval mirror for evidence of repairs. The backs and underside were usuallynot painted by the manufacturer. If paint is present it is proof the piece has been repainted and may have been repaired.

Cheval mirrors remained popular until about World War I. By that time, the cheval mirror had become obsolete because most people had dressers or dressing tables with mirrors or used wall hung mirrors.

Some Cheval mirrors for sale today started their life attached to a dresser or dressing table and have been modified to make them look like cheval mirrors. Check the bottom and lower front of the mirror frame. If there is evidence of screw holes, or filled screw holes, the piece was once attached to another piece of furniture and is not an original cheval mirror.

Mirror boxes took portability one step further than the cheval mirror. Mirrored dressing boxes were used by travelers so they could have a mirror with them wherever they stayed. These boxes also contained space for shaving accessories and toiletries and often had a drawer underneath the box. The box opened to reveal the mirror which was propped up on the front edge of the box during use. Mirror boxes were often custom made and were decorated with gilding, ivory, stenciling and expensive veneers.

Mirrors were added to a vast number of pieces of furniture – dressers, vanities, dry sinks, sideboards, hall trees, armoires and many more pieces. The mirrors were held in place by backboards usually made from the same unfinished wood which was used for the other secondary wood on the furniture. The backboard was attached to the case of the furniture with small tacks or nails. The backboard protected the delicate silvered mirror backing and provided support to keep the mirror frame square and rigid.

Manufacturer's labels were often glued on the outside of the backboard, but can also be found on the inside of the backboard or on the back of the glass itself. A manufacturing date can also occasionally be found stamped on the back of the mirror. The presence of a label or stamp can increase the value of the mirror and help to date the piece if it is suthentic.

It is easy to determine whether a mirror is made from old glass or more modern glass. A little detective work will easily uncover the differences. Tap a coin on a piece of old glass and you will hear a definite, sharp tinny ringing sound. Tap a coin on a modern mirror and you will hear a more muted dull sound. Old mirror glass seldom exceeded 3/16" and is considerably thinner than glass used today. Very old glass is always thicker at the bottom than it is at the top because it had a tendency to sag. Modern glass is nearly double the thickness of old glass – averaging between 1/4" to 3/8" thick. You can check the thickness of the glass by placing the edge of a coin or a business card against the surface of the mirror. The distance between the reflection and the coin or card will equal the thickness of the plate of glass.

Many older mirrors had beveled edges. The beveling process on pre-Victorian mirrors was done by hand with a pumice stone and the beveling often appears irregular, uneven and soft-edged. Modern beveling is achieved by using a machine with a sandstone wheel. This results in a hard, sharply defined edge. If the beveled mirror edge produces prismatic colors when viewed from an angle this is usually an indication the mirror has been made from new glass.

Old glass will have a yellowish or grayish reflective color. New glass has a colorless very clear reflective quality. To check the color, hold a plain white card against the mirror's surface. If the reflection is a close match to the true color of the paper it is probably Victorian glass or modern glass. If the reflection has a yellow, blue or gray tone to it the glass is old. This dark tone is caused by the high tin content of the glass itself, not from the silvering on the back.

The backing on an old mirror was silvered by pouring on a combination of mercury and tin and then spreading it with brushes towards the edges. When all of the backing was coated, the mirror was tipped so the excess solution could run off the edges. Some areas of the mirror would retain more solution than others which would result in an uneven finish. You can often see evidence of the brush marks or unevenness showing through the mirror as the silvering starts to age and deteriorate. Modern glass is coated with a thin layer of silver or aluminum and then finished with an application of lacquer.

Mirrors exposed to moisture or humidity (and some-times just time itself) will eventually develop age spots which will appear as non-reflective grey spots on the mirror's face. This will occur regardless of the technique used to create the backing. On old glass, these spots will often appear as large swipes or blobs. These are a result of the uneven application of the mercury and tin during the silvering process.

Silvering on old mirrors will break down and deterio-rate from the center of the mirror to the outer edges and even-tually from one end to the other. These defects can be removed by having the mirror professionally re-silvered. But be forewarned – re-silvering can be very expensive. Ask around your local antique stores or contact some local appraisers for the name of a professional who specializes in re-silvering and ask to see samples of their work *before* you have your mirror done.

If your mirror is old or a true antique it should not be re-silvered. A perfect antique mirror is usually concealing a previous repair or could possibly be a fake. Very few perfect antique mirrors exist, and most of them are in museums. Imperfections add to the authenticity, and may actually add to the value. In some cases, original glass in a mirror may increase the value by as much as 25-50%. If the silvering has deteriorated to the point where a mirror's usefulness has been diminished by the defects, remove the mirror, store the original, and fill the mirror frame with a quality replacement. In most cases replacement glass will not significantly detract from the value of the piece.

Some new mirrors are given an "aged" "antique look" by scraping the mercury amalgam from the back of old mirrors and then applying it to the back of the new mirror. This gives the new mirror a mottled look that duplicates the look of an aged mirror. Mercury is poisonous, costly and extremely difficult to work with and is no longer used commercially in the United States for mirror backings. It has been replaced by the silvering process. You can often tell what has been used for the backing on the mirror by looking at the color of the glass. Mercury backings will create a blue-toned reflection. Silver backings result in a brighter warmer reflection.

Some refinishing books recommend you strip the silvering off the back of a mirror yourself before taking it to a professional for re-silvering. They suggest this will save you money and will be appreciated by the professional. It won't save you money, and it probably won't be appreciated by the professional either. Some may not even accept the job if the mirror is stripped when you bring it to them, as they will have no knowledge what chemicals you have used or to what contaminates the mirror may have been exposed. If the mirror is old, it deserves to be taken to a professional and have the job done right or leave well enough alone.

Some mirrors may look like they are in perfect condition – no flaws, no age spots, and yet something just doesn't seem right. In those cases you might want to remove the backboard and check to see if someone may have stripped the silvering completely off of the old mirror until it was a clear piece of glass, and then had a new mirror cut to put behind it in the frame. The old, usually beveled glass in the front will give the illusion of a beveled glass mirror. The give-away here is the added layer will usually provide a different depth to the mirror. It is cheaper to have a new unbeveled mirror cut and put behind a stripped piece of beveled glass than to have a replacement beveled glass mirror made. This is not an uncommon practice.

In the early 1800s mirror frames covered in gilding were quite popular. Some of these frames had large carved crests and many used patriotic motifs (eagles, flames, laurels, etc.) and had attached candle brackets. Some of these frames incorporated a chain with a small hanging ball suspended in front of the mirror. This was supposed to help keep flies off of the mirror and gilding to prevent fly specks and damage. Unfortunately, when central heat started to become popular in the 1900s the gilding on the frames was exposed to a fluctuation of temperature changes which eventually destroyed many of the gilded surfaces. Damaged frames were often painted with gold or bronze paint instead of regilding to conceal the damaged gilded finish. If the frame was finished with *water gilding* you may be able to remove the paint without damaging the gilding underneath. Of course, once the paint is removed you will be faced with whatever damage caused the frame to be painted in the first place.

To test the finish to see if you can safely remove the paint, use a cotton swab dipped in mineral spirits and lightly rub the surface in an inconspicuous area. You should not see paint or finish on the swab but you will probably see dirt. Next dip a swab in denatured alcohol and rub in an inconspicuous area. Again, you should not see paint or finish on the swab. Finally dip a swab into a paint stripper containing dichloromethane and methanol. Lightly rub in an inconspicuous area. The paint stripper will start to remove the paint but will not damage the gilding *if the gilding is water gilding.* If the gilding is oil gilding it will also be removed by the stripper and you will start to see the *gesso* or *bole* underneath the gilding, or possibly bare wood.

Gilding involves applying expensive sheets of gold leaf to a surface primed with gesso and bole. Bole is a type of burnishing clay used to smooth out irregularities in gessoed surfaces and it adds a color base under gilding which enhances areas where the gold leaf is missing or could not be applied such as carved areas and crevices. Gilding requires special tools, lots of time and patience and a substantial amount of money. If you have a frame that needs to be regilded, you would be better off seeking professional help with the project rather than attempting to do it yourself, especially if the piece is old or valuable.

Cleaning a mirror - Carefully rub the surface of the mirror with a ball of newspaper or white paper towels dampened with denatured alcohol, or rubbing alcohol diluted with water. Rub and buff until dry. To avoid damage to the mirror backing always apply the moisture to the paper towel or paper and *never* directly to the mirror. Never allow the cleaner to run around the edges.

Commercial window cleaners are not recommended for use on new or old glass mirrors because they can cause the silver backing to oxidize almost immediately on contact. Virtually any cleaner including vinegar, ammonia or alcohol can potentially damage the backing, but the high alkaline content in commercial spray cleaners makes them the harshest and most dangerous of all.

Many newer mirrors are made with a sealer over the silvering to help prevent damage to the backing. A light coat of clear spray varnish can be applied to the back of an older mirror to help protect the silvering and prevent potential moisture damage.

Patching the silvering on a mirror - A non-permanent non-damaging repair can be done to most older mirrors which have thin spots and streaks. Carefully remove the wooden backboard from the mirror. Measure the size of the damaged area on the silvered backing. Cut a piece of reflecting foil (available at crafts supply stores and some woodworking supply stores) or a piece of reflective film (the kind used for tinting windows) so the patch is the size of the repair plus 1/2" on all sides. Carefully place the foil over the damaged area and use your fingers to smooth the foil over the backing. Use tape only if necessary to hold the film in place. Replace the wooden backing.

Replacing the backboard on a mirror - The wooden backing on a mirror is usually the same unfinished secondary wood used for backboards on dressers, chests and desks. The backboard protects the silvering on the mirror from damage and provides support to the frame to keep it square. Old mirror frames often have a collection of screwholes in the wood from attachments used to secure the mirror to walls or furniture during the course of its lifetime. If the holes have begun to join together and break the wood, or the wood dries out and begins to crack, the backboard will need to be replaced. If you believe your mirror is a true antique, consult a professional for this job to prevent damage to the old glass.

To replace the backboard: lay the mirror on a blanket or other padding on a firm surface such as a large table or on the floor. Use a tack puller and needle-nosed pliers to remove the tacks or staples. Be careful not to damage the mirror frame. Use the old back as a pattern and trace the shape on to a piece of plywood the same thickness as the original piece of wood. Cut the board along the traced lines. Carefully align the replacement board on to the back of the mirror. Fasten with tacks or small nails. You may want to pre-drill the holes a few sizes smaller than the tacks you are using to make it easier to hammer in the nails or tacks. Be careful the nails are not driven in too close to the mirror's edge as this can chip or crack the glass.

Mirror frames - Mirror frames can be made from a variety of materials – metal, plastic, ceramic and wood, just to name a few. Older mirrors (especially those produced before the 19th century) were almost always framed with wood. Many frames appear to be elaborately and decoratively carved, but the "carving" is often *gesso* (a hard, plaster-like substance) or plaster imposed on to the wood rather than carved into it. Gesso and plaster decorations are easily dented and chipped and can develop fine hairline cracks as the material ages.

During the 19th century, some "carved" frames were made from "compo". Compo consists of layers of putty-like stucco applied over a wirework frame, and then finished with gilding. These frames are easy to detect with a simple test. Stick a sewing needle into the reverse side of the frame. Compo will be easily penetrated by the needle but wood will not.

Many old frames become "out of square" causing the mitered corners to separate and the small nails holding the frame together to protrude from the surface. *Do not* be tempted to remove the nails. Once removed it can be difficult if not impossible to reassemble the frame. Squirt some glue into the corner and then use a tack hammer to tap the nails back into place. Be certain the frame is square up when you do this. If you do not have a carpenter's square available you can use a sheet of paper. Put a corner of the sheet of paper under a corner of the frame as you are reassembling it.

Reconstructing missing decorative pieces on mirror frames - Missing pieces of carved wood or gesso can be easy to repair or replace if the area is small. Larger areas are more difficult to repair and the repaired area is usually very obvious once the repairs are done. Broken or missing wood and gesso decorations can be repaired using the same techniques. If the mirror frame is a true antique the repair job should be left to a professional restoration service.

Remove any dust or flaking finish from the frame by lightly brushing with a soft, clean paint brush. Apply a thin layer of undiluted all purpose white glue to the damaged area on the frame. Allow the glue to dry while you mix up the gesso. This glue layer will act as a foundation for the repair.

Gesso is made by mixing together plaster of Paris, water and water-soluble white glue. A small glass dish or shot glass is usually the perfect size for mixing the ingredients. The mixture will begin to set very quickly, usually within three minutes, so you will want to mix small amounts at a time and work quickly. If the mixture dries to the point where it begins to crumble it will not adhere properly to the frame and you will need to discard it and mix another batch.

Use a measuring spoon and measure 1/2 teaspoon of plaster of Paris into your container. Add a little bit of water (use an eye dropper if you have one) and a little bit of water-soluble white glue. Stir the mixture with a popsicle stick or other small piece of wood to combine the ingredients. Mixing gesso is one of those "learn as you go" kind of things. Too much water will make the mixture too runny, too much glue will make the mixture too glossy or shiny and will make it brittle and difficult to sand when it dries. Add a little more plaster of Paris to correct a runny mixture or a little more water to help correct the addition of too much glue. If all else fails, throw away the batch and start over.

When the gesso is properly mixed, remove it from the container and roll it between your fingers like putty. Form it into a ball and quickly apply it to the damaged area on the frame. Use your fingers to shape the gesso to match the surrounding design. Tools used for creating pottery, popsicle sticks, toothpicks and a variety of other household items can be used to shape the gesso into the approximate shapes of the missing decorations.

Allow the gesso to dry overnight. When completely dry, it will have a chalky consistency. Sand any rough areas very gently with super-fine sandpaper. Use a small chisel, file, or emery board to help define the design if necessary. Brush any sanding dust from the area with a soft clean paint brush. Carefully wipe the frame with a *tack rag* to remove any traces of dust, then seal the repair with a coat of shellac to protect it from moisture.

If the damaged area is large, repeat the process, mixing additional small batches of gesso until all of the repairs have been made.

Blend the repair to the rest of the frame by matching the color and finish of the frame.

If you are trying to repair a large area on a frame you may want to make a mold so you do not have to sculpt the designs freehand.

To do this, buy some soft modeling clay (the kind that does not harden when it is exposed to air and can be reused over and over). Break off a small piece of clay and knead it between your fingers until it is pliable. Flatten the clay until it is about 1/2" thick and big enough to cover the damaged area you want to duplicate. Chose an area of the design which is intact and matches the damaged area. Dust it with a thin coat of flour. Place the piece of modeling clay over the design and press down firmly. Wait a few minutes, then carefully peel the clay away from the frame. Be careful not to distort the shape.

Mix a batch of gesso, but make it just a bit thinner than usual. Spoon the gesso into the mold. Allow the gesso to dry overnight before removing it from the mold. Use an X-Acto knife or single edged razor blade to trim off any excess dried gesso and to make the molded part fit properly. If you do not end up with a perfect match, thin gaps can be filled in later with dabs of another batch of gesso.

Apply a layer of white glue to the frame then position the replacement part in place. Use pieces of masking tape to hold the pieces in place until the glue has a chance to set. When the replacement is set, mix up a thin batch of gesso and fill any gaps or small holes which may have appeared as the molded pieces dried. Lightly sand any rough spots with superfine sand paper or use an emery board. Remove any sanding dust with a tack rag, then apply a thin coat of shellac to the molded parts. When the shellac is dry, match the finish of the repaired area to the rest of the frame.

Repairing the finish of the frame -

This can be a broad topic, because the techniques used to repair the finish will obviously depend on the type of finish on the frame.

Repairing frames with a painted finish -
If the frame has a painted finish, and the area to be repaired is small, you can often *stretch the paint* to cover the chipped areas. Properly done, the repairs are almost imperceptible, and the color match is as close as you can get to the original paint – because it *is* the original paint. If the damage is extensive, the frame will need to be repainted.

Thoroughly clean the damaged area with white paper towels dampened with mineral spirits to remove any traces of dirt, wax or grime. Next, pour a small amount of paint stripper into a small glass jar or dish. Dip a very fine artist's brush into the stripper. Wipe off any excess on the rim of the dish, then very lightly brush the paint at the edges of the chip to soften the paint and then pull it over the cracked area. Repeat the process until the crack or chip is filled. Feather the edges to blend the repair.

Stained wooden and clear finished frames -
If the frame is made of stained wood, you can use oil paints or wood stain to stain the gesso to match the existing color of the frame.

Apply the colorant with a cotton swab, a small artist's brush or use your fingertip. Allow to dry completely. Seal the color under a light coat of shellac. Felt tip markers, (used to conceal scratches on furniture) can also be use to color gesso.

Scratches in the clear finish of a frame can be repaired by using a small artist's brush to lightly stroke shellac or varnish over the scratched area. Or, as a replacement, you can use clear nail polish to cover the scratches. Lightly feather the edges of the repair so they blend with the rest of the finish.

Less expensive wooden frames were often "grain-painted" or "false-grained" to imitate expensive figured wood. These grain-painted pieces were less expensive than their veneered counterparts during the 19th century, but are rare today. They can now be worth considerably more than veneered or solid wood frames if the paint on the frame is original and in good condition. Make sure any figured wood on your frame is really wood and not paint before attempting to repair it. Once damaged it can be difficult if not impossible to repair and the damage can significantly reduce the value of the piece.

Repairing frames with a gilt finish - If the frame has a gilt finish, and the damaged area is small, the gilt can be successfully repaired and blended into the undamaged area. Regilding small repairs on an antique mirror frame does not usually detract from its value *if* the gilt and the workmanship are of good quality, and the frame does not appear to be "new" or over-gilded as a result of the repairs. Old gilt will have a patina or rubbed sheen, and can add as much as 30-50 % to the value of the frame if left intact.

Prepare the surface before applying the gilt. A light coat of shellac applied over the gesso or the frame itself will provide a good base coat. Next, use a small artist's brush to apply a thin coat of liquid gold leaf paint. Work on a small area a time, but work fast – the solvent in the paint evaporates quickly and it will dry sooner than you expect. Gold leaf paint should not be used on large flat areas as this will accentuate the brush marks in the paint and make the repaired area very obvious. Allow the paint to dry completely before proceeding with the repair.

Do not use "gilt paint" or gold metallic paint in place of the liquid gold leaf paint. Paint is very runny, difficult to work with, and most brands contain no real gold. Gold leaf paint will also help blend the repaired area with the original finish on the rest of the frame and draw less attention to the repair.

To complete the repair, wax gilt should be applied over the gold leaf paint to highlight the frame and help duplicate the original finish. Wax gilt is made from real gold suspended in a wax and turpentine base. It is available in yellow gold and many other colors including brass, silver, rose gold, and white gold. Choose the color or combination of colors you will need to duplicate the original finish.

To apply wax gilt, dip a soft cloth in a little turpentine to moisten the cloth, then into the jar of wax gilt. A little wax gilt goes a long way so don't attempt to load-up the cloth with wax or apply it too heavily to the frame. Spread the gilt over the gold leaf paint and blend the edges of the repair to the undamaged area with light feathering strokes. Use light pressure during the application to help bring out the full color of the gilt. Work on a small area at a time, and brush back and forth to help bring up the sheen of the gilt. When all of the gilt has been applied, use a clean soft cloth to buff the finish to a sheen to match the original finish.

Check your local arts and crafts store or woodworking supply store for wax gilt and gold leaf paint.

If you encounter stains on a gilt frame, you can often remove them by gently dabbing the stained surface with a raw onion.

Genuine golf leaf - Genuine gold leaf is made from 22 to 23-1/2 carat gold beaten into very thin sheets – often less than 1/1000th of an inch thick. It is very expensive, very fragile and the prices can change with the fluctuations of the gold market. But it is one of the most beautiful types of furniture decoration available since the furniture is literally covered in real gold. You will want to carefully clean a golf leaf finish so you can retain as much of the original finish as possible. Use a new paint brush to clean the frame and remove accumulated dust and grime from the carving.

Gold leaf is sold in small squares which have a thin paper backing. Peel the backing off of the thin sheet to reveal an adhesive surface on the underside of the gold leaf. The sticky surface is then carefully applied to the frame, and then tapped into place with a small brush. The application of real gold leaf requires skill and very steady hands, and is not recommended for amateur refinishers. If you have an antique with gold leaf that needs repair, contact a professional.

Repairing cracks or dents in frames - Small cracks and dents can often be removed from mirror frames using the same techniques used to remove dents from any other type of furniture. Lay the frame down so it is flat and horizontal. Use a fine needle to poke a few small holes in the wood in the dented area, in the grain if possible. Use an eye dropper to apply a drop or two of water and allow the water to remain until it swells the wood fibers and raises the dent. Wipe off any excess water when the repair is complete.

Larger dents away from glued joints may require steam swelling to raise the dent. Steam will usually do a better job of raising the dent than just water alone. Place a small piece of moist cloth over the dented area, then touch the tip of a clothes iron set to the "cotton" setting to the cloth. Hold the iron on the cloth for only a few seconds. The steam will penetrate through the cloth and down into the wood to swell the wood grain and raise the dent. The procedure made need to be repeated several times. Do not leave the iron on the cloth too long or you may end up with a burn in the finish instead of a dent. Be careful if the piece has a water sensitive finish, or you may create water damage spots.

Repairing separating corner seams on wooden frames - Old or antique wooden frames will, more often than not, show evidence of separating seams on the inside edges of the corners. This is a natural occurrence caused by the wood shrinking across the grain due to a combination of time, changes in temperature and humidity. Newer wooden frames should have tight seams because, theoretically, the newer wood should not have been exposed to enough elements or had enough time to shrink. If the corner seam is loose on a newer frame, it has probably been severely mistreated or was poorly made in the first place.

Separated corner seams can often be successfully filled with either shellac or lacquer sticks or wax touch-up sticks. If the frame is a gesso covered frame, a small batch of gesso can be mixed up and used to fill the cracks.

A separated corner seam on a wooden mirror frame.

The Finish

The older the piece of furniture, the less likely it will still have its original finish. Furniture was made to be used, and use causes finishes to wear off, regardless of the type of finish. Older furniture, unlike modern furniture, was made with the intention of eventually needing to be refinished. Many pieces of furniture with clear finishes today were never intended to be clear-coated and were originally painted. If the wood did not have a nice figured grain pattern, or could not be stained to make it imitate a more expensive figured wood, it was coated with paint.

Almost all turned chairs, Windsor chairs, tavern tables, the majority of dining tables, and many beds, stands and chests were originally painted. These pieces of furniture were often constructed of several species of wood (Windsor chairs could be made from as many as five to seven different species of wood) and paint would conceal the differences in the wood grains.

Original paint can help you determine the age of furniture, if you are lucky enough to find some remaining in an out of the way place where stripper did not reach. Look under chair seats where it would not have been sanded and where the wood would have been more porous and more absorbant. Other good places to look are in the corners of panels or edges of drawers where stripping tools may not have been able to remove every last trace of stubborn old paint. Red, yellow and black were popular paint colors during the 17th century. The blueish-green color so often associated with Early American furniture was commonly used at the end of the 18th century. During the 1830s gray, white and red milk-based paints were used in abundance. Grain painting was very popular during the 19th century.

Old paint was often handmade and the formulas contained ingredients which would almost certainly be outlawed today. Lead, mercury, and arsenic were common ingredients and colors were achieved from natural ingredients including berries, clay and blood. Lime was added to homemade paint to increase the durability. Egg whites were added to give paint a semi-gloss sheen.

In addition to a regular coat of paint which would completely cover furniture and disguise the wood grain, many cabinetmakers used a thin coat of paint to color the wood yet allow the grain to show through. Thin red paint could be "washed" over the furniture to give wood the appearance of mahogany or cherry. Old paint colors were originally very bold and bright and bear no relation to the muted conservative tones we see today. Old paint mellows with age. Our forefathers liked bright colors to perk up their homes.

Age will cause painted finishes to become very dry and cracked and they will begin to show a maze of fine lines. Old paints were generally oil based and dry out very slowly, but once dry, they will come off in flakes instead of small chips if the surface is scraped.

As they age, old shellac finishes will often separate into little circles that darken and eventually conceal the grain of the wood underneath. Shellac finishes expand and contract with changes in heat and humidity and trap dirt and pollutants in the finish. This causes the surface to develop a bumpy "alligatored" texture and an overall dark, opaque look.

An old varnish finish will slowly dry out as it loses its oil content and will check into squares, often across the entire piece of furniture.

Clear lacquer, (which is a 20th century invention) tends to check into rectangles. Shellac and lacquer finishes can both be dissolved by their solvents and smoothed out and repaired. This process is technically referred to as *reamalgamation*. Varnish is a generic term for a variety of clear finishes, not a specific finish, and can not be dissolved once it has been completely cured.

An "alligatored" finish. You can see the bumps and texture on the surface of the finish.

Section Two

A Brief Overview of Furniture Styles and Periods
What to Look For and What to Look *Out* For

Furniture styles do not generally make radical changes. There is usually a transitional change as a new style gains in popularity and an old style begins to fade. For a period of time, the two styles will be popular con-currently. Some styles had a more widespread popularity than others, and some were more regional. Some lasted for many decades, others for just a few years. But even when the style had passed, the furniture remained. Most homeowners could not afford to dispose of their furnishings and start over again with every new furniture whim. New pieces might be incorporated into the decorating scheme but the old ones remained in service for many years.

A piece of furniture can be classified in a *style* and a *period*. The style of the furniture is determined by the design characteristics. The period of the furniture is determined by when the piece was produced and was popular. Periods are often identified with the reign of a king or queen, or an historical event and acquire their name from this association. To make things even more confusing, furniture styles tend to overlap, and some styles, like the "Victorian style" for example, consisted of a variety of design movements which were all popular concurrently.

Many of the styles were popular in Europe before crossing the Atlantic ocean and becoming popular in the United States. As a general rule, Americans were always ten or twenty years behind the Europeans. Furniture made in the fashion of an earlier period, but made at a later time than the original period are referred to as "in the style of". If a piece of furniture has design elements of a particular period and was manufactured during that era it is called a "period" piece.

Colonial Furniture (or Pilgrim Furniture)

The earliest American settlers made very crude furniture. Tools and time were scarce, and what they did make was very rough and utilitarian. The few remaining examples of furniture from this time period are in museums and private collections. Most people had very plain simple, functional furniture. A few of the more wealthy settlers hired craftsmen to attempt to reproduce the furniture they had left behind in England.

By the mid 17th century "turners and joiners" (the name given to early cabinetmakers because they constructed furniture by turning the wood on a lathe and then joining the pieces with mortise-and-tenon joints) were creating massive furniture with bulbous legs and deeply carved cabinet fronts. Many case pieces consisted of a frame made of grooved stiles and rails, and panels. The panels were often decoratively carved. Paint was the most popular furniture finish but few pieces exist today with their original paint still intact. Some Colonial furniture was decorated with applied split spindles and egg-shaped wooden ornaments called *bosses*. Bosses were often painted with black paint to make the wood resemble ebony.

Native woods from local forests were used for furniture construction. Oak and pine were the most common woods, but ash, walnut, hickory, maple, apple and cherry were also used if they were available. Oak and pine were in abundance in the new colonies and American cabinetmakers used them as the primary wood for a majority of their creations. Pine, ash, maple, or hickory were used as secondary woods. Maple or hickory were often used to make the turned components on furniture.

Early American homes had few chairs, and they were

generally massive stocky pieces of furniture constructed entirely of turned posts and spindles. Native woods were used and the chairs often had rush or cane seats. These chairs were called *Great Chairs* because of their size, or *Carver chairs* (named after John Carver the first governor of Massachusetts Bay Colony) and were reserved for important guests and senior members of the household. Other family members sat on a variety of stools, benches or chests which were more commonly found in the average home. Cromwell chairs (named after Oliver Cromwell the 17th century English leader) and Farthingale chairs (named after a type of Renaissance skirt) were the earliest forms of American upholstered chairs. The chairs were covered in needlework (occassionally in leather) and were dubbed with the knickname *turkeywork chairs* because the needlework patterns were based on "turkie carpets" (Turkish carpets).

A piece of furniture called a *settle*, which was a long bench with a high back, became a standard fixture in front of the fireplace in most houses because it provided seating for a number of people and shielded them from cold drafts while capturing as much heat as possible from the fireplace (much like the wing chair would do many years later).

Colonial houses were very small, and pieces of furniture were expected to do double-duty, or be folded away when not in use. Small tables and candlestands often had tilting tops. This not only allowed them to be stored compactly against a wall when not in use, but also permitted them to be used as firescreens in front of the fireplace. Rotating tables also made it easy to adjust an unevenly burning candle without spilling hot wax on the table or on someone's hands. Tilt-top tables generally had a small, round or hour glass-shaped cast brass spring lock used to secure the table top in place. Like most early brass hardware, these locks were usually imported from Birmingham even though the tables were made in the United States. The locking device made a "snapping" sound as it was fastened into place, and small candlestands and tilt-top tables gained the nickname "snap stands" or "snaps". A surprising number of these original brass locks can still be found under old tilt-top tables.

Gate-leg tables and drop leaf tables were the most popular table styles because they saved valuable space. Some tables had tilt tops and could double as chairs. *Chair-tables* consisted of a chair with a round top made from two boards with flattened ends which was attached to the rear stiles. The chair could be converted to a table when additional table space was needed or folded up and pushed back against a wall to provide additional seating. Regardless of the style, all tables were made with wide heavy boards.

Bible boxes and chests were the most common case pieces of furniture. *Press cupboards* were simple enclosed chests used to store clothing and household linens and were found in almost every Colonial home. *Court cupboards* were more open and usually more ornate and decorative, and were used to display precious items and utensils. They were predominately found in the homes of the few wealthy Colonial families until towards the end of the Colonial period. Colonial beds were usually high, four poster beds which were draped with curtains to retain heat during the winter and keep insects away in the warmer months.

The Puritan philosophy was very strict about worldly pleasures and Colonial furniture was not built for comfort nor was it excessively decorative. Some pieces, however, show the native influences of the country from which the various immigrants had previously resided.

* An important clue to the age of a chair is its proportions. Especially the size of the slats. Generally speaking, the larger the slats the earlier the piece.

* A chest-on-frame was a paneled lift top chest used by early Americans to store their valuables. Fewer than one hundred of these American chests are known to exist

today, although similarly constructed European chests can be found. Reproductions can be created by adding a set of legs to a box or chest. Check the wood under the chest for wear. If there is evidence of wear, then the chest portion has probably not spent its entire life on the frame and has been "created" into an antique.

* A *chest-on-drawers* consisted of a chest with a top that opened for storage and a full sized drawer underneath. The chest-on-drawers was almost always painted in bright colors (red, green and black) and was often decoratively carved. The carving can help pinpoint the area in which the chest was made. Chests with original paint are obviously worth more than repainted ones. Do not remove the paint on a very old piece.

William and Mary Furniture

William and Mary furniture was named after the king and Queen of England, William of Orange and his Queen, Mary, who reigned from 1689 to 1694. They preferred lighter and more graceful furniture with more elegant lines than their predecessors. The court and the English people followed suit and elegance and a more genteel style of furniture, replaced the utilitarian furniture of the past.

The William and Mary style in America was an interpretation of the Baroque mode popular in Europe earlier in the century. Dutch colonists brought this new style to the United States and the graceful, tall and slender furniture became widely accepted on both sides of the ocean. Walnut, maple and fruitwoods replaced oak. Vertical lines and heighth became trademarks of the William and Mary period. Furniture was decorated with paint and fancy grained veneer, inlay, arched panels and elaborate low-relief carving. Turned trumpet, scroll or spiral shaped legs replaced the blocky, squatty legs of the past. Even simple chests had bulbous ball, bun or turnip feet. Furniture was well constructed using dovetails, pegged mortise-and-tenon joints, and nailed and paneled construction techniques and was extremely sturdy. Most of the William and Mary furniture was also more comfortable and attractive than the previous Colonial pieces.

Hardware was usually imported and was made of cast brass instead of wood. It became decorative as well as functional during the William and Mary period. Pulls and escutcheons were primarily scrolled plates and with tear-drop shaped handles.

Chair backs became taller and narrower and stiles and legs became thinner. Seats were woven of rush or cane, or covered in leather. Leather upholstered chairs were often called "Boston chairs" even though the chairs were made all over New England. Many chairs were originally finished with a coat of paint and have been repainted numerous times since.

Slat back chairs, also known as *ladder back chairs* were first introduced during the 17th cetntury. (Ladder back chairs were called *scrolled-splat chairs* in earlier furniture design books.) During the 18th century these chairs took on a lighter look and had thinner dimensions. The ladder back chair is one of the most commonly reproduced pieces of furniture. Reproductions will lack pegs at the juncture of the slats and stiles of the chair, and the slats will usually be produced by machine and be uniform in size. The turnings on a reproduction will be more crisp and even than on an original.

An important point to look for when determining the age of a chair is the overall proportions of the piece, but particularly the size of the slats. Larger slats are characteristic of earlier pieces. Eighteen century chairs featured lighter proportions and the 19th century featured more delicate detailing. Be on the look out for sharp edges at the turnings (they should have been worn down by a century or so of use and wear) and any form of construction other than mortise-

and-tenon joints. These are sure signs of a fake.

Corner chairs were very practical and were not confined to use in one room. They could be placed out of the way in corners for use as needed, and were handy as desk chairs. They were even used in the bedroom to hold a chamber pot. Corner chairs generally had maple frames and woven rush seats.

Daybeds were introduced during the William and Mary period and looked like chairs with radically extended seats. They had iron chains attached to a movable back to allow it to be adjusted for comfort. Wing chairs (also called "easy chairs") were introduced and were the first chairs really designed for comfort, with their fully upholstered and well padded frames. The wings would help ward off drafts from cold poorly heated rooms and helped retain heat from a fireplace. An interesting side note, wing chairs were used more often in bedrooms than in parlors according to household inventories of the day.

Colonial life was becoming a bit easier for the middle and upper-middle class, and furniture started to be designed to meet their new needs. Letterwriting became a popular activity and small desks were created to offer a place to write, and to store pens, quills, ink and paper. The earliest desks were based on the basic box design of the traditional Bible box which was a standard fixture in every home. Bible boxes did not have locks (because, afterall, who would steal a Bible?) and they did not have internal compartments. The simple box was modified with a slanted top to be used as a writing surface, and internal compartments were added to hold writing accessories. Later, a frame and four legs were added.

A Bible box.

The slanted top desk opened on hinges at the upper edge, and provided access to the writing accessories stored inside. There are only a few dozen authentic examples of these pieces known to exist. In later variations, the hinges were put on the lower edge of the writing surface and the lid folded down and the inside of the lid became the writing surface. Sliding rails pulled out of the desk and supported the lid to stabilize and support the writing surface. Drawers were added to the lower frame of the desk and cubby holes and drawers were added to the top section.

Examine the underside of the desk where it connects to the frame. You should not see signs of wear if the piece is a true desk-on-frame. Wear marks are evidence the writing box portion was not originally attached to the frame.

The William and Mary slant front desk was a combination of both a desk and a chest of drawers, and became the prototype for most later desks. It was the first desk form used for storage that could be used from a comfortable seated position. The interior of the desk could contain a simple grouping of cubbyholes (or pigeonholes) or an elaborate arrangement of drawers, cabinets and hidden compartments. Desks as well as some of the internal compartments often had locks. A top of the line desk could often be determined from a less costly one by the number of storage spaces on the interior of the desk. Check the wood on the interior compartments to make sure they are original to the desk. The wood, stain and finish on the cubbyholes, compartments and internal doors should be the same as on the rest of the desk. New, more elaborate interiors can be attached to the inside of an old desk in an attempt to increase the value of the piece.

* Check the desk frame to make sure the upper desk parts were not added to an existing bureau to create a slant front desk. The wood should be of similar type,

color and finish throughout the piece. Look for screw-holes that do not match up and wear in unusual areas.

Small and medium sized tables came into common us-age for tea, playing cards, and displaying family heirlooms during the William and Mary period. Tables with slate or marble tops, four turned legs with an X-shaped stretcher connecting them to strengthen the legs, and often a shallow center drawer or side drawers were used for food preparation. The marble topped tables were called *slab tables,* the slate topped ones were called, *slate tables.* Ornate dressing tables also came into vogue with similar turned legs and X-shaped cross stretcher.

Butterfly tables (named for their wing-shaped table leaf supports) always had tops constructed of single boards. Reproductions will be made from several boards glued together and will be assembled with nails and screws. European butterfly tables have more elaborately carved turnings than American examples. Gate-leg tables which were introduced in the United States in the 17th century, were constructed similarly to the butterfly tables. The difference is in the leaf support. In general, thick legs and thick turnings indicate an older table. Both the gate-leg table and the butterfly table are commonly reproduced. Examine the underside of the top for evidence of replacement or repairs.

Hutch tables had oval tops which lifted up to provide extra storage space. The top was mounted on a trestle base with solid feet and a plain board stretcher mortised through the side planks.

Smaller tables, often called *candlestands,* were used for many purposes in an early American home. Maple candlestands were often painted black to immitate ebony, or were stained and had gilded trim. *Joint stools,* simple jointed rectangular stools, were used for seating and also as small tables. Game tables or card tables had hinged tops which opened up to reveal circular depressions at the corners of the table to hold glasses and oval ones to hold game counters.

The high chest with three or four tiers of drawers attached to a table was a variation of the dressing table or slab table. More drawers slowly evolved on to the bottom half of the piece of furniture which by now resembled a chest-of-drawers on a chest-of-drawers. This new tall piece of furniture called a *highboy* became the common storage area for clothing and linens. The highboy consisted of two sections which made it easier to move around than one large piece of furniture. The upper class could custom order gilt stencils and fine lacquerwork to decorate their highboys and tables.

Some "highboys" are faked today by marrying pieces from two double chests or two chests of drawers together. The top of a highboy can also be married with a chest of drawers to create a highboy. Only a few of the original William and Mary highboys are believed to still be in existence.

Lowboys were smaller dressing tables, typically with three drawers, the center one being smaller and shorter. Some very rare early examples have just one full length drawer. The legs were always joined with an X-shaped cross stretcher which allowed the user to sit closer to the dresser. Lowboys were often made as part of a set and had a matching highboy. Highboys and lowboys were constructed using either nails or dovetail construction.

Today some "lowboys" on the market started their life as a highboy. If the top of the highboy is damaged, the top of the base can be veneered, stained and finished to make it look like a lowboy. Pieces of old veneer are often used when creating fake furniture. Check the grain on the top to see if the grain pattern and color truly matches the rest of the piece. Check the patina and wear on the top. It should be comparable to the rest of the piece. Also check the style of the top to make sure it matches the rest of the piece. The value of a newly created lowboy will will obviously be considerably less than an original.

Be on the look-out for replaced finials or feet on lowboys and highboys. Also check the legs and feet to see if they have been repaired. Dowels and screws are often used to repair cracked legs, and worn legs may have been lengthened.

The size of the piece can be a tip-off as to whether you have an original or a fake highboy or lowboy. Low-boys can be 1/5 to 1/4 smaller all the way around than a comparble highboy. Another tip-off may be the price. Low-boys are rare and hard to find. A very reasonable price on a low-boy may be for a very good reason.

* Inlay was an expensive and very time consuming process during the Colonial period. If a piece of furniture has inlay (and the inlay is original), it was probably quite valuable in its day.

* Many pieces of Colonial furniture may have lost their original feet with the passage of time. Look underneath the furniture for holes or other evidence of previously applied feet. If the furniture currently has feet, check to make sure they were not added to a piece which was not originally designed to have feet.

* William and Mary furniture with painted floral designs (or other painted designs) are very rare and valuable. Check the decorations to determine if they are original or if they were applied at a later date to increase the value.

Queen Anne Furniture

The Queen Anne style of furniture was named after Queen Anne of England who reigned from 1702 to 1714, but the furniture style was popular long after her reign ended, and did not influence American cabinetmakers until ten years after her death. The furniture style lasted from 1725 to 1750. Queen Anne furniture is most noted for its delicate curving lines, sinuous "S" curves and restrained decorations which often consisted of carved shells or fan shapes. The shell design became the single most popular motif of the period and classic open shell carvings were carved into just about every type of furniture and into architectural details such as fireplace mantles and cupboards as well. The use of carving, however, was less elaborate and more restrained during the Queen Anne periodthan in preceeding years.

Furniture from the Queen Anne period was generally small, richly finished and highly polished. The flat top on case pieces was replaced with broken pediment tops with elaborate central finials. Decorative batwing brasses replaced tear-drop pull hardware.

An exotic foreign wood called "mahogany" was imported from the Carribean and introduced to Americans during the Queen Anne period. It has remained a popular wood for formal furniture ever since. Mahogany was easy to carve and had a beautiful color and grain pattern, but was expensive, and was predominately used by cabinetmakers in large port cities. Most cabinetmakers continued to use native woods like walnut or maple, and cherry wood was often used on later pieces. Furniture was contructed using dovetails and paneled and pegged mortise-and-tenon construction.

Inlay and marquetry lost their popularity during the Queen Anne period, and veneer and lacquer were used instead to decorate plain furniture. *Japanning* (a western adaption of Oriental lacquerwork) was used as a finish on some Queen Anne pieces. Japanning involved applying many layers of lacquer darkened with lampblack, and resulted in a distinctive hard, dark, glossy surface. Decorations consisting of birds and fruit, and sometimes animal and human figures were added to the blackened background using gold and vermilion powder. Black was the most common color for side chairs and many of them were Japanned or ebonized, rush seats and all.

During the beginning of the 18th century, cabinetmakers began using the *cyma curve* – a classic double curve which got its name from the Greek word for "wave form". The cyma curve was often used on chair backs and pediments. The popularity of the cyma curve lead to the evolution of the S-shaped *cabriole leg*. The two curves on the cabriole leg (which was modeled after an animal's leg) produced a sturdy but decorative support for furniture, and it became a hallmark of furniture design for much of the 18th century. The cabriole leg made it possible to support heavy pieces of furniture on slim legs without the use of stretchers. Cabriole legs could be found on tables, chests, chairs and just about every other type of furniture. The pad of the foot was often carved into graceful spade, trifid, claw, or claw and ball shapes.

Folding card tables and game tables with hinged folding tops, and some dining tables with hinged folding tops were useful, decorative, and saved space. Tables could be pulled away from the wall, opened and used, then closed and returned to their place. *Breakfast tables* were small drop-leaf tables with one drop leaf the same size as the rectangular top of the table. When the leaf was opened, the table would be perfectly square. These tables got their name because they were used for serving breakfast in bedrooms.

Delicate tea tables and candlestands with recessed tops (which were supposed to resemble trays), valanced skirts and tripod cabriole leg bases were introduced during the Queen Anne period. The kneehole desk also came into use during this time, but the narrow opening area made it unpractical and uncomfortable for many people who tried to use them.

Chairmakers began inserting flat sections of wood called "splats" into the back section of chairs. Splats were often cut to resemble fiddles, classic vases or other shapes. Chair backs began to be shaped to conform more closely to the curve of the human body and were designed for comfort, unlike many earlier chairs.

Corner chairs, which were also called "roundabouts", served various purposes during the Queen Anne period. They could be used at a desk or placed in the corner of a parlor or bedroom. If the chair had a deep wooden skirt attached to the seat it may have served yet another purpose. The upholstered seat was designed to lift up and contained an inner support for a chamber pot. Some skirts have been shortened over the years in an effort to make the chairs more stylish. Turn the chair over and feel the wood. Shortened skirts will generally have a rough unfinished feel.

Newport, Rhode Island was one of the major cabinetmaking centers in the 18th century, and some of the finest most simplistic Queen Anne furniture was made there. Newport pieces had very restrained, elegant designs and plain legs which were usually straight rather than curved. Curved cabriole legs and carved shell designs were not usually found on pieces of furniture made in Newport.

American furnituremakers were making their own mirror frames by the Queen Anne period, but they still more often than not, imported the mirror glass from England and other parts of Europe. *Dressing glasses* were placed on small tables or dressers and were the forerunners of bureau mirrors. The framed mirror was mounted on a wooden base containing a swivel device which allowed the mirror to be viewed from different angles. Queen Anne mirrors seldom had small drawers in the mirror base. The drawers became popular in later periods.

Mirrors from the Queen Anne period, in original mint condition, are rare. Frames are often broken or have been repaired and may have pieces of the ornamentation missing. Replaced parts are often easily identified by looking at the back of the frame. This is also a good way to find evidence of repairs as the seams are often more obvious on the unfinished side.

* Feet are occasionally added to the top section of a Queen Anne highboy which has lost its base to transform odd furniture parts into a chest of drawers. The clue to the transformation is in the upper drawers. Most Queen Anne chest of drawers had full length drawers. If the upper drawers on the "chest of drawers" are less than full length, you probably have a "created" piece.

* Highboy bases without their top section can be "made" into lowboys. The top section is fitted with a new piece of wood which slightly overhangs the edges and is finished to match the color and finish. The clue here is in the size. An original Queen Anne lowboy was one-fifth to one-quarter smaller all the way around than a comparable highboy.

* Queen Anne flat top secretary desks had, as their name implies, flat undecorated tops. There were no broken pediments or bonnet tops. Just a molded cornice and a flat top. Some of these pieces are thought to have been made by cabinetmakers who did not want to deal with the complexities of crafting those extra details. Others were made for people who did not want to pay for the extra detailing. Authentic examples of Queen Anne flat top desks are rare. But a two door cupboard can be added to a Queen Anne slant front desk and the resulting piece will duplicate the look of a rare flat top secretary. Check the wood throughout the piece of furniture to make sure the wood, color and finish are consistent. Check the backboard for evidence of joinings.

* Queen Anne side chairs should be evenly proportioned with restrained decorations. Unusually tall chair backs and carved detailing on the knee brackets and feet are usually obvious signs of reproductions.

* Country pieces or pieces from more rural areas are easier to fake from just about every period because the original cabinetmakers could not afford to spend as much time making them or decorating them. Fashionable details required special tools, special skills and time. The authenticity of most furniture can be confirmed by checking underneath the furniture and inside the furniture. This will provide evidence of repairs, newer wood or inappropriate furniture construction.

Probably the single most important contribution of the Queen Anne period was the *Windsor chair*. Ironically, it did not reflect nor really represent the Queen Anne style in any way.

Windsor chairs - One of the most durable chair designs ever devised arrived in the United States from England around 1725. Windsor chairs were light weight, sturdy, comfortable and inexpensive. They originated around the town of Windsor, England and were originally designed to be tavern or coffeehouse chairs. The Windsor chair appealed to American homemakers and furnituremakers and distinctively different variations on the basic English chair began appearing around 1730. The American chairs varied greatly from their English counterparts in the shape of seat, back and legs.

There are six basic styles of American Windsor chairs: the *low back* or *captains chair* with a flat semicircular top rail set on short spindles doubling as an armrest; the *hoop-back* which was a modified low-back chair with an arched piece topping the central section; the *comb-back* which was also based on the low back chair. Comb-back chairs had a series of spindles extending above the arm rail and fitting into a serpentine top rail. The *fan back* was a side chair with a serpentine top rail like the comb-back, but no dividing arm rail. The back consisted of long spindles flanked on each side by heavier turned stiles. The *continuous arm* chair had the arms and the arched top rail both made from a single piece of bentwood, but had no mid-rail. The *loop-back* was a side chair with a sharply bowed back rail enclosing long spindles.

High back Windsors are considered more collectible than low back Windsors and can often sell for as much as 25% more. Some other variations on the Windsor chair were the addition of writing arms, or angled braces behind the back.

The legs on Windsor chairs were turned in a variety of shapes. The thickness of the legs and the pattern of the turnings will often give clues to the geographical origin of the chair and its construction can be used to some degree to help date it. Vase-shaped turnings were more commonly used before the American Revolution and bamboo shapes were more commonly used afterwards. Cabriole legs on a Windsor will date it between 1740 and 1770. Hooped-back Windsors were made after 1740. Wheel-splat Windsors were made after 1790. Gothic splat and pointed arch back Windsors were made between 1760 and 1800. Bulbous turnings on the posts will date the chair to after 1830. Classic Windsor chairs were made until about 1830, then the chairs began to be mass-produced, and have been machine-made and reproduced ever since.

A label from a Windsor rocking chair manufactured by a company that has been producing Windsors since 1857.

The Windsor was an all wood chair with delicately turned or simply cut interlocking parts. They were built for comfort and fit well into any setting from modest homes to millionaire's homes. Windsors were used in many variations inside the house and outside on the porch. They were one of the most popular chair styles during the 1800s and remain one of the most popular styles of chairs today.

The back of a Windsor chair was made of turned or whittled spindles (often a dozen or more) which were enclosed by a curving or straight rail. The seat was constructed of solid wood and shaped to fit the body. The turned legs spread out at a 20° angle and were reinforced by turned stretchers. Windsor chairs were sturdy because the parts were made from green wood which would later shrink to create naturally tight joints. Early Windsor chairs were put together without using nails or screws. The legs and spindles were carved from well seasoned wood. These pieces were then set into well-fitting holes in plank seats carved from green wood. After a few months, the green wood would dry and contract, and would grip the ends of the legs and spindles creating a tight bond which did not let go with the passage of time. Sometimes wedges were set into the ends of the spindles to spread the round tenons and secure the joints. As the wood aged, the wedges would often "pop" out of the wood like wooden pegs tend to do and for the same reasons. Later chairs were constructed using glue and screws to hold the chairs together, and the chairs were often made from one type of wood not an assortment of woods like earlier chairs.

Windsor chairs were made from a variety of woods so the components of the chair could be made from the most appropriate wood for a particular purpose. Pine or poplar was used for the saddle seats because softwood was easy to shape and carve. Spindles, arms and legs needed to be strong, so hardwoods like hickory, ash or birch were used. The hardwood used in the construction of the chairs varied by region and it was not uncommon for a chair to be constructed from a combination of hardwoods.

Because an assortment of woods was used in the construction of Windsor chairs, they were almost always painted to protect the wood and camouflage the mismatched natural wood colors and grain patterns. Some Windsors were embellished with painted designs applied by stencilling or painted freehand. Green, red, black and yellow were popular paint colors for early Windsors. White was in vogue during the 18th century. Black was popular during the 1900s but many of the black painted chairs were stripped during the 1920s by people trying to make the chairs look more modern and less dated.

Some Windsor chairs were originally manufactured with upholstered or padded seats. Many of these chairs no longer have their original padding or upholstery, but you should be able to see tell-tale holes across the front or back and around the sides of the seat, or under the chair seat. The holes are evidence the chair has had an upholstered seat at some point in its life. They do not, however, tell you whether the upholstery was original or was added at a later date. The shape of the nail hole can help to identify the type of nail used to attach the upholstery fabric, and that in turn can help to date when the upholstery was applied.

The value and quality of a Windsor chair can often be determined by the number of spindles in its back. The more spindles it has the older and more desirable the chair is usually considered to be. The 19th century brought an increase in the production of Windsor chairs but a decrease in the quality and in the number of spindles they contained. The wood on the later chairs was of an inferior quality and the edges of the wood are sharper and less mellowed than on older chairs. As the Windsor chair gained popularity and craftsmen began modifying the design, the splay of the legs became highly esteemed. Many collectors feel the wider the splay the better.

The spindles start in the seat on a Windsor chair, go up through the arm rail, and continue up through the crest of the chair. These pieces should follow a straight line, even though it may not necessarily be a vertical line. Any variation from a straight line is an indication the chair has been broken and repaired or a section of the spindle has been replaced. There should be a total of six mortises on the underside of the seat – four for the legs and two for the arm supports if it is an arm chair. If there are more holes, or the holes have been redrilled and mortised you will have evidence of a repair.

Splats were occassionally used in the center of a Windsor chair in place of the centermost spindles. Splats were carved in a variety of shapes including Prince of Wales, wheelback, feathers and many other ornate patterns.

A replacement piece on a chair is not always made with the correct type of wood, especially on a painted piece of furniture. Many repairers feel it doesn't matter what type of wood is used for the repair because once paint is applied it will blend the repair and make it un-noticeable. Unfortunately, different woods will age at a different rates, and a repair which was undetectable when it was originally done will become glaringly obvious given some time.

Windsor chairs came in a variety of forms – straight-backed, fan-backed, curved backed, arm chairs, rocking chairs and side chairs. The New England Windsor chair has a small writing shelf attached. The most valuable styles, as far as most antique collectors are concerned, are examples with two to four braces behind the back spindles extending from the seat to the upper edge of the back of the chair.

Because of the popularity of the style, Windsor chairs

were made in large quantities and sold in very large sets (by today's standards). Such a large quantity of chairs were manufactured, that it is very easy today to acquire odd chair parts to use to repair a damaged chair or reassemble orphaned pieces into a new chair. These "hybrid chairs" which are created from pieces of various old chairs are often difficult to recognize from a genuine unmodified antique because all of the components are generally from the same time period and from a similar style of chair.

Original Windsor rockers are rather rare and are most commonly found in the "arrow-back" style. Windsor rockers usually have thicker legs than regular Windsor side chairs or arm chairs. Some Windsor chairs have been converted into rocking chairs by fastening the rocker to a ledge cut in the side of the foot. The rocker had to be attached in this manner because the lower leg lacked the thickness required to attach a rocker in any other manner.

Windsor chairs have been made continuously around High Wycombe in Buckinghamshire, England, since the 18th century. The style of the chairs remains basically the same, but the construction techniques have changed and the chairs have been produced by machines for the last one hundred years.

The Windsor chair achieved wide-spread popularity in the early 19th century, and they began to be mass-produced in in factories in the United States and abroad. Many of these factory-produced chairs had wide top rails. They were called *arrow-back* or *rod-back* chairs depending on the shape of the spindles. Some chairs had a rectangular projection above the top rail and were called *step down Windsors*. The Windsor style was not limited to chairs and some styles from the late 18th century and early 19th century were modified to produce stools and settees.

* Painted surfaces can sometimes conceal repairs and damage. Carefully check painted Windsor chairs for

163

evidence of damage or repairs. Cracked spindles or other damage may be camouflaged under several layers of paint.

* Many chairs have been repainted a number of times during the course of their life, and the paint you see may not be original. Look into the grooves of the stiles or spindles, at the joinings of the stretchers or under the seat for evidence of original paint the stripper may have missed.

* Some restorers will attempt to duplicate designs and decorations the chair may or may not have originally had. Check pictures of similar chairs to verify the authenticity of any decorations.

Chippendale Furniture

Chippendale furniture is a combination of many styles including William and Mary, Queen Anne, Rococo, Georgian and Gothic and was influenced by the Spanish, French and Chinese. Thomas Chippendale was an English cabinetmaker who influenced furniture designs from the middle to late 18th century and for many years afterwards, and who published *The Gentleman and the Cabinet-Maker's Director* in 1754. The most distinguishing elements of the Chippendale style are claw-and-ball feet, cabriole legs and open back splats on chairs. It is believed most of the "Chippendale" furniture in the United States is not original Chippendale but rather "Chippendale inspired".

The actual American Chippendale period lasted from 1750 to 1780. American cabinetmakers duplicated the Chippendale style, but the American version was elegant and generally more simple than the English originals. American furniture often reflected trends already out of style in England. *Highboy dressers* were popular in the United States during the

Chippendale period even though they had fallen out of favor in Europe by that time. The American highboys were decorated with urns, fans or shell shaped inserts, broken *pediments,* and carved finials. Other case pieces were decorated with carved acanthus leaves, swags, shells, and scrolls.

Leather was one of the most popular upholstery fabrics throughout the 18th century, and upholstery tacks began to serve a decorative as well as a functional purpose. Borders of upholstery tacks were added to upholstered furniture as a means of decoration. Camel backed sofas with arched backs, (which were a fairly simple design for the Chippendale period) were covered in silk damask and other elaborate fabric. Sofas had simple separate legs, or legs which were connected with stretchers. The stretchers served a dual purpose: they were decorative and they added extra support which stabilized the furniture.

American furniture had regional differences which influenced the design of various pieces. New York Chippendale furniture was often more restrained than pieces manufactured elsewhere. Chairs had solid splats instead of decoratively pierced ones. They used flat scrolled handholds on arms instead of knuckle carving, and generally had claw-and-ball feet. Tables produced in New York were proportionately heavier than tables manufactured elsewhere. Straight table skirts, simply curved heavy legs, and claw-and-ball feet with talons at 90° angles to each other are characteristics of New York craftsmanship. New York also manufactured the sturdiest and most beautiful card tables, many of which had five legs. Four legged card tables were more commonly produced outside of New York.

Furniture made in Boston had minimal carving but lots of curves. Furniture made in Philadelphia was usually elaborately designed. Chair splats were carved and pierced, and stiles were often inticately carved. Philadelphian chairs often have a distinctive feature of seat rails which are mortised into the rear legs so the narrow rectangular tenons are evident behind the rear legs. Tables made in Philadelphia had distinctive depth to the table skirts, elaborately carved tops often with scallloped edges, large over-hang on the tops, a distinctive curve to the cabriole legs and unique detailing on the carving of the claws on the feet. Philadelphia was the largest American city preceeding the Revolutionary War, and the rich and affluent people of Philadelphia wanted fashionable furnishings. Thomas Chippendale's design book arrived in Philadelphia shortly after it was published, and Philadelphia society was quick to adopted his designs.

Furniture manufactured in Connecticut was more rural and conservative and featured rush seats on chairs and simple turned legs. New Hampshire produced furniture with a combination of traditional and fashionable designs.

Mahogany became the primary wood of choice for cabinetmakers in larger cities. Native woods – cherry, pine, maple, walnut and poplar – were used by cabinetmakers in smaller more rural areas. The native woods were used as a secondary wood by craftsmen in both large and small cities. The type of wood used for the furniture often made a major difference in the price of the finished piece, then as well as now. A cherry or walnut piece was generally worth less than a similar piece made from mahogany.

One of the most notable pieces of furniture from this period was the *knee hole dressing table*, which was a chest of drawers with a set of drawers on either side of the kneehole opening and a small center drawer above the opening. *Breakfront bookcases, Pembroke tables* and rocking chairs also made their appearances during this time period.

Rocking chairs originated in the United States some-where around 1760. The idea for the rocking chair has been credited to Benjamin Franklin but no one seems completely sure who first came up with the idea of attaching rockers on a chair or where the first rocking chair was made. Americans loved the idea of a chair that rocked almost from its inception, but Europeans thought it was nonsense and just an American folly.

The earliest rocking chairs did not start out as rocking chairs, but were regular side chairs with rockers glued to the legs. Notches were cut into the inner or outer side of the bottom two or three inches of the chair legs. Rockers were then fitted into the notches. Early rockers were thin and deep (some measuring 1/4" in width but three inches or more in depth) and consequently earned the name "carpet cutters".

Regular chairs usually have slightly tapered legs cut wider at the upper edge and narrower at the lower edge. A side chair converted into a rocking chair will show proof of its former life because it will still have its tapered legs. When furnituremakers began creating chairs intended to be rocking chairs, they eliminated the tapering and cut the legs with the same circumference from the top to the bottom. A notch was then cut into the center of the lower edge of the leg and the rocker (which was now similar to the dimensions of today's rocking chair rockers – about 1" wide and about 1-1/2"-2" deep) was placed on the notch. Then, a pair of pins was driven through the legs and rockers to secure them to the chair. As production of rocking chairs increased, the notching system was replaced by applying the rockers directly to the base of the chair leg.

A round tilt-top tea table with a unique support called a *birdcage* was produced by New York and Philadelphian cabinetmakers during the Chippendale period. The birdcage device (consisting of two planks joined by columns at each corner with a hole in the lower plank fitted over a tripod base) allowed the table top to be rotated as well as tilted. Small furniture that could be easily moved about and folded to take up less space was very practical and common in the 18th century. The top of the table was manufactured from a single board. A table top made from multiple boards is either a reproduction or a fake.

Most of the chairs (both side chairs and arm chairs) from this time period had splats instead of chair rails and they were more ornately decorated than previous chairs. Carved pierced slats, yoke-shaped top rails and carved stiles added decoration to chairs. Ladder back chairs with scrolled horizontal slats were quite popular. *Cabriole legs, claw and ball feet* and *bracket feet* were also populardecorative effects during this period.

The Chippendale period is noted for elaborately carved curved parts. Case pieces were shaped into *bombé* (a kettle shape with an overhanging molded top), *serpentine* (bowed at the center and hollowed out at each side), *oxbow* (a hollow center with a swell on each side), and *block front* shapes.

Bombé chests are extremely rare and expensive. The sides and drawer fronts were often carved from a single piece of wood. The front and sides curve outward and then curve back in sharply at the base. They often had four full length drawers, the three lower ones having sides conforming to the curve of the case. Reproductions will often use smaller pieces of wood glued together instead of a single piece of wood, and if you look closely you will see the seam. The bombé form was only used on three types of American furniture: chest of drawers, slant-front desks, and for a brief time on the slant-front secretary. English pieces were made in a greater variety of pieces of furniture.

Oxbow drawer fronts are found almost exclusively on Chippendale and Federal chests. The oxbow shape is usually worth considerably more than a straight front. They were made in limited quantities because the work involved in shaping the front made it difficult to produce and quite expensive. The sides and front were made from single boards which were then carved. The chest consisted of three or four equal or graduated full length drawers. The brass hardware was cast not cut.

The oxbow chest has been reproduced since the late 1800s and continues to be reproduced today. Reproductions can be detected by looking at the large pieces of wood and locating the seams. Smaller pieces of wood are often glued together to make up the larger boards on a reproduction. Hardware on a reproduction will be stamped or cut instead of cast brass. Wire nails are often used on reproductions instead of the dovetailed, pegged, and nailed construction of the originals.

The serpentine front is more common than the oxbow and by comparison is less expensive, but they are still rare and can be quite pricey. The serpentine shape was difficult to produce and was always more expensive than a straight front piece. A serpentine chest usually contained four or five full length graduated drawers or two half length drawers over three full length ones. These pieces were generally made in major urban centers by very skilled craftsmen.

The most unusual feature of the block-front form is the shaped front which was often carved from a single board. This was extremely challenging for the craftsman. Block front chests began to be reproduced in the early 1900s and the form is still being reprduced today.

Some block front chests had unique decorations. Chests from the Newport, Rhode Island area often had carved shell decorations. The shells were either carved directly into the wood or were carved separately and glued on later.

* Chest of drawers and chests-on-chests were more popular in urban areas than low chests. Low chests were more common in rural areas because they were easier to produce. On a chest of drawers of any size, check the sides of the drawers and the runners for wear. The wear should be even on the side of the drawer and the side of the case. If you do not see signs of wear, this could be an indication repairs have been made, pieces have been replaced, or the piece is a fake.

Candle-stands, which have been a popular piece of furniture throughout many different furniture styles over the years, remained popular during the Chippendale period. In fact, so many remain available today they must have been produced in enormous quantities. These small tables were used, obviously as the name indicates, as candle-stands, but also served as small tables for other functions. Round tops were the most common shape, but square topped tables were also made. Tilt-top versions were also available.

Federal or Classical Furniture

Federal furniture, which was popular from 1780 to about 1830, was an American style influenced by Phyfe, Adam, Hepplewhite, Sheraton and Regency furniture. The Duncan Phyfe style originated in the United States. All of the other styles originated in Europe and later found their way to America. Salem, Massachusetts was one of the major centers in the country for fine cabinetmaking during the Fedreal period. The affluent clientele in the area included many wealthy shipowners and custom furniture was often manufactured specifically for them.

The ornate carving which had been popular in previous periods was replaced during the Federal period with decorative columns of molding and simple turnings called *reeding.* Straight lines replaced the curving lines which were so popular in the preceeding styles and classical decorations such as the Greek key, urns, inlaid ovals and lyres were popular motifs of this period. Some feel this more simple style of furniture was a revolt against the excesses of the Rococo period. Others believe it was directly related to the discoveries in the excavations of Pompeii, Herculaneum and other ancient sites between 1738 and 1748.

Plain chest of drawers came back into style during the Federal period, and some chests and desks had slightly bowed fronts. Federal furniture designs were more simple than they had been in years and this allowed craftsmen to produce quality furniture at a much greater rate. Round or square tapered legs and spade, French, bracket or arrow feet graced the bottoms of Federal furniture. Hardware pieces were stamped brass shaped into round, oval or rectangular shapes.

Pieces of furniture from the Federal period covered a

broad spectrum from elaborately grained mahogany furniture to plain simple painted pieces. Painted furniture manufactured in the Federal style was produced for more than fifty years. Unfortunately, most painted furniture was often less stylish than furniture made of fine woods. Furniture could be made from inexpensive pine or a mixture of woods and then have the evidence concealed under a coat of paint. Some painted furniture was false-grained to make it appear to be a species of more expensive wood. Paint can also conceal damage, repairs and new wood. Painted pieces will need to be checked in corners and crevices and inside the case work to determine if the paint is original and if the furniture is original.

The most elaborate American painted furniture was manufactured in Baltimore. The furniture itself was made of simple turned parts which were factory-made. But the painting was painstakingly done by hand.

The Federal period is noted for painted "fancy chairs". These chairs had elaborately painted scenes on the back slats, and gilding, stencilling, piercing and carving were occassionally added for additional decorative effect. Some chairs were originally sold unfinished and could then be painted or finished by the purchaser.

Painted "fancy" furniture is difficult if not impossible to find in its original condition. Some painted pieces had the paint added decades after the original manufacture date of the furniture. Added decorations can affect the value of the furniture based upon the quality of the painting and the age of the addition.

"Fancy" painted furniture is much more vulnerable than furniture with just a regular painted surface and presents a double problem of caring for the furniture and the paintings. Painted pieces should be kept in areas which do not get too hot, too dry or too damp. Heat and dampness will adversely affect the painted surface.

Restoring painted areas is difficult and can radically affect the value of the furniture. When in doubt, consult a professional. Do not attempt to repair a valuable piece of furniture. Shiny areas in the middle of a painted scene or areas where the sheen appears too "flat" could be evidence of a previous repair. Paint can also be used to hide cracks and other damage to the furniture.

Federal country furniture, like country furniture from other periods had simple lines and subtle decorations, if any. But while the furniture may have been simple, it was not crude. Country furniture was not necessarily made in the country. "Country" furniture can be made anywhere anytime. It was often produced by large factories in urban areas along with more sophisticated decorative pieces. Country furniture was made to be functional. Excessive decorations made the furniture less utilitarian. The best country furniture has simple lines and subtle details like tapering legs and plain functional hardware.

Unfortunately, the simple lines and designs of country furniture make it easier to fake. When in doubt turn the piece upside down. The wood underneath the furniture should be a uniform aged color. Remove the drawers and look inside the casework. The inside wood should show the same uniform aging. Look for tell-tale circular saw marks and other modern tool marks, and evidence of new or replaced wood. Look for screwholes which do not match up. Check to make sure modern screws or nails have not been used. New "old" furniture is often made from old wood. Painted pieces may be covering up new wood. Check the unfinished wood for signs of age. Many "new" old pieces of country furniture are crudely and carelessly made. That is an obvious sign of a fake. Drawer interiors made from polished maple are another sign of a fake. Reproduction hardware will be thinner and less carefully made.

The two most notable innovations of the Federal period were the sideboard and the commode. Sideboards were medium to large-sized case pieces which contained drawers to hold cutlery and linens, and shelves behind cabinet doors to hold china, crystal and silver serving pieces. The commode was a small chest with drawers and shelves that resembled a small sideboard. The tops on sideboards and commodes were made from either wood or marble. A commode could be used in the parlor or the bedroom and was often used as a washstand because it provided a storage area for toiletries and a place to use them. When used in a bedroom, the cabinet of the commode could be used to discreetly store a chamber pot. Commodes varied from plain and strictly functional, to what would have been considered quite decorative for their time.

Separate rooms set aside for dining were at one time only found in homes belonging to the rich upper class. During the Federal period they started to become a standard fixture in most middle class homes. Tables designed specifically for dining became more popular including styles which could be opened up to make them larger or folded to make them smaller as needed. Dumbwaiters or serving tables were based on English designs and were very utilitarian extra pieces of furniture in formal dining rooms. The shelves and drawers could be used to hold extra serving pieces. American dumbwaiters were more simply designed than English pieces and were made using mahogany as the primary wood and pine or tulip poplar as the secondary wood. English pieces were also made from mahogany but ash wood was used as the secondary wood.

Sewing tables were introduced during the Federal period. They were made to compliment other larger pieces of furniture and usually contained drawers, often divided up into small compartments, or hanging fabric bags to hold necessary tools and accessories. These tables were often called "square work tables" but they are actually rectangular in shape, not square. Oval and kidney shaped tables were also made.

Drop-leaf tables with one or two leaves to open and extend the table top were used in drawing rooms, parlors and libraries. These tables usually had a small drawer (some had two) and occassionally you can find one with a drawer that can be opened from either side of the table. *Pembroke tables* were first made in England in the 1760s. The term refers to small, elegant tables with rectangular leaves. They supposedly got their name from the Countess of Pembroke in Wales who ordered a table with similar specifications to be custom-made for her. Pembroke tables were made in the Chippendale style in the United States before the Revolutionary War, but they increased in popularity during the Federal period.

Federal side tables were multi-function tables which could be found in many rooms serving a variety of different purposes. They were relatively tall tables designed to stand against a wall as a pier table in a hallway, as a serving table in a dining room, as a decorative accent, or as table ends to be placed at either end of a dining table to extend the table to accomodate additional people. Most side tables had wooden tops but some tops were made from marble. Marble topped side tables are rare and are quite valuable.

Candlestands remained popular in the Federal period as both a place to hold a candle to light a room and as small serving tables or tea tables. A very tall version of the candlestand with a long carved pillar mounted on a tripod claw-foot base was called a "pillar and claw table".

The Federal period featured a greater number of tables in a wider variety of shapes and sizes than any other period. Game tables remained popular, and it is said card tables were never more popular than during the Federal period. The most elegant and elaborately made card tables were manufactured in Rhode Island where they were known for producing unusually shaped tables with beautiful intricate inlay. New York was known for producing dark wood tables with contrasting shiny bright brass decorations.

American cabinetmakers produced a variety of card table shapes during the Federal period, and the round table was the least popular shape of all. Many round Federal card tables attributed to American manufacturers were actually made in England. An English table can be distinguished from an

American one by checking the secondary wood. American cabinetmakers predominately used pine as the secondary wood. English cabinetmakers used oak and ash.

Card tables usually had a hinged top which would fold open to enlarge the size of the table top. Some tops would open and then turn at a 90° angle. The legs on card tables were usually long and slender and because of the weight placed upon them, they were susceptible to breakage. Carefully check legs for evidence of repairs. A poorly repaired leg can cause permanent structural damage.

Stools were a staple item in American households almost from the very beginning. They are a very basic form of seating. Stools during the Federal period were frequently made with green wood, using construction techniques similar to those used in the Windsor chair making process. Pieces of the stool were carved from green wood and the legs and stretchers were inserted into place. As the wood dried out and shrank, it would tightly grip the surrounding wood. No glue or nails or other joinings were required on the originals. Reproductions, on the other hand, are usually glued together.

Pianos stools were produced in significant numbers during the Federal period. Americans had more leisure time and were quite receptive to appreciation of music and the arts. The adjustable piano stool with its cylindrical screw mechanism which adjusedt the heighth of the stool, was made from a variety of woods and in many different styles. Most had plain seats – with or without upholstery – but others had curved backs attached.

Side chairs were made to match dining tables and were used to decorate hallways and parlors. These chairs often had a center splat carved into an urn and feather pattern or carved into a series of columns. Chair backs took on plain shield, oval or heart shapes. Square-back chairs became popular in the early 1800s. The square-back style became popular again during the early 1900s as part of dining room sets. Reproductions generally have less detailed carving and the reeding is flattened not rounded on the top.

The thin pieces of wood used to create shaped backs and delicate carved splats on Federal chairs are easily broken and many have suffered damage and been repaired over the years. Some repairs were professionally done, but most were not. Carefully check wood for evidence of repairs. Once broken, the chair back will be difficult to repair and will usually be permanently weakened.

An unusual style of rocking bench, called a *rocking settee* or a *mammy's bench* was popular towards the end of the Federal period. The benches were predominately produced in rural areas and were made of ash, pine or cherry wood, then painted and usually stencilled with decorations. They were constructed like a normal bench but had short rockers attached to the sides and a small, removable guard rail consisting of two stiles and two rails that attached into holes in the front of the seat on one side. The guard rail was used to protect children rocking in the settee. These pieces are hard to find today, and should be carefully checked to make sure the rocking settee is not a modern "creation" made from rockers from a rocking chair and a removeable rail constructed from another piece of furniture. The more rare the piece of furniture – the more money can be made by faking it.

Another unusual bench design invented during the Federal period was the *convertible settee* which was patented in 1827. The convertible settee had a two part seat. The top seat was either rush, or covered in upholstery, stuffed with horsehair and outlined with brass upholstery tacks. The bottom piece of the seat would slide under the top when closed. When the bottom was pulled out, it would covert the settee into a bed.

Tester or canopy beds were the most common style of bed well into the Fedreal period, but low-post beds were made throughout the 18th century. The shape of the leg can often help to date a bed. Early beds had thick turned legs and tapered legs could be found on beds made later. Low-post beds were often covered in drapings hung from the ceiling of the room, which closed in the bed area, contained warmth and kept drafts off of the occupants. Because the coverings concealed the bed frame, and the bed itself was not visible, it was not necessary to replace the frame to keep up with changing furniture fashions. The bed frames were usually rather plain and had simple lines. The bed hangings, on the other hand, could be very expensive and often quite elaborate.

The mattress was supported on hemp ropes tightly strung across the bedframe and attached to knobs spaced an equal distance apart on the inside of the wooden sides, head and foot of the bed or was woven through holes in the bedframe. Hemp rope, being a natural product, had a tendency to sag and stretch out of shape, and had to be occassionally tightened with a *bed key*, a wooden contraption used to provide leverage. The mattress, which was usually stuffed with feathers and was called a "feather bed", was fitted between the wooden frame. This frame was called a *bedstead*. The term was later shortened to "bed". An original bedstead should have holes in the frame where the rope would originally have been woven through or should still have the wooden pegs (or at the very least, evidence of them).

Canopy beds consisted of two curving rods with five or six thin stretchers supporting the sides and the covering (which was often lace or netting). The headboards were simply shaped and low. There was no footboard. Beds with easily removable arched canopies were called "field beds" because they were considered portable. Four poster canopy beds could run the gamut from simply-shaped painted pine to elegant mahogany headboards and footboards with silk draperies and swags. Bed draperies did not just serve a decorative purpose. Houses were poorly heated and exposure to the night air was considered a health hazard. Draperies could be closed around the bed to keep drafts off of the occupants and to help keep them warm.

Folding beds were made throughout the 18th century.

These beds often had simple arched headboards and had hinged siderails to allow the bed to be folded. They were usually plainly decorated and had simple carving.

The *day bed* which was based upon the designs of the Grecian or Roman couches and the French *récamier* was an interesting addition to the Federal era. Today this piece of furniture is often called a *fainting couch*. That name was not used during earlier time periods and is a rather new term. The legs on the day bed were shortened from the original designs to suit American tastes and style preferences in the early 1800s. Day beds could either be upholstered or have caned seats and backs. Caned pieces often had cushions made for them to make them more fashionable and comfortable. Some day beds had plain maple wood frames painted to resemble expensive mahogany. The low wooden headboards of similar heighth on each end of the bed made it appear like two chair backs facing each other. Wooden slats were dropped into the side rails to support the mattress. This type of bed was often called a "hired man's bed" and served as an extra bed in a room not necessarily designated as a regular bedroom.

Simple box-like cradles with rockers attached to the bottom were popular throughout the 17th and 18th century. The construction varied very little except that earlier ones were made with tongue-and-groove construction and later ones used iron-nails. Pine was the most common wood but cherry and other fruitwoods were also used, especially for cradles made by amateur cabinetmakers. Cradles often had a hooded enclosure at one end which partly covered the top. This was more practical than decorative. The hood helped to keep drafts in a poorly heated room off of the baby and helped to keep the child warm. Some previously hooded cradles have lost their hood over the years. Look at the top edges of the cradle for evidence of holes used to attach a hood.

Trestle-base cradles had a base made of a long stretcher connected to two low curved legs. Two turned stiles were connected to the ends of the trestle base and went vertically up to a horizontal stretcher which connected them. The cradle was attached to side stiles with brass mountings and the cradle was swung back and forth rather than rocked.

Most cradles were made of local wood and were very simple and traditional looking. They were not affected by style changes and did not usually change their shape or design to accomodate current styles. The upper class would occassionally have a cradle custom-made in a fancy and fashionable style, but these were rare exceptions to the rule.

Gilded mirrors decorated with patriotic motifs were popular decorative accents during the Federal period. Eagles with spread wings, shields, wreaths, sheafs of wheat, cornucopias and stars were created with gesso and added to wooden frames which were then gilded and painted. Gesso is quite delicate and many of these mirrors have been broken and repaired over the years. Very few undamaged examples remain today. Check the inside of the frame for evidence of repairs.

Girandole mirrors were popular with the upper class during the Fedreal period. These mirrors had elaborately carved gilded frames and a special piece of convex mirrored glass which

179

allowed a wide-angle view. They were often placed in large dining rooms or ball rooms so hostesses could keep an eye on all of their guests. Very few of these pieces were produced and they are very valuable today.

* Federal style corner cupboards were made with either solid wood doors or glass doors. Pieces with glass doors are more rare and consequently more valuable. Carefully check the glass, the muntins and the frames. The same type of wood, stain and finish should be used on the cabinet and the frames, and all parts should show equal signs of age. Some cabinets have had glass doors added to replace their original solid wood ones in an effort to increase the value of the piece.

* *Washstands* are small, narrow pieces of furniture designed to hold a pitcher and bowl, a soap dish, a glass and often had a shelf or a drawer to store toilet articles. They were common fixtures in almost every bedroom before the advent of running water and indoor plumbing. Because of their small size they are popular pieces for collectors, and are also popular pieces for reproductions. Look for signs of wear on an original. There should be water damage, or at least evidence of water usage on the top. Some washstands had a round cut-out area in the top where the lip of a washbowl would rest, and there should be watermarks around this area and marks on the back piece from the handle of the pitcher and from splashed water. Water will leave a white mark on most clear finishes, but will leave a black mark if it penetrates through the finish and into the wood.

American Empire Furniture

Empire designs were first introduced in France around the beginning of the 19th century, but did not become popular in the United States until about 1815. Once introduced, American Empire furniture remained popular for almost fifty years. An immigrant named Charles-Honoré Lannuier was one of the first cabinetmakers to introduce the Empire style to Americans. He worked in New York between 1803 and 1819 combining early Empire and Louis XVI style elements into his designs. The new style was enthusiastically accepted by American consumers, and other cabinetmakers eager to capitalize on the trend copied Lannuier's ideas, but with more restraint. New York became known as the center for stylish furniture and people came from all around the country to buy furniture manufactured in this new furniture mecca.

Early pieces of American Empire furniture, made between 1815 and the 1840s, were handmade. They were very symmetrical and had heavy lines and rectangular shapes. Late American Empire pieces, made between 1840 and 1850, were mainly produced with steam-powered circular and band saws. These machines replaced handcarving on all but custom-made pieces which were produced in smaller shops. American Empire furniture was massive, heavy and imposing, and featured "C" and "S" shaped scrolls. John Hall's book *The Cabinet Maker's Assistant,* published in Baltimore in 1840 illustrated how the use of veneer, and band saws, circular saws and other machines could create elegant furniture which could be easily afforded by the average middle-class household.

The American Empire style was a revival of ancient Greek and Roman forms which were adapted to the 19th century way of living. Popular motifs of the period were the Greek scroll, classical columns and the lion's claw foot. Empire furnishings had wavy scroll designs balancing heavy geometric shapes. *Ormolu* (a decorative trim using bronze or brass mixed with a thin layer of gold) was used in place of gilding to decorate elaborately designed pieces of furniture. Gilded caryatids as well as other forms of columns were used as supports for tables and chairs. Elaborate cornices graced the tops of case pieces of furniture. Wooden furniture was deeply carved, and stencilling and brass or bronze decorations replaced wood inlay as decorative elements.

As the Empire period progressed, furniture became more curvilinear and the decorative effect relied more on the shape of the sawn pieces and not on the carving. The over-all line of the furniture was more important than decorations, and if carving was used, it was to add emphasis to the outlines of the furniture. Furniture feet were carved into balls, scrolls or to resemble animal feet. Mahogany, rosewood and other rich, elaborately grained woods were favored by designers of Empire furniture. Veneers were used where solid wood was not practical, and marble was used as a decorative accent on tables, dressers and sideboards.

One of the most common pieces of hardware from the American Empire period is the brass drawer pull shaped like a lion face with a ring in its mouth. Wooden and glass knobs were also used.

Machines and advancements in mass-production techniques allowed Empire furniture to be made in just about every price range. Simple painted furniture and veneered furniture was available for modest homes and budgets, and elaborately gilded, marble-topped pieces made from exotic figured woods were available for the wealthy clientele. Laborers using steam-powered machines produced row upon row of chairs, tables, chests, beds and other pieces of furniture. Machine-made furniture was mass-produced and made available to anyone for purchase at any time. In the past, cabinetmakers would consult with clients and build furniture to their specifications. Now, customers could go to a shop where stock was kept on hand, readily available, and at a lower price. Machines put many of the smaller cabinetmakers out of business. Not only did the 19th century signal the end of the small cabinetmaker and the entrance of mass-production, but it was also the beginning of purchasing power for the masses. No longer were the rich and affluent the only ones who could buy on a whim.

Sleigh beds are probably one of the most popular pieces of furniture from the American Empire period and remain popular today. In the late 1790s Juliette Récamier, a French society leader, commissioned Francois-Honoré Jacob-Desmalter, a French furnituremaker, to create a custom bedroom set for her. The highlight of the set was a mahogany bed with flared ends shaped like swans' necks which were decorated with bronze mounts. The bed was originally designed to be placed horizontally against a wall, sometimes on a special platform, and was decorated with bed-draperies which hung around the bed from an overhead canopy.

American sleigh beds were rather reserved, with little decoration, and relied on the basic shape of the bed and the wood from which it was created for its decorative effect. But the European examples became increasing elaborate as the nobilty tried to out-do each other with intricate marquetry, bronze mounts, and carved legs and platforms.

Sleigh beds (which gained their name from the similarity of its appearance to the front of a sleigh) were manufactured in almost every major cabinetmaking city in the United States from the East coast to the Mississippi. The basic form is a couch adapted into a bed. The headboard and footboard were usually identical in heighth and were topped with curved rounded rails. The headboard curved inward towards the mattress and the footboard curved outward away from it. The French had several terms for the sleigh bed design: if the head board and footboard were of equal heighth, the bed was called *lit a la turque* (Turkish bed), if the sides of the bed curved to resemble a boat or a basket it was called *lit bateau* (boat bed), or *lit gondole* (gondola bed), or *lit en courbeille* (basket bed). It was not until the beds were shipped to the United States that they acquired the name *sleigh bed.*

Some early sleigh beds were intricately carved, others were quite plain. Mahogany, rosewood and veneers were often used in the construction. During the Art Deco period designers reinvented the sleigh bed by using exotic woods and high polished lacquer finishes. The basic silhouette remained the same, but the platform, ornaments and fancy feet were not added.

The dimensions of reproduction sleigh beds are quite different from original antique beds. Newer beds can be purchased in king or queen sizes which would not have been available in the early 1800s. Rooms in modern houses have gotten smaller and most beds are no longer designed to be positioned against a wall like the originals. This could result in one of the occupants becoming trapped in the bed and unable to climb out without climbing over the other occupant. The curving of a traditional sleigh bed takes up more floor space than a conventional bed, so some manufacturers have reduced the curviture of the ends and, in some cases, have reduced the size of the footboard as much as seven to twelve inches lower than the headboard. One of the reasons for this modification is so people can lay in bed and watch TV without having the footboard stick up too far to interfere with the view of the TV.

Cradles changed into decorative pieces of furniture and became more like miniature beds during the American Empire period and continued to be made to match bedroom suites during the next few major furniture periods. Early cradles were simple boxes, made from local wood and occassionally had a hood or added rockers. Empire style cradles were made from walnut or pine and often had decoratively carved stiles and rockers. Cradles were finished with either paint or a clear finish.

Some early cribs or cradles have been modified and made into chairs or settees by removing one of the sides. The alteration will destroy the value of the piece of furniture and quite often can destroy the furniture itself, since it was originally designed to hold an infant and not one or more adults. The extra strain on old joints can cause them to break or become loosened in their sockets.

Klismos chairs, based on the ancient Greek chair form (with a broad, straight top rail and curved side stiles and legs) were one of the most popular chair styles during the American Empire period. They were sturdy, functional and attractive. Duncan Phyfe made more of this type of chair than any other identified furnituremaker. Klismos chairs were epecially popular in New York, Duncan Phyfe's home state. The chairs had a sturdy wooden frame and an upholstered or caned seat. Mahogany was most commonly used for the frame, but tiger maple (a rare beautifully grained wood) was also a favorite because the unique grain pattern of the wood served as a decorative element on the curving lines of the chair.

Klismos chairs were often part of a set of furniture including armchairs, sofas, center tables and console tables. Sets of matched dining chairs were often sold in groups of six, eight or more. Some klismos chairs were very simple and plain others were ornate almost to the point of being gaudy. Later chairs were taller than the originals and were constructed from darker wood. The detailed carving will have a sharper edge to it on a later chair and there will be evidence of 20th century screws or nails used in the construction.

The French originated upholstered furniture with coil springs in the 1700s, but American furnituremakers did not incorporate springs into their furniture until around 1826. Prior to that time, furniture was stuffed with feathers, wool or hair placed over a webbed frame. "Sofas" originated in France in the late 1600s and got their name from the Arabic word "sopha" which means "cushion". A *sofa* usually had an upholstered back and seat and was made to accomodate a number of people. *Love seats* were also called "courting chairs" and resemble two chairs which have been pushed together and are missing the inside legs and extra arms. They were designed to accomodate two people. A *settee* was larger than a love seat and usually twice the width of a regular chair. The seat and back were usually covered with upholstery, but some examples had exposed wood on the back, often with decorative carving.

Sofas manufactured towards the end of the American Empire period often combined elements from two different styles. These pieces were called *transitional pieces*, although the name is somewhat misleading. "Transitional" implies one style was on its way out and another on its way in to take its place. That was not always the case. Many rural craftsmen continued to manufacture furniture in a style that was familiar to them and in which they were comfortable long after it officially went out of style. They would combine elements of the old style with the new. These transitional pieces were often less expensive than pieces of a singular popular style. Combinations of Empire and Rococo Revival elements were popular from the late 1820s to around 1860. Reproductions of this combined style were made from 1890 through the 1920s.

Juliette Récamier, who introduced the sleigh bed to the world, is probably better known for bringing popularity to yet another piece of furniture. In her 1800 portrait painted by Jacques-Louis David (which now hangs in the Louvre), she is seated on a chaise lounge or French bedstead. The piece became associated with her and was dubbed "the récamier" and the name stuck and remains in use today. *Récamiers* and *méridiennes,* were examples of the continuing popularity of the daybed, and were available in a variety of styles – from plain and understated to extravagantly adorned. Some Empire style daybeds, especially ones with caned-backs and sides, were made in China to American specifications and then exported to the United States. The carving on Chinese export pieces is generally more intricate than on American examples. The wood used in the construction can also help to identify Chinese export pieces since some of the woods used are not available in the United States. Caned-back récamiers often had a removable front guard which fit over one arm and was held in place by small wooden dowels which fit into corresponding holes on the front of the sofa frame.

At the opposite end of the fashion spectrum from the fancy récamiers was the country style settle. The American settle dates back to the Pilgrim and Colonial period. They were simple utilitarian pieces of furniture designed for seating and, if the seat was hinged, for storage. Empire settles were often constructed of pine, finished with a coat or two of paint, and reflected some of the detailing of the Empire period.

Country Empire furniture had some of the stylish elements of the Empire period, but for the most part, it was a simple interpretation of the style. Country furniture was sturdy and restrained. Legs on country pieces were often thicker than on urban pieces and stretchers and stiles had simple turnings. Urban furniture had more carved detailing on stiles, stretchers and legs.

Rural cabinetmakers used pine and other native woods and stained or painted the furniture instead of following the practice of urban cabinetmakers who concealed these rather plain or unattractive woods with veneer. Figured woods such as mahogany, tiger maple or flame maple were occassionally used for country pieces but these pieces are the exception not the rule. Country furniture made from figured wood is worth con-siderably more than a similar piece made from unfigured wood because these woods were so rarely used on country pieces.

Window seats were first introduced during the Federal period and were an evolution of the simple stools used in parlor sets. During the American Empire period some window seats had arms, most did not, and they ran the gamut from simple designs with plain finishes to carved scrolled shapes and gilded decorations. The legs, arms (if they had them) and frame of the window seat were made from wood or base wood covered with veneer, and the seat was upholstered. Window seats were designed to be placed in front of windows, as their name implies, but they were also used in the center of rooms or against walls. Few window seats have survived from either the Federal period or the American Empire period and today they are quite rare.

Bed frames changed during the American Empire period and began to be fastened together with an iron bolt which passed through the bed posts into a nut set in the rail instead of the mortise-and-tenon joints which were previously used on bed frames. The head of the bolt was hidden behind a small brass cover which could be swung aside, and the bolt could be tightened with an iron *bed wrench.*

In 1820, a New York cabinetmaker named John Hewitt invented a cast iron hook to replace the bed bolts and mortise-and-tenon joints. The hook was designed so the weight of the occupants of a bed forced the joint down and tightened it to make it secure. Modern beds still use this concept today.

Card tables remained popular in the American Empire period. The most popular style had a pedestal base with a tapered column ending in a base mounted on small feet. The rectangular top was hinged and unfolded for use. Other styles were also popular during this period including double pedestal tables with flat-carved curves mounted on a support with flat-sided legs or X-shaped base with circular ends. The rectangular top on these tables was hinged and could be turned 90° when opened.

Center tables were a standard parlor fixture in most homes during the American Empire period. A plain slab of marble was the most common table top. Wooden tops often had elaborate designs inlaid into the wood. The round top was mounted on a pedestal and a base. An interesting example of the center table was the *specimen marble table* which featured various colors and types of marble arranged in a geometric pattern on the top of the table.

Furniture made during the American Empire period was proportionately heavier than the Sheraton and Hepplewhite furniture which preceeded it and center tables seemed to be the epitome of this. Furniture was being mechanically mass-produced and was available to a larger group of potential customers. Some pieces were simply produced and decorated and the price reflected this. Other pieces of furniture took elegance to excess and these pieces were reserved for the wealthy upper class. Many pieces of American Empire furniture were destroyed towards the end of the 19th century because of its large size, "dated" look and heavy, cumbersome appearance. A limited number of quality examples from the period remain today and they are quite valuable.

American Empire drop-leaf tables were designed with the middle class in mind. When the leaves were down the table could serve as a center table. When the leaves were raised it would become a dining table. The table had a rectangular top and two rectangular leaves attached by hinges on the underside. The table top was mounted on a pedestal which was mounted on legs. The pedestal and legs could be carved or left plain. The top of the table was often made of mahogany. The base and legs were usually made of pine and were painted to look like mahogany.

Pro Tip: The stains used to color mahogany furniture during the early 1800s were much darker than the stains used in the 1830s and beyond. These stains penetrated very deeply into the wood, dyeing the wood fibers and are difficult if not impossible to remove.

The *console* or *pier table* was another standard of the American Empire period starting around 1810 and lasting for about thirty years. These tables with large mirrors attached were placed between windows in the parlor, or in a hallway, and were the perfect heighth and size to use in a dining room as an extra serving piece. The top of the table was usually made from marble. White marble was most common, but other colors of marble tops were also used. Beneath the marble was a wooden skirt (sometimes decorated with gilding or ormolu.) supported on four carved columns. On some examples, the columns are also made from marble. The columns attached to a shelf (which may have been decorated with gilding or ormolu) and beneath the shelf were decoratively carved feet which were occassionally gilded. Drawers were seldom found on pier tables. Pier tables made in New York were generally simple designs which were elegantly embellished with ormolu or painted decorations. Tables made in Philadelphia had more elaborate designs with scrolls replacing the columns and bottom shelves cut into complex patterns.

Expandable dining tables with circular tops opening up to contain one or more leaves became popular during the later part of the American Empire period. On some examples, the top and the base expanded. The base consisted of clusters of columns set on a small platform or a cylindrical base. The inner mechanism on the table often contained a manufacturer's label or mark. You can use this information to help date the piece of furniture.

Sewing or work tables were abundantly produced during the American Empire period. Not all of the pieces were well designed or well constructed and many of these pieces are still around today. (Just because a piece of furniture is old, does not make it valuable or beautiful. Our fore-fathers made junk too.) Some pieces were quite plain and others were liberally embellished with carving, but all American Empire pieces were heavily proportioned. American Empire sewing tables were made from both solid wood and veneered wood. Mahogany and mahogany veneer were the most commonly used woods. The basic sewing table was rectangular shaped, often with leaves on the sides attached with hinges and could be opened to increase the work space. The casework of the table contained two or more drawers (one of which was often compartmentalized to hold needles, thimbles and smaller accessories) and often a fabric bag hung from the lower drawer to hold fabric and larger accessories. The case was mounted on a pedestal (square, round and turned, or carved) attached to a base (of various shapes) with four carved feet. The feet were carved into the shape of animal's paws, scrolls or balls. Sewing tables usually had brass casters attached to the feet to make the piece easier to move.

Dressing tables were just beginning to appear during the Empire period and few of them were made with attached mirrors. If you should find one with an attached mirror, examine the wood around the mirror frame to make sure it matches the wood used on the table. The finish and stain should be the same. Examine the mirror attachments (which should be brass) to make sure they are not replacements and the hardware is of similar age to the rest of the piece.

Most Empire dressers originally had mirrors attached to the casework, however, many of them today are often missing. Check the backboard on the dresser for screwholes and for the shadowed image left from the support boards of a mirror.

* Check the back of chests of drawers to make sure the backboard and other wooden components are original and have not been replaced. It is easier to see the replaced pieces from the back than the front.

* Check the drawers on the dresser to make sure they fit properly. If the drawers have been repaired, check the backsides to see if they have been shortened, reworked or are from another piece of furniture.

Empire sideboards were often shorter and bulkier than their Federal style counterparts. Pieces made in more rural areas did not have drawers to contain silver and serving pieces. Empire sideboards are less elaborately decorated than their predessors. Part of the reason behind this is the increase of the mecahnical production and reduction of hand-done work. The increase in mass-production lead to a gradual decline in the craftsmanship of most furniture. As a general rule, Empire pieces have few drawers and cupboards.

Empire ogee-frame mirrors are one of the most commonly available antique mirrors. They are wide framed rectangular mirrors with two narrow bands of gilding flanking a wide "S" shaped curved molding of figured wood (i.e.: mahogany, rosewood, or walnut) or wood painted to look like a figured wood. In the 19th century, the more expensive mirrors were made of solid mahogany or veneer, but today, the false-grained pieces in good condition are actually more valuable because they are now more rare.

China Trade Furniture

There was a wide-spread fascination in the United States with anything Oriental during the early part of the 18th century. Some furniture, called *China Trade Furniture*, was specially manufactured in China for export to the United States and combined both Chinese and Western elements. The designs were a combination of the American Sheraton, American Empire neoclassical styles and Oriental styles. The furniture was manufactured from bamboo, cane and exotic woods like Oriental rosewood.

China Trade furniture is relatively rare and is generally found in port cities and other areas which were centers of the China trade. At first glance, many China Trade pieces appear to be fake Sheraton or Empire pieces because the wood and the decorations do not match those used on Western pieces. Carving on Chinese export pieces is often excessive and more elaborate than the carving on American pieces. China Trade furniture featured the traditional leaves, shells and scrolls of the Sheraton and Empire periods but also occassionally contained Oriental motifs. Not all pieces of China Trade furniture were carved and some plain examples do exist.

Some newer pieces of furniture may look similar to China Trade pieces and may be confused for antiques. Original China Trade furniture should show signs of wear and age. Newer pieces are generally not as well constructed as the originals.

Shaker Furniture

Shaker furniture is very popular because its simple lines allow it to blend easily with other styles of furniture and it is just as popular today as it was when it was conceived over 150 years ago. It is probably the most perfect example of pure country design. Reproduction Shaker furniture is very common and original pieces can be difficult to find.

The Shakers were a separatist religious sect who came to the United States in 1794 and settled in the Capital District of New York state. The full and proper name of the sect was United Society of Believers. They were dubbed "Shakers" because of the shaking dance movements they made as a part of their religious celebration. Shaker colonies were set up in Mount Lebanon, near the Massachusetts border and in Niskayuna which is located between Troy and Schenectady in New York. The movement eventually spread all the way to Maine and Kentucky, but in spite of how wide they spread geographically, even at its height there were never more than 6,000 members.

The Shaker communities depended on agriculture and various craft industries to sustain themselves. Work was a form of worship for the Shakers, and they took great pride in what they produced.

Simplicity and utility were the two major concerns for Shaker furniture. The form of the furniture was designed around the function of the furniture and all unnecessary ornamentation was omitted. Furniture was often made with a specific room in a specific building and often a specific person in mind when it was designed, and the dimensions of Shaker furniture can vary because of these tailor-made tendencies.

Original Shaker pieces may have lacked decorations but they were perfectly proportioned, consisting of classic lines and balance and showing superior workmanship. Furniture forms were based on simple designs, from Windsor chairs and slat-backed chairs, to plain tables and benches and low post beds. The Shakers made a variety of tables, cupboards, and hanging cupboards intended to contain small kitchen items, personal items or work related items. Hanging cupboards were often quite shallow. Cupboards were made for many different purposes and each piece was designed uniquely for its purpose. The size of the piece, the number of drawers, the placement of the drawers and doors, and the interior arrangement all depended on the intended purpose of the furniture.

The Shakers were very organized and disliked clutter, and their furniture designs featured a variety of drawers and storage areas, some in places where you would not normally expect to find them. Shaker furniture generally had tall, narrow proportions and was very simply designed. Inexpensive local woods like pine, birch, ash, hickory and maple were used for the construction. Turned elements were kept plain and slender, there were no carved rings or added detail. Slats and stretchers were kept simple and had no unnecessary carving. The boards used for construction were of uniform size and good quality. If the Shakers came across a board with a knot in it, they would remove the knot and plug the piece of wood with a matching wooden patch. Shaker furniture was always constructed with evenly spaced, well cut dovetails and not nailed construction. Wooden knobs were used as drawer pulls.

Furniture was produced for domestic use and for work. (The seed industry was a mainstay of the Shaker communities and tables for sorting seeds and high stools were produced in large quantities.) A large majority of Shaker furniture was produced during the period between 1820 and 1870. The production of all pieces of furniture – with the exception of chairs – started to decline after 1870.

Shaker furniture was originally produced for personal use within their own communities. But by the middle of the 1800s the membership of the sect was shrinking and the extra furniture was no longer needed. This furniture was offered for sale to the public (or "The World's People" as they referred to outsiders) as well as other pieces which were made with the specific intent of being sold.

Shakers were among the first in America to produce chairs for sale on a large scale. The first chairs were sold in New Lebanon, New York in 1789 and they continued to produce chairs at their factory well into the 20th century. The Shakers refined their designs over the years to include high and low stools, a variety of chair styles and tables of various shapes and sizes. But they kept the basic principle that "the most simple things are the most beautiful". It is said some Shakers believed their furniture was originally designed in heaven and the patterns were transmitted to them by angels.

The chairs were crafted from maple and cherry wood and had clean simple lines. The back on a genuine Shaker ladderback chair will have a noticeable incline towards the rear to make the chair more comfortable. If the chair is perpendicular to the floor it is probably a reproduction and not genuine Shaker.

Almost from the beginning of the public sales, the Shakers warned people about competitors who made furniture similar to the Shaker style, but who did not produce furniture equal to its quality in materials and workmanship. The same still holds true today. Not all furniture that looks like Shaker furniture is genuine Shaker furniture. Original furniture will have a stamp or a gold tag identifying it as being manufactured by "The United Society of Believers". Some pieces made for sale outside the community were marked with metal mounts attached to the rear legs to identify them as original. Other pieces were branded as a form of identification.

Furniture salesmen travelled the country selling Shaker furniture and its popularity quickly spread. Unfortunately, as the furniture was growing in popularity the Shaker population was declining, and it was drastically reduced by 1900. A very limited amount of authentic Shaker furniture has been made since that time.

The Shakers were very creative, industrious people and invented clothespins, dependable circular saws, the stereoscope viewer and, of course, a very simple but practical style of furniture. They believed industrious work was a form of worship. Their baskets, wooden boxes and furniture items were highly sought after in their time and even more collectible today. However, if the Shakers had truly made everything ever attributed to them, every member of the sect would have had to have worked non-stop year round, and never slept in order to do it.

The Shakers were a chaste religious group and because of their vow of chastity there was seldom a need for cribs or cradles. They liked children and were concerned about their welfare and occassionally babies and young children were taken to the Shaker colonies to be left in their care. Cribs were made for these circumstances but were not intended for use for offspring of the Shakers themselves. Some infant and child-size furniture was made by the Shakers for others and given as gifts. But a genuine Shaker crib or cradle is a rare find.

As for adult bedding, Shakers predominately made low, narrow single beds. Double beds were made in small quantities up until 1830 and were not made after that date. Shaker beds were made from pine or maple and were usually painted. The headboards were low and undecorated and the stiles and legs were tapered cylinders. Footboards were occassionally used, but they are not common. The frame of the bed had evenly spaced holes drilled into the wood and tightly strung rope was woven through the holes and used as a mattress support.

What we call bedrooms the Shakers called "retiring rooms" and each retiring room could accommodate as many as four Shakers. The room would usually contain a bed for each person, a rocking chair, a small table with a single drawer, one or two candlestands (small round tables about 18" diameter and about 25" tall), a sconce, and sometimes a mirror. Free-standing floor racks were also commonplace in retiring rooms, kitchens and wash houses. They were usually about 3' wide by 3' high and consisted of four round rods connected to footed sides. These all purpose racks could be used for drying clothes, holding towels, storing clothes and for a variety of other purposes.

The other rooms of the house contained an abundance of shelves and pegged racks. The racks were used for hanging just about everything, including clothing, baskets, shelves and furniture. Chairs would be hung on the pegs to make it easier to clean the room and to make room for religious services.

There are no genuine Shaker card tables or game boards. The Shakers did not play cards or games and would have had no use for that type of furniture. They were very concerned with functuality and would not have wasted the time or materials on an item that could not be used.

In the early 1860s, the Mount Lebanon Shakers designed a line of chairs sized specifically for the people who would use them. The sizing started with 0 for infants up to the Number 9 which was designed for large adults. The number 5 chair was the most common and was usually used as a dining chair. Number 0 and Number 1 pieces were made in very limited quantities and are very hard to find. The numbers were impressed on the back of one of the slats of the chair to indentify the type and size of the chair. A gold transfer trademark imprinted with the "United Society of Believers" was also put on furniture to identify it.

In typical Shaker style, the height of the seat and the overall dimensions of the chair were carefully planned. The backposts on a Shaker chair were bent slightly towards the rear and the back rails were curved so the chair fit a tall or a short person, perfectly. Some Shaker chairs had a small maple button fitted into the bottom of the rear legs allowing the person sitting in the chair to adjust the tilt of the chair. Another interesting innovation was the ball-and-socket feet on the rear legs of some armchairs and side chairs which allowed the person sitting in the chair to tilt the chair back for comfort.

The seat of a Shaker chair can be either solid wood, or woven with splint, cane or Shaker chair tape. The Shakers preferred fabric tape over other woven seating materials (like rush, wood splint, or cane) because it did not dry out and break, did not pinch or snag their clothing, was strong and long lasting, and was comfortable and colorful.

The most popular Shaker chair was the "slat back" or straight chair. It was a ladderback style chair with tall back posts ending in rounded finials. There are many reproductions of this now classic-shaped chair, but it is often the finial that catches the eye and raises the question of the chair's authenticity. Reproduction chairs often have more decorative finials than would be found on a traditional Shaker chair.

The Shakers also created the forerunner of today's swivel office chair. The Shakers called it a "revolving chair" or a "revolver". They were first produced at Mount Lebanon, New York around 1860, but these chairs were also made in Shaker communities in Massachusetts and New Hampshire. Revolvers were made almost exclusively by the Shaker communities. The chair had a solid wood seat, and an arched spindle back. The wooden spindles on the back of the chair were sometimes replaced with metal ones. A threaded steel rod allowed the chair to be raised or lowered by spinning it.

 Pro Tip: Shaker rocking chairs have the rocker mortised into the chair posts. If the rocker is attached in any other way it is not an original Shaker rocker.

The Shakers manufactured settees similar to Sheraton or Windsor styles, but they added their own unique touches. The back was constructed of plain panels, the arms were usually plain and simple with rounded ends, and the legs were simply tapered. The seat cushion was supported by ropes woven back and forth and then tied to knobs on the sides, front and back of the seat frame.

The candlestand form has been popular throughout every furniture period and style. The Shakers were no exception and produced several variations on the candlestand. The small round topped tables with tapered cylinder pedestals and tripod bases were used to hold candles and other household items in various rooms throughout the house. Rectangular variations of these tables, with a gallery around the top, were used to sort seeds. Some Shaker candlestands have drawers suspended from the top.

Shaker mirrors are unique in that they were mounted on "T" shaped hangers. The hangers are pierced at the top so they could be hung from nails or pegs. A cord runs from the hanger to the back of the mirror allowing it to be adjusted to the proper heighth needed by the user. Shakers were quite modest, and most mirrors were hung high on the wall so only the upper part of a person's head could be reflected in the mirror. The mirror frame had pegs across the bottom of the frame which were used to hold brushes and combs.

Victorian Revival Furniture

There is no singular "Victorian style" of furniture. The term "Victorian Furniture" is based upon the styles and sub-styles of furniture manufactured during the reign of Queen Victoria of England who became a symbol of the fashions and attitudes popular throughout much of the 19th century. There was some historical basis of design during the Victorian period, but some of the revival styles were quite liberal in their interpretations. The Victorian Revival period lasted from 1840-

1880 and covered several revival styles: *Gothic Revival, Rococo Revival* and *Renaissance Revival.* Furniture manufacturing was in full swing by this time, and factory production made it possible to produce a huge variety of furniture for the increasing number of customers, and furniture once again took on mid-size to massive proportions.

Gothic Revival style - The Gothic Revival style was the first of the mid-19th century styles to be called a "revival" style. It contained two completely different approaches: the first one was strictly decorative and used details from historic monument, the second and later approach, was influenced by designers like William Morris who wanted simple functional forms.

Gothic furniture regained popularity in England around 1830, and by 1840 it had crossed the ocean and made an impact in America. This medieval inspired furniture featured such Gothic motifs as arches, tracery (a delicate intersecting of lines and carving), and *quatrefoils* (a carved design with four lobes, like a flower with four petals or a composition of four small leaves). Gothic Revival furniture was designed to be used in Gothic Revival homes. A number of architectural details like the pointed arch, the rose window and tracery were modified and incorporated into furniture designs. Chair backs were good candidates for these details and were often designed using more than one of these dominate features.

Chairs often had balloon-shaped backs and, like most other pieces of furniture, cabriole legs. They were produced with a wide variety of molded and carved decorations. The curved braces or low arms on balloon-backed chairs are rumored to have originated because of the full skirts worn by women between 1840 and1860. The chair allowed the women to sit on the chair more comfortably. Balloon-backed chairs were made in just about every price range, and the type of wood used and the amount of carving and decoration were often relative to the price. Gothic Revival side chairs were often made in large sets.

It is not unusual to find sets originally consisting of eight, ten or even twelve chairs. Beware of sets that may have recently been "created" out of pieces from broken chairs. Upholstered seats on side chairs were often covered with tapestry done in small geometric or floral patterns.

> **Pro Tip:** Balloon-backed chairs were blatantly repro-
> duced in the 1930s and continue to be reproduced
> today. Reproductions are generally smaller than originals
> and the details are not as rounded.

Gothic Revival furniture was very extravagant with exaggerated curving shapes, emphatic carving and cut-out areas displaying the popular motifs of the period. Upholstered furniture was often deeply tufted and inner springs (which were perfected during this period) made the furniture extremely comfortable. Footstools were often found as part of a parlor set. It was believed elevating the legs could cure rheumatism and gout, and footstools were implemented to raise legs to the proper elevation for good health. Small footstools are sometimes called *gout stools.* Footstools often had upholstered seats and decorative upholstery tacks, but some were made from un-upholstered carved wood. Another type of small footstool was the *slipper stool,* which had a hinged top which could be lifted to reveal a storage area for a pair of slippers.

In contrast to all of this excess and exuberrance were the more simple, straight forward lines of furniture from designers such as William Morris. The *Morris chair,* for which he is most remembered, was a simple rectangular oak mission style easy chair. It was upholstered with leather and contained the unique ability to adjust the angle of the back of the chair for the comfort of the person sitting in it. Wooden support rods were held in place by knobs behind the arms of the chair and could be moved to adjust the angle of the back of the chair. Furniture from this part of the Gothic Revival period was simple and uncluttered and contained minimal decoration. Oak replaced the rosewood, mahogany and walnut woods which were so popular in the extravegant Gothic Revival furniture.

A Morris chair

Rococo Revival style - The Rococo Revival style was not introduced in the United States until around 1840 even though it had been popular in England for some time before that. Once here, it remained the dominant style in the U.S. for about twenty years. It was referred to by people at the time as the "Louis XV style" not as Rococo Revival. The style is based on the European Rococo style, but the carving was much more "in your face". Rococo Revival furniture was some of the most elaborate furniture created during the 19th century. Fruit, flowers, shells, cupids and scrolls were carved in higher relief than on their European predecessors, and the carving was much more realistic. Rococo Revival pieces were smaller than the European pieces, but still duplicated the curving shapes. The furniture had cabriole or scrolled legs, often with casters to make it easier to move the large pieces of furniture.

Rosewood was the most fashionable wood of this period, but mahogany, cherry and walnut were also used on pieces of lesser quality. Boxwood was used on mass-produced factory pieces and was made to look like rosewood with an application of stain and some false-graining techniques using special combs with rubber teeth or special rollers. Marble tops were common on many types of furniture during the Rococo Revival period and scalloped shapes were preferred to straight edges. But marble tops can also be recently added to furniture to increase the sales price and desirability. If possible, remove the piece of marble and take a look underneath it. The furniture frame should look old, rough and unfinished. It should also show signs of wear from the marble rubbing against the wood during years of use. There should be marks on the underside of the marble from where it has been in contact with the wood.

The Rococo Revival style was most commonly used to create bedroom furniture and parlor furniture. Parlor sets could be quite elaborate and contain sofas, settees, chairs, center tables and other smaller accessory pieces. The tête-à-tête, a new form of conversational sofa, with two seats facing in opposite directions with backs forming an S-shaped curve, was created during this period.

The carving and pierced wood which comprised the intricate motif of the Rococo style was made possible by a new technique invented by John Henry Belter, of New York. Belter was a German immigrant who is credited for bringing the wood-bending techniques and carving style that defines Rococo Revival furniture to the United States, and many of his competitors quickly copied his pieces. He was just one of many craftsmen who used laminated wood to create the intricately carved Rococo forms. Rococo Revival furniture was produced all over the United States, but the most documented pieces were made in New York, Philadelphia and Boston.

There are three quality levels of Rococo Revival sofas: the first level contains the John Henry Belter-style laminated sofas, the second the J. and J. W. Meeks-style laminated sofas, and the third level contains sofas made from solid wood bent into Rococo shapes. Solid wood pieces of furniture cost more when they were manufactured and they are worth considerably more today. Both Belter and Meeks had their shops in New

York. New York and New Orleans were known for producing the most elegant Rococo Revival furniture. Alexander Roux and Charles Badouine were two other prominent New York cabinetmakers who helped define fashionable Rococo Revival furniture.

John Henry Belter made the finest and most elaborate furniture with intricate carving and well-executed lamination. He loved rosewood and used it to carve roses and leaves and pierced the surface of the wood to create ornamental designs. He also used mahogany, *blackwood* (hardwood painted to emulate ebony) and stained oak. He introduced improved methods of lamination to the furniture industry and was the only manufacturer to receive a patent for his lamination processes. He used six or more layers of wood in the manufacturing of his furniture while his competitors used only three to five. Layers of wood were glued together so the grain of the successive pieces were at right angles to each other. This pattern was followed until the desired thickness was attained. Then, steam and a special matrix was used to curve the wood into the desired shape.

Belter is considered the most important American cabinetmaker during the Rococo Revival period. His chairs all had small brass rollers on all four legs, unlike most Victorian furniture which had rollers or casters only on the front legs. Some of his pieces still have the paper label under the seat identifying them as having been made by John Henry Belter. If the upholstery is original, the paper label may be hidden under the protective cambric fabric under the seat. Genuine Belter pieces have extraordinary carving and detail, and superior laminated wood surfaces, with prices to match. John Belter produced a large quantity of parlor furniture, but he also made furniture for bedrooms and dining rooms.

Charles Badouine was a cabinetmaker in New York from the 1830s until the 1850s. He took frequent trips home to his native France, and brought back the current styles and motifs from the Continent. It is reported at one time he employeed nearly 200 workers to help him produce parlor suites, ètagéres and a variety of styles of chairs.

Rococo Revival sofas were usually made as part of a parlor set and were seldom sold individually. They often had intricately carved top and bottom rails with piercework, and carved arm supports. Rosewood and other exotic woods were used and the seat and back were lushly upholstered. Rococo Revival pieces with simple frames were also made in just about every furniture manufacturing area in the country until around 1880. The more simple Rococo Revival pieces had an understated attractiveness widely accepted by the public, and they continued to be adapted for use long after they went out of style. Rococo Revival furniture was originally upholstered with damask or velvet, but few pieces still have their original upholstery. Reupholstering a piece of furniture does not noticeably reduce the value of the piece *if* it is properly done with material appropriate for the period and style of the furniture.

The *méridienne* was a type of high-backed settee that was part of the parlor sets which were so popular during the middle of the 19th century. Méridiennes were often manufactured in pairs and were made to face each other. They had intricately carved rosewood frames and a single arm on one side. John Henry Belter produced méridiennes with piercework frames. The back of the settee was deeply tufted and the upholstery was usually rich silk or damask.

Rococo Revival piano stools with screw mechanisms to adjust the heighth were mass-produced in factories during the 19th century. The stool usually had a pedestal base with four legs underneath. Mahogany was a popular wood choice and the stool often had carving on the pedestal, seat base and legs. Low backs were occassionally added to some stools. If the seat was upholstered silk, damask or other fine fabric was used and it was well padded.

Rococo Revival center tables are some of the most

distinctive pieces of furniture from the period. The oval tables with white marble tops and intricately pierced and carved skirts and cross stretchers are quite easy to recognize. The laminating process developed by John Henry Belter helped other cabinetmakers to create intricately carved furniture, but Belter's pieces were the most elegant and elaborate and have always been in greater demand.

Papier-mâché furniture was made in England between 1810 and 1870. American Rococo Revival furniture was easily interpreted using papier-mâché as the medium. Small tables with gilded scalloped edges and tilt-tops were decorated with painted pictures of still lifes or landscapes. The table top was mounted on a pedestal attached to a flat, four footed base. Papier-mâché furniture was delicate when it was created and age makes it even more so. Check the furniture very carefully for evidence of repairs which may have been done and covered with additional coats of paint.

The Rococo Revival style was not exclusively used for indoor furniture. Cast-iron furniture was made for use on porches or in the garden. J. L. Mott of New York was a major producer of cast-iron furniture and published a catalogue of different styles of Rococo Revival furniture well into the 1870s. Chairs, settees and tables were manufactured in foundries all over the country. Cast-iron furniture was primarily made for outdoor use and many pieces were produced for cemeteries and other public outdoor areas. Cast-iron reproductions are common. Check the undersides of the furniture for signs of age and wear and for previous coats of paint or repairs.

Renaissance Revival style - Renaissance Revival furniture was popular at the same time as Rococo Revival furniture, and some feel its popularity may have been *because* of the Rococo Revival furniture. Renaissance Revival was everything Rococo Revival furniture wasn't. It was a return to straight lines, but was decorated with applied moldings, veneered panels, and on the more expensive pieces, inlay and piercework. Some Renaissance Revival furniture had gilding, ormolu and applied porcelain or ivory decorations. Architectural elements such as pediments, columns, and balusters were decoratively used but served no structural purpose. Gone were the over-done carvings and excesses of the Rococo style. Medallions, cartouches, flowers, fruit, classical busts and animal heads became popular motifs. Walnut was the wood of choice and lighter woods were more popular than the darker somber woods so popular in preceeding styles.

Renaissance Revival furniture can be divided into two catagories: pieces made in traditional workshops using techniques such as fine carving by skilled craftsmen and marquetry, and pieces which were made using machines to cut and turn elegant parts which could be easily assembled into fashionable furniture, in lieu of fine craftsmanship.

Factories in Pennsylvania, New England and Grand Rapids, Michigan (which became the leading furnituremaking center) mass-produced furniture from pine and other inexpensive local woods and false-grained the wood to make it look like expensive figured woods. This furniture became known as "cottage furniture" because it was inexpensive enough so the average worker could afford to buy it to put in their cottage home, but was also used in vacation cottages of the upper class. Cottage furniture was often sold as a set. The bedroom set would usually include a bed, a washstand, a dresser, a chair and sometimes other matching pieces.

Factories also mass-produced furniture made from walnut and other better woods and used matching veneer for decorative panels. The furniture was large and imposing and had intricate carving and turnings.

Renaissance Revival tall chests of drawers fit into homes at the time they were manufactured, but few homes today can accommodate such large pieces of furniture. This makes them difficult to sell today. Tall chests could be seven feet tall from the top of the finial on the pediment to the feet. Some pieces have been shortened to make them more saleable. Check the backboard to see if there are visible saw marks. Look for evidence the backboard has been removed or replaced. Check the feet and legs to see if they have been shortened. An altered piece will have variations in the color and finish when closely examined. These tall chests were often part of a set or a *bedroom suit* or *bedroom suite* consisting of a bed, the dresser, a chest of drawers, possibly one or two nightstands, and one or two chairs.

Many pieces originally had porcelain and iron casters which may have since been removed. Caster removal can alter the overall lines of furniture and can make chairs too short to be used comfortably at a matching table. Look underneath the feet. If you see holes or filled holes, you will know the piece was originally designed to have casters. Period hardware is available from some mail order catalogues and at many antique stores or secondhand stores. If you decide to replace the casters, try to replace them with casters from the correct period to retain the value of the piece.

Wooden side chairs were designed with either solid backs or pierced wooden backs and had either solid wood seats or caned seats. Upholstered armchairs were mass-produced in factories throughout the midwest and in smaller workshops in major cities across the United States. Mass-produced chairs kept up with the latest fashions and had good lines and detailing. They often had gilding, ebonizing, ormolu or applied brass decorations.

Pro Tip: Reupholstering can completely change the shape of a cushion and the overall lines of a chair if too much or too little stuffing is added. Look at pictures in old books or company product catalogs before reupholstering a piece of furniture to get an idea of how the furniture would have originally looked. This will allow you to more closely duplicate the original look of the piece.

Folding chairs were produced by numerous companies between the 1870s and 1880s. They consisted of an iron frame with upholstered cushions and optional wood trim on the arms and top rail. The chairs were advertised as being useful for invalids and for helping to cure gout and rheumetism. The bottom section of the chair cantilevered forward from the seat and elevated it to serve as a footrest, and the chairs could be folded up compactly when not in use. These chairs often contain labels with the manufacturer's name, city and state, and patent dates and numbers. This information can be very useful in dating a piece of furniture or establishing its value, IF the label is original and genuine. A patent date does not mean the piece of furniture was made on or even shortly after the patent date. But it does make it easier for you to learn more about the piece of furniture and its design by obtaining a copy of its patent description.

Rocking chairs have been a popular piece of American furniture since their invention. Victorian rockers had wooden seats and backs, upholstered seats and wooden backs, upholstered seats and backs, and woven seats with wooden backs. Even the President of the United States, Abraham Lincoln, was fond of rocking chairs. Lincoln's favorite rocking chair at his home had a padded seat and back, and rounded arms. Rockers similar to this style became known as *Lincoln rockers*. The owner of the Ford Theater in Washington, D.C. placed a rocker in the Presidential box at the theater for President Lincoln to use, and Lincoln was sitting in the rocker the night he was assassinated.

Carpet rockers are small folding rocking chairs with the seat and back made from a carpet-like material. These chairs are lightweight and portable, and could be carried from room to room or tucked away when not in use. *Slipper rockers* were low rockers with wide seats used by the lady or gentleman of the house for putting on or removing shoes without having to bend over. A lady or gentleman from the Victorian time would never think of exposing their feet and would always put on slippers after removing their shoes.

Pedestal-base revolving armchairs were a late 19th century innovation. They were preceeded by the Shaker "revolver" and piano stools with turning mechanisms. Revolving armchairs became popular as desk chairs and remain so today. Revolving armchairs often had leather upholstered seats, but some were constructed from wood and had no upholstery. The revolving mechanism will often have the company name and/or a patent date cast into the metal parts. This information can be used to date and authenticate a chair and help identify where it was made.

Stools were used in front of chairs or sofas as foot supports and as backless chairs during the Victorian period. They were used as accent pieces in various rooms and were often part of a bedroom suite or parlor set. Victorian stools were decorated with gilding or ebonized decorations. Tapestry, carpet upholstery, embroidery and needlepoint were used to upholster the footstools. Some stools had tops which lifted, to reveal a small storage area. Homes in the late 1800s were furnished quite eclectically and could feature a variety of stools in different styles.

* During the middle of the 19th century, architects often designed some or all of the furniture for the houses they designed. Many of these pieces are signed, labeled or marked in some other way with the architect's name. This type of identification can greatly increase the value of a piece of furniture.

Infant's beds changed between 1870 and 1880. The new style, called a "crib", was similar in appearance to the cribs we still use today. They had a headboard and footboard and side galleries of spindles. Iron-framed springs were used to support the mattress. Cribs also had an added bonus: they could be folded up for easy moving or storage.

During the late 19th century, pedestals became popular as a means of displaying sculptures, ceramics and knick-knacks. Pedestals were luxury items and frequently had elegant detailing. Ebonizing and gilding were often applied in geometric patterns or in Oriental or other exotic motifs. Inlay, contrasting woods and paint were also used as decorations. The American middle-class was becoming wealthier, and they wanted a prominent but tasteful place to display sculptures and artwork as proof of their new wealth and sophistication. Countless pedestals were mass-produced in factories throughout the United States and they are still in abundance today.

Small round or oval tables with marble tops were also mass-produced by factories during the Renaissance Revival period. Reproductions of these tables were quite common in the 1930s and they are still imitated and reproduced today. Evidence of dirt, use and wear can help separate the originals from the fakes.

Renaissance Revival style furniture was not just found inside the home, but appeared outside in the garden and on the porch as well in cast-iron form. Cast-iron furniture was manufactured in foundries all over the country during the late 1800s. Cast-iron contains a high carbon content and, unlike most metals, can not be shaped no matter how hot it is heated. Furniture pieces are formed by pouring liquid metal into molds, then allowing them to cool. Once cooled, cast iron becomes extremely hard and durable. The resulting hardness and low production costs made it a very popular furniture material.

Some Renaissance Revival cast-iron furniture imitated rustic wooden furniture, but many of the popular pieces had naturalistic "grape and leaf" patterns done in piercework on the seats, chair backs and table tops. Cast-iron furniture was designed to be used both indoors and outdoors, but indoor pieces were not as widely accepted and were popular for a much shorter period of time.

Most cast-iron furniture was originally painted with dark colors; green, gray and brown being popular choices. Today, white and black are the most popular colors. Check in the corners and crevices of the furniture and around the nuts and bolts holding it together for evidence of the original paint color.

Some manufacturers cast the company name directly into the piece of furniture under a chair seat or in a medallion on the back of the furniture. The company name or patent date can help to determine the age of the furniture.

* Cast-iron furniture can be broken and repairs can be camoflagued under multiple coats of paint. Check the furniture carefully for signs of a repair. Also, be aware old layers of paint on the chair may contain lead.

Neo-Grec (or Neo-Greek) and Egyptian Revival - The Neo-Grec and Egyptian Revival styles were substyles of the Renaissance Revival style. They were very elaborate and exotic but never popularly accepted by the masses and the furniture was produced in small quantities. Because of the limited production, these pieces are usually more valuable than others from the period. Neo-Grec or Neo-Greek furniture featured Greek motifs such as columns, leafy scrolls and palmettes.

The Egyptian Revival period lasted from 1870 to 1880 and was triggered by Napoleon III's resumption of the French archaeological excavations in Egypt. Egyptian motifs such as sphinx heads, animal heads, Egyptian masks and other Egyptian themes were used on furniture in place of the typical classical Renaissance Revival elements of the period. Egyptian motifs had been briefly popular between 1820 and 1830, had a resurgence of popularity during the Renaissance Revival , and then became popular again during the early 20th century.

Corner cupboards declined in popularity during the Victorian periods and glass-front china cabinets took their place. They were used as display cases for anything from china to knicknacks. Middle-class Victorians were eager to show off their collectibles as a statement of their financial status and social breeding. Victorian homes would have been cluttered by today's standards, but many Victorians believed more was never enough and they proudly displayed all of their possessions. Elaborately carved cabinets and cabinets with mirrors and shaped cornices were originally more expensive to purchase than plain ones because they were more labor-intensive and usually constructed of wood of a higher quality. Because of this, plain cabinets may be "gussied up" today with components they did not originally have in an effort to fetch a higher price.

During the late 19th century, bent-glass panels were used on the sides of cabinets so the contents could be more easily displayed and seen from more angles. There are few companies who still manufacture curved glass today, and it is expensive and difficult to replace if it is broken. Check the frame of the cabinet to make sure the glass is secure and is original to the piece. Also check to make sure the curved glass has not been replaced with straight glass panels. If the doors are curved, chances are the glass in the door was originally curved.

Vitrines were also used to display collections and knicknacks. A vitrine is different from a china cabinet or a bookcase in that it has a mirrored back inside the cabinet and thinner shelves. There would be no reason to reflect books in a bookcase, and the thin shelves of a vitrine would not be able to support the weight of books. Vitrines were often decoratively carved and had glass panels in the doors. Some contained drawers beneath the cabinet doors. Vitrines were not as common as bookcases or cupboards and consequently are worth more today. Because of their rarity and value they are prime candidates for being "created". An orphaned top section from a piece of furniture can have a mirrored backing installed and some thin shelves attached inside and – voila! – a vitrine is born. Check for consistency in the wood, the color and the finish. Look for screwholes that do not match up on the piece. Carefully check the piece to determine authenticity.

Another large piece of furniture which was used to display collections and knicknacks in Victorian homes was the *étagère*. Cupboard base étagéres were almost always custom-made. They were elaborately decorated with gilding and veneer and were intricately carved. Because they were usually quite large, they consisted of several smaller sections which fastened together to make the whole unit. Pieces of these larger units are often "married" to other pieces of furniture or modified to create another piece of furniture.

Wardrobes and *armoires* were large storage pieces used to hold clothing. Most houses did not have built in closets during the Victorian era and the wardrobe or armoire served this purpose. Early Victorian wardrobes were very cumbersome, heavy and hard to move and many of them were dismantled and discarded when they were no longer needed. A large number of wardrobes were manufactured in England or in other parts of Europe and sent over to the United States. Foreign pieces were often more intricately carved than their American counterparts and can be identified as imported by the wood used in their construction. If the wood is not native to the United States, there is a good chance the piece was imported.

Another large piece of Victorian furniture which was found in almost every household was the sideboard. Sideboards became smaller during the Victorian periods than they had been in the past, but they were still a substantial piece of furniture. A Victorian home would be considered cluttered judged by today's standards, but excess was the norm during the Victorian period. An average size room in a Victorian home could have as many as six tables and a dozen or more chairs. Sideboards were reduced in size just so they would fit into the room. The side-board contained drawers to hold silverware, serving pieces, or linens, and had cabinets to hold china and silver pieces. Some were designed with special cabinets to hold wine.

On a much smaller scale, *shaving stands* became popular during the Victorian period. Shaving stands were basically a dressing glass mounted on a pedestal placing the attached mirror at a comfortable height for grooming. The wood framed mirror was attached to the frame with iron or brass swivels. There was usually at least one drawer in the cabinet to hold shaving accessories, and the top of the cabinet could be made from either wood or marble. Both wooden and marble tops should show damage from water and wear. The legs usually had casters so the stand could be moved easily. Today, the casters may be missing and the mirror or hardware may have been replaced. Some shaving stands have lost their pedestal somewhere along the way and are now being passed off as dressing glasses or cheval mirrors. Look on the underside of the cabinet where the pedestal would have been to see if the piece has evidence left from a former life.

Spool furniture - Spool furniture was an unpretentious style of machine-made furniture. It was manufactured by both large factories and small furniture shops. *Godey's Magazine and Lady's Book* published by Josepha Hale first introduced this simple style of furniture around 1815 and it remained popular for almost fifty years. Pieces of wood were turned on a lathe and carved until the wood resembled a symmetrical row of spools, balls or buttons strung together. Earlier pieces of furniture were created with straight elements and later ones were curved. The resulting carved wood could be used to create almost every conceivable piece of furniture, but beds were the most popular pieces of spool furniture. Spool beds are often called "Jenny Lind" beds. In 1850, P.T. Barnum introduced Jenny Lind, "The Swedish Nighingale", to American audiences. She was a popular attraction wherever she toured and clever marketing people immortalized her by naming merchandise in her honor. The spool beds were co-incidentally growing in popularity at that time and were dubbed "Jenny Lind". The name stuck and they are still called Jenny Lind beds by many people today.

Spool furniture was produced from just about every type of wood. Cherry and walnut pieces were coated with a clear varnish. Inexpensive woods like pine and poplar were often stained to look like mahogany or rosewood. Many spool beds have been painted over the course of their life time, and needless to say, removing coats of paint from them is a tedious task. Turning wood on a lathe creates lots of open end grain which can trap small specks of paint in the wood pores. It is almost impossible to remove all traces of paint from spool furniture once it has been painted.

Eastlake furniture - Charles Lock Eastlake was a prominent English author and architect who believed mass-produced factory furniture was responsible for the overall decline in the quality of furniture workmanship and design. He wanted to raise awareness to the lower standards which had become commonly accepted by the furniture industry and the public. Eastlake promoted the honest use of materials, quality craftsmanship and a return to furniture which integrated form and function. He thought the furniture from the preceeding periods had become both excessively decorated and poorly produced and he disliked the darkly stained woods, and mechanical carving. He wanted a return to simple sturdy furniture and felt curves wasted wood, and created uncomfortable furniture which did not have the strength of straight line furniture. He presented his new ideas in his book *Hints on Household Taste in Furniture, Upholstery and Other Details* which was published in England in 1868 and in the United States in 1872. This was the beginning of the Eastlake style which lasted until around 1890.

The Eastlake style did not rely on excessive decorations and focused instead on the natural beauty of the wood. Walnut, cherry and maple were used for earlier pieces. But the supply of American walnut was quickly becoming depleted because the trees had been over-harvested, and golden oak soon replaced walnut as the most commonly used wood as the style grew in popularity and the quality of the furniture decreased.

Eastlake promoted flat surfaces, squared-off corners and rectangular shapes arranged in straight lines. Decorations were simple, usually geometric or floral and were either incised into the wood or carved from a different piece of wood (sometimes of a different species) and then glued in place. "Carving" was often stamped or cut out by machine resulting in a very uniform design. Automatic fret-saws and gouging devices provided an inexpensive and quick way to decorate mass produced furniture. Chip carving and parallel lines called "railroad tracks" were frequently used as decorations. Furniture was also decorated with turned stiles and spindles, and inset veneered panels. Some washstands and hall trees had ceramic tile inserts. The legs on Eastlake furniture were straight, not curved like former furniture styles.

Unfortunately, many large factories throughout the East and Midwest did not share Eastlake's integrity for quality materials or craftsmanship and modified the style so they could churn out Eastlake furniture. Furniture was mass-produced to try and keep abreast of the changing tastes and fashions of the time, and was often poorly manufactured and called "Eastlake" when it really bore little resemblance to the style.

A very small number of pieces of furniture from the Eastlake period are labeled. Herter Brothers and a few other quality, up-scale cabinetmakers of the time labeled their work. These pieces are quite rare and valuable today. Most of the furniture was anonymously mass-produced as factories churned out furniture to try and keep up with the demand.

Furniture was often sold in sets or "suites". A *parlor suite* often consisted of three to seven pieces of matching furniture. More expensive sets could consist of even more pieces. A large parlor set could contain a sofa or love seat, four side chairs, an armchair and a chair with partial arms. A small set would include at least a love seat and two side chairs. The upholstery fabric, carving and legs would all be identical within the set. *Bedroom suites* would include a headboard and footboard, a commode, a chair, one or two night tables and an assortment of other pieces. The furniture would be identically carved, have identical hardware and identical marble or wooden tops.

* Parlor sets often included a *gentleman's chair* and a *lady's chair*. The gentleman's chair was a wide upholstered chair with upholstered arms or partially upholstered arms. A lady's chair was generally not as wide and did not have arms. This allowed a woman to fit into the chair while wearing a full hooped skirt without causing the skirt to ride up and reveal her "underpinnings".

Eastlake chest of drawers often featured bonnet cupboards. The bonnet cupboard was a small square cupboard built into the dresser providing a place for a lady to store her bonnet or a gentleman to keep his hat. The built in cabinet replaced the cardboard bandbox previously used for storage. Cherry and walnut were often used for the earlier pieces. Occassionally mahogany or rosewood would be used. Oak was used on mass-produced pieces later in the period.

Eastlake dressers were mass-produced in factories through-out the East and Midwest between 1880 and 1910 and then shipped all over the country. Many of them were made with cheap materials and shoddy construction. The oak was cut very thin and the frames were often constructed from inferior wood. At the time of its original purchase, a typical oak Victorian dresser would have cost about five dollars. Dressers made from maple or walnut (instead of oak) were usually produced earlier in the period and are generally of better quality. Eastlake dressers often had full length wooden framed mirrors attached to the top of the chest and were surrounded on one or both sides by drawers.

Early Eastlake commodes (from approximately 1875 or so) were manufactured by large factories in the East and Midwest and were often made from oak, a wood which did not come into wide demand until around 1890. Early Eastlake styles can easily be mistaken for the golden oak furniture popular from the turn of the century until around 1920. Earlier pieces had plain fronts, later pieces often had bowed or serpentine fronts, and they were often veneered and not made of solid oak. Later pieces were also held together with nails and generally poorly constructed.

Folding chairs were popular pieces in the small parlors of middle class homes during the end of the 19th century where space was at a premium. They were inexpensive to buy, very sturdy and comfortable. Spare chairs could be folded and put away when not in use and brought out when needed. Many of the folding chairs from this period were patented and several companies specialized in manufacturing them. The manufacturer's marks can usually be found under the seat or on the back of the chair. George Hunzinger and Sons of New York patented several styles of folding chairs in the 1860s, and patented a new style of folding chair in 1876 with steel mesh webbing on the back and seat covered with fabric. Hunzinger furniture originally had a label identifying the manufacturer, and if the label is still in place today it can greatly increase the value of the piece.

Plywood arm chairs were another popular chair style from around 1870 until the end of the 19th century. Plywood was used for the backs and seats of the chairs. Hickory, ash or another local wood was used for the frame of the chair. These mass-produced chairs were very economical and could be found in lower-class homes, and in public places such as churches and schools. Different types of plywood were used and a variety of designs were pierced into the plywood as a form of decoration. This style of chair was often adopted into bench size for church and school seating. Public benches often had cast metal frames instead of wooden frames. Plywood does not hold up well if exposed to dampness or water and many of these chairs have been damaged or destroyed over the years. Even though they were mass-produced during their heyday, there are few remaining examples today.

The tête-à-tête (the S-shaped conversational sofa first introduced in the 1820s) continued to become more common-place as the 19th century continued. They were comfortable and practical and fit in with the eclectic furnishings of late 19th century homes. Eastlake tête-à-têtes often featured braiding, tassels and fringe, and exotic velvet or silk upholstery. Wooden spindles were frequently ebonized.

Small tables, plant stands and fern tables were produced in massive quantities by factories all across the United States during the Eastlake period. New York, Boston and Philadelphia produced the finest furniture of this period with the most outstanding detailing. Ebonizing was very popular, but many pieces were also painted or made from light wood and left in a natural state. Some unusual Eastlake examples have upholstered table tops and feature brightly colored, exotic embroidered fabric fastened to the table with brass tacks.

Center tables and other mid-sized tables although decoratively cut and shaped by today's standards, were constructed of machine-cut pieces and put together on an assembly line. Center tables often had marble tops mounted on a table with a cutwork skirt. The top was then mounted on a carved pedestal which was attached to elaborately carved legs. Tables usually had iron casters to make them easy to move around the room.

Marble tops appeared on a variety of different types of furniture during the Victorian period. The most valuable pieces of marble have fancy scalloped edges. The second most valuable pieces have plain-edges with decorative corners cut on the marble. Straight line edging was the easiest to produce and was the most common. The value of the furniture is affected by the cut of the marble. The value can also increase or decrease based upon the color of the marble. As a general rule, reddish, rose and brown marble are considered to be the most valuable. Black and gray are in the middle range and white marble was the most common so it is considered to be the least valuable today.

One of the most common tables from the Eastlake period is the parlor table or gypsy table. More recently these tables have come to be known as "lamp tables". These simple square parlor tables with slanted legs were produced in great quantities after 1880. The table top often had a skirt or decorative carving or molding on the edges. The legs were turned in various designs, and there was a shelf fastened about halfway down the legs that may or may not have had decorative carving on the edge. The table could have simple carved feet with casters attached or have tapered legs which fit into shoes of brass claws clutching glass balls. Some parlor tables had fabric tops and others had legs which unscrewed to make the table easier to move and store.

In 1875, while Charles Eastlake was still in England planting the seeds of change in furniture design and manufacturing, John D. Larkin was starting the Larkin Soap Manufacturing Company in New York. His brother-in-law, Elbert Hubbard, was a member of the creative staff for the company and came up with a marketing idea for a premium plan based on purchases. They created an organization housewives could join and urged them to get their friends and family to start Larkin Clubs. The more Larkin products customers bought the more points they could acquire. Points were redeemable for rugs, silverware, furniture and other household necessities. The furniture was manufactured by Larkin in Buffalo, New York and shipped to the customer directly from the factory. For the most part, the furniture was flimsy and inexpensive. They often had very explicit instructions attached to the backboards telling the recipient how to unpack and care for the furniture. Of course, the instructions included using Larkin Furniture Polish and other products to maintain the "like new" appearance.

Elbert Hubbard visited England in the early 1890s and converted to the Arts and Crafts Movement. He rejected the over-use of machinery to create furnishings, metalwork, pottery, jewelry, textiles and leatherwork. He returned to Buffalo, New York and left the Larkin Company to start a colony for handicraft artisans at East Aurora, New York. This group took on the name the *Roycrafters* and they wove textiles, created jewelry, made pottery and metalwork and furniture emphasizing handiwork and craftsmanship. They marked their products with a *Roycraft* stamp.

On May 7, 1915 a German submarine sunk *The S.S. Lusitania*. More than one thousand one-hundred ninety-eight people perished aboard the ship. One of them was Elbert Hubbard. The Roycrafters had lost their leader and the Larkin Company had lost the best marketing person they would ever have.

Anglo-Japanese style - The Anglo-Japanese style is a Victorian substyle which appeared in the United States between the late 1870s and 1900 following an Oriental trend in England called the "English Aesthetic Movement". The Anglo-Japanese style never really gained widespread popularity in the United States like it did in England, but the importation of Japanese woodblock prints and other Japanese objects and the display of Japanese art objects at the Philadelphia Centennial Exhibition in 1876 motivated a few manufacturers to produce a limited amount of furniture. Japan had been closed to foreign travellers for two centuries prior to the Exhibition so few Americans had ever been exposed to the Japanese culture or its furniture and decorations prior to that time.

The most common pieces of Anglo-Japanese furniture

were folding chairs, galleried tables and stands and screen-like hall racks. Cherry or maple were the predominate woods used and they were occassionally stained to imitate mahogany or ebony. Anglo-Japanese furniture featured stiles and rails turned to resemble bamboo, and the wood was often ebonized or fumed. Incised carving featured Oriental patterns and motifs such as bamboo, plum blossoms and pagodas.

The fabrics on upholstered pieces mimicked rich Oriental silks. Many Anglo-Japanese pieces resemble Eastlake furniture in their basic shape and style and they both have incised carving and saw-fretwork as decorative elements. The major differences are the Oriental themes of the carving and the fact few Eastlake pieces were originally painted.

Art Nouveau Furniture

The Art Nouveau style was very well received in Europe and affected just about everything from furniture and glassmaking to architecture. But it was not appreciated in the United States until 1904 when the French brought an exhibit to the World's Fair. The French Pavillion at the Fair in Saint Louis (dubbed "The Grandest Fair of All") had an exibition of Art Nouveau furniture, and shortly afterwards a limited number of furniture manufacturers in the midwest began producing small quantities of pieces somewhat resembling the French furniture.

The new style was noted for its traditional craftsmanship, simple fluid lines and tight "S" curves called "whiplash" curves and elongated flowing natural forms. American furniture makers used isolated motifs from the Art Nouveau style – stylized flowers, leaves, fruit and other organic forms – and incorporated them into Eastlake or Rococo Revival styles to create American Art Nouveau furniture. Few pieces of furniture were created entirely in the unadulterated Art Nouveau style.

Oak was the most popular wood for turn of the century furniture and was used to produce just about every style of furniture. Art Nouveau furniture was no exception, and mass-produced pieces were primarily made from oak. Mahogany, rosewood and walnut were used for higher quality or custom-made pieces. Inexpensive furniture was often constructed using gumwood as the base wood with a walnut or mahogany veneer.

* Rosewood is very brittle and tends to crack easily. The thinner the wood the more likely it is to develop cracks. Art Nouveau furniture made from rosewood should be carefully examined to determine if it has been cracked and repaired.

* Bentwood was used to construct some Art Nouveau furniture and reproductions of these pieces have been made over the years. Reproduction bentwood will usually have legs which are flatter than the turn-of-the-century pieces. The wood and finish will also lack signs of wear and age.

Colonial Revival Furniture

The American centennial brought about a renewed wave of patriotism and an interest in early American furniture. The earlier pieces manufactured during this period were often referred to as "Centennial furniture" and were usually better made than pieces from later in the period. Most of the furniture produced during the Colonial Revival period (which lasted from 1876-1925) was not literally based on actual pieces of furniture but was instead, loosely based on the earlier style.

The most faithful Colonial reproductions were made in the late 19th century. People seemed more interested in having furniture resembling older pieces than owning pieces with strict historical accuracy. Manufacturers created their own blended Colonial style which was a mélange of different styles from the past. Colonial Revival furniture differed from the originals not only in style, but also in the materials used and in the proportions of the furniture.

Most Colonial Revival furniture was mass-produced and veneered basewood was used instead of solid wood, decorative carving was pressed into the wood by machine instead of being carved by hand, and hardware was stamped brass instead of cast brass. Oak was the primary wood used for the majority of the furniture, but mahogany and walnut were used on high quality pieces. The boards used on revival furniture will be thinner than those on original furniture. The top of a piece of furniture will be made up of several boards glued together on a Revival piece instead of one solid board on an original. Boards on Revival furniture will also have circular saw marks which would not appear on the original furniture since the circular saw did not come into common usage until around 1840. Inexpensive wood was also often stained to resemble walnut and mahogany. Pine was used as the basewood for veneered pieces and plywood was commonly used for the backboards.

Most Colonial Revival pieces have different dimensions than the originals and are generally not as high or as wide. Larger pieces like sideboards were often scaled down from the original dimensions to fit into smaller more crowded 20th century rooms with limited space. Furniture manufactured at the beginning of the Colonial Revival period may have used dovetails or pegged construction to hold the furniture together, but furniture produced at the end of the period was held together with wire nails, screws or factory-cut dowels.

A few cabinetmakers, such as Wallace Nutting, manufactured furniture which was a strict reproduction of actual pieces of Colonial furniture. Nutting used pieces from his own collection to ensure an authentic look. He used appropriate wood and construction methods so his handmade furniture imitated the original as closely as possible. His reproductions were so authentic that even today it can be difficult to differentiate between his reproductions and the originals. Nutting used a brand to mark his furniture and also a paper label. Obviously, if they are intact today they will add to the value of the piece.

* As a general rule, the more closely a piece of furniture resembles the original the more desirable and valuable it is.

* An original Colonial desk-on-frame would have consisted of an upper and lower section which were not permanently attached to each other. A Colonial Revival desk-on-frame will have the upper and lower sections permanently attached to each other. Eighteenth century drawers would have been chamfered to make them fit into the drawer slots in the case. Reproduction drawers will be square-cut. Dove-tails, if they were used, will be narrow, uniform and machine cut, not uneven and hand cut like on an original. Hinges and hardware will often be made of iron on a reproduction.

* Most antique tea carts were made during the Colonial Revival period. The earlier pieces generally were more detailed with shaped drop leaves, and more carving on the stiles or handles than pieces made towards the end of the period. Tea carts were manufactured with and without removable glass trays. Replaced glass does not necessarily lessen the value of the tea cart. A missing tray on a tea cart which originally had one, however, will reduce the value of the piece. The large wooden back wheels had rubber tires, and the front wheels (which were usually made of brass) also had rubber tires. The rubber may be brittle and cracked, or may have been replaced. Many tea carts had a drawer on one of the shorter ends to store silverware and accessories. Check

under the top for evidence of an original drawer if it is missing.

Arts and Crafts and Mission Furniture

The Mission style of furniture was supposedly based on furniture used by monks in the old California missions which were founded by Father Junipero Serra during the Spanish Colonial times. It is unlikely this was the true inspiration for this style of furniture and very few original pieces of furniture from the missions have survived to support this claim.

Oak was the predominate wood used for this style, and the furniture was designed with function not decoration as the primary concern. It was the belief of the Arts and Crafts Movement that only useful and beautiful things should be in a home and neither price nor fashion should determine art or quality. The American Mission style was an adaption of the Arts and Crafts style which had evolved in England. Both styles stressed simple construction, with obvious signs of handwork such as exposed mortise-and-tenon joints. The exposed pegs were often the only decorative elements on the furniture. Simple flat boards were used in the construction, minimal decorations were used and stains and finishes were kept to a minimum.

Grand Rapids, Michigan became the major manufacturing center for oak furniture, but Mission style furniture was mass-produced in factories all over the country between 1900 and 1915. Paper labels, metal tags and brands burned into the wood were used by manufacturers to identify their furniture. Brand name furniture was popular in the early 1900s just like it is today. If the furniture has retained its identification it will usually increase its value.

Patent dates on mechanical parts of the furniture can also be used to help date a piece of furniture or even to help identify the manufacturer. While this may not pin-point the actual date of manufacture, it will give you a reference point as to when the furniture was made. Furniture was usually manufactured around the time of the last patent date on the mechanical parts.

The Arts and Crafts Movement was not welcomed with open arms by the masses. Machines and mass-production had allowed middle-class Americans to afford furnishings and other household items which were once reserved for the rich upperclass. Many people were not willing to give up these newly attained luxuries to return to simple undecorated handcrafted-looking furniture.

Charles Rennie MacKintosh of Scotland, Josef Hoffman of Austria and William Morris of England championed the Arts and Crafts Movement in Europe. William Morris was an artist, architect and poet who researched church history as a student and later established a business in 1860, specializing in ecclesiastical furnishings. His company also produced murals, tapestries and stained glass windows. When the company expaded, they added secular items and furniture, metalwork, carpets, bookbinding and wallpaper were among the items in their inventory. William Morris worked hard to raise public awareness and appreciation of handcrafted furniture and quality construction. A decade later the concepts spread to the United States but the Arts and Crafts Movement was never as popular here as it was in Europe. Few original pieces of American Arts and Crafts furniture exist outside museums and private collections.

Morris was a dedicated worker, successful businessman and champion for social change, but he is probably most remembered for being the inventor of the "Morris chair" – the first recliner. It was a plainly constructed, undecorated chair made of square-edged rectangular slats of wood, with an upholstered seat and back. A moveable rod could be placed in a groove in the base of the chair and the back could then be slanted at various angles and would retain the desired incline.

John Ruskin was born into an affluent English family and grew up to become a professor at Oxford University. He was a very religious, very wealthy man and was one of the founding fathers of the American Arts and Crafts movement. The Arts and Crafts movement stressed function and unadorned beauty over the ornate excesses of the Victorian era. Ruskin was a social reformer and writer and strongly believed in the biblical doctrine of caring and sharing. He used his inheritance to help improve the conditions of the poor and believed quality in architecture was closely related to morality and therefore related to religion. He sought a return to simple values and a less mechanized society.

Mass-produced and machine-made furniture often had rounded edges on the wooden slats instead of simple carved rectangular boards like the original Arts and Crafts pieces. Machine-made pieces also frequently had applied wooden decorations which was contradictory to the original concept of function not decoration.

The biggest problem with the Arts and Crafts movement was lack of widespread public acceptance. The second biggest problem was trying to produce well-constructed handmade furniture from quality materials, at a price which was affordable to the average person. Most Arts and Crafts furniture manufacturers produced such a limited number of pieces their prices were too expensive for all but the upper class clientele. It was Gustav Stickley who found a compromise between mass-production and and handcraftmanship.

Gustav Stickley and his four brothers manufactured conventional Victorian furniture for a little more than 10 years from around 1880 until the mid-1890s. They produced typical walnut late-Victorian furniture in the appropriately over-decorated style which was popular at that time, under the name "The Stickley Brothers Company" in Grand Rapids, Michigan. Unfortunately the native American walnut trees were quickly becoming depleted towards the end of the 1800s because they had been over-harvested by greedy furniture manufacturers. Gustav did not care for what he considered the flimsy furnishings which had become so commonplace, and in 1895 he and a partner opened a shop in Eastwood, New York and started manufacturing plain, comfortable, solid and durable furniture. He wanted to improve the quality of furniture while reducing the cost and christened the resulting furniture designs "Craftsmen".

Gustav worked for two years to perfect his new style of furniture and finishes and officially presented it at the Grand Rapids Furniture Exposition in 1900 and again at the Pan-American Exposition the following year. His furniture was predominately made from white oak because he liked the way the flakes in the grain were highlighted when the wood was quartersawn. But he felt the oak needed to be darkened and aged to make it even more attractive. Quartersawing exposes the wood's medullary rays and creates a decorative wavy flake pattern distinctive to quartersawn wood. But quartersawing is an expensive process because it yields a limited quantity of usable top grade boards and creates a lot of waste wood. It also requires extra time, tools and skills. Oak was the predominant wood used in Gustav's furniture but other indigenous woods were also occassionally used.

Stickley's furniture was constructed from thick planks of wood and assembled with the simplest of construction methods. Joints were assembled square end to square end and then fastened with screws, pegs or glue. Mitered corners and dove-tail joints were too fussy and time consuming to be used on this simple furniture. Any designs carved into the furniture for decoration were square or rectangular in shape – no curves. A geometric design was occassionally glued on to the furniture as a decoration. For the most part, the furniture consisted of straight uncluttered lines.

In keeping with his philosophy, the furniture had cushions made of natural products. Genuine leather, usually cowhide or sheepskin, which was specially treated to make it durable and waterproof and to prevent it from crazing and cracking. Imitators would eventually copy Gustav's designs and use imitation leather, homespun fabrics and cheaper woods and finishes. But Gustav Stickley stuck to his high standards.

Stickley invented a technique for darkening and mellowing oak by moistening the wood to open the pores and then placing the assembled furniture in an airtight area where it was exposed to strong ammonia vapors for several days. The length of exposure depended on the color of the desired finish. The furniture was then lightly sanded, followed by a coat of brownish or silver-gray oil stain, and then given a coat of lacquer to protect the wood and seal in the color. The finishing touch was an application of "Craftsman Wood Lustre" which was applied to each piece before it left the factory. Stickley was compulsively concerned with quality. He encouraged purchasers to return any piece that did measure up to their standards.

Gustav Stickley sold "do it yourself" furniture kits so homeowners could create their own furniture. Patterns to create Stickley furniture were even published in popular magazines. He believed "do-it-yourself" projects around the home would improve the moral fiber of the household and help to shape honest men and women.

Stickley's biggest competition came from (of all places!) his two younger brothers, Leopold and John George. In 1900 Leopold and J.G. purchased the Collins, Sisson & Pratt Furniture Company in Fayetteville, New York. They copied Gustav's designs and then began producing furniture on their own near their brother Gustav's location. Four years later the company was incorporated as L. & J. G. Stickley, Inc. The furniture they produced was imprinted "The Work of L. and J. G. Stickley". Gustav's brothers used his diversification into architecture against him in promoting their products. They claimed crafting furniture was their only business, and they manufactured furniture customized to meet the needs of the customer and not standardized to meet the needs of the average person.

Gustav Stickley marked his furniture in three places to make sure it could be identified as his. He felt this protected both the designer and the purchaser. His mark showed a red joiner's compass and between the prongs of the compass he inserted a Dutch motto "Als ik Kan" which translates to "As I Can". Beneath the compass was his signature. He also placed a Craftsmen label on the furniture. But beware – labels, like everything else, can be faked.

By 1916, Gustav Stickley was bankrupt and out of business and his competition "Hand-Craft", "Mission", "Quaint", "Arts and Crafts", "Stickley Brothers" and "Roycroft" were producing furniture similar to his designs, but more often than not, with lower quality and standards. This simple style of functional oak furniture which was now widely available in various price ranges began to be called "Mission furniture".

Gustav Stickley lived to see his furniture style stolen by his brothers and other competitors and then go out of style a few years later. But he may have postumously had the last laugh. He always said his furniture was so well designed and so well proportioned that even *he* could not improve upon it, and it would be worth many times its original cost in fifty to one hundred years. A small dresser which Gustav would have originally sold for less than fifty dollars will often sell today for several thousand dollars.

Stickley's brother's company, The L. & J. G. Stickley Company is still in business today. It was purchased by Alfred and Aminy Audi in 1974 and continues to produce quartersawn oak furniture made in theArts and Crafts style. The company remains dedicated to the original principals of the Arts and Crafts philosophy – clean lines, honest comfortable designs and strong simple construction. The furniture is still produced and finished using the same techniques Stickley perfected more than 100 years ago.

Roycroft Industries was founded in 1895 and began producing Mission style furniture in East Aurora, New York in 1900. Elbert Hubbard, (See also *Larkin Soap Manufacturing Company*) the owner of Roycroft Industries, visited Arts and

Crafts designers in England and brought back many of their design concepts which he used to create his own furniture. Each piece was entirely crafted by hand, but his company did not produce the quantity or the variety of furniture that Stickley and some of the other Mission furniture manufacturers did. Roycroft produced some larger pieces of furniture, but most of their product line consisted of smaller pieces. Roycroft marked their furniture in conspicuous places – usually on the side or the top of the piece.

Two furniture designers on the West Coast, Charles Sumner Greene and Henry Mather Greene of Pasadena, California, adapted the English Arts and Crafts style with an Oriental influence. They created a limited number of pieces of Arts and Crafts furniture to be used in houses they designed. Their custom-made furniture influenced a following of imitators who made less expensive reproductions of their designs.

Charles Sumner Greene used round wooden bosses to cover the heads of screws which held the furniture together. This was later adapted into the designs of mass-produced Mission style furniture to give the pieces the illusion of being handcrafted. Greene and Greene constructed their furniture of mahogany, ebony, and fruitwood in lieu of traditional oak and decorated their furniture with inlay consisting of a variety of materials including gemstones.

Frank Lloyd Wright was another architect/furniture designer who incorporated Mission, Arts and Crafts and Art Nouveau elements into his furniture designs. His pieces could often be distinguished from the run-of-the-mill Mission style furniture because of his unusual decorative additions. He duplicated the straight lines and functional forms of the Mission style, but his interpretations included subtle architectural elements such as moldings and feet created by solid boards placed at a 180° angles to the base of the furniture. Furniture designed by Frank Lloyd Wright during the early part of the period is generally considered more valuable than pieces made between the 1940s and 1950s when the furniture was produced in greater quantities.

Designer pieces with labels or other forms of identification which can prove their heritage are quite rare and valuable. Architect-designed furniture can often be documented by looking up articles in period newspaper and magazines about homes for which the furniture was made. Room plans and architect's renderings were often included in the articles. Custom-made, limited edition furniture was quite expensive to produce and is obviously rare, expensive and quite collectable today.

Mass-produced Mission furniture can usually be easily identified by the inferior construction techniques which were used. A large majority of this furniture was poorly balanced and designed, and was joined together with glue, angle irons set on the inside of the frames where they would not show, or with screws (the heads of which were then concealed under wooden bosses). Little or no attention was paid to details. Stickley's styles, conversely, were carefully balanced and designed, had the utmost attention paid to details, and were constructed using pegged, dove-tailed and mortise and tenon construction.

Mission style settles or settees were common fixtures in parlors, libraries and halls furnished in the Mission style from about 1900 well into the 1920s. They were sturdy, practical and inexpensive. Settees, like other mission style chairs, were constructed of straight rectangular oak boards, and occassionally had leather cushions added for comfort.

Stools were a very popular piece of Mission style furniture. They were inexpensive, useful throughout the house and epitomized the informal spirit of the Mission style. The stools were made from straight-edged rectangular oak planks and fastened together with mortise-and-tenon joints. Leather was used for the cushion if there was one.

Tables of all sizes were constructed using the same oak plank and mortise-and-tenon construction. Table tops were made in a variety of shapes as were the legs. The simplest shapes were often the most popular. Mission furniture could be found in informal settings in homes in the big cities as well as in the country. Oak provided strength to the furniture and the Mission design made it utilitarian. Cross stretchers were often mortised through the table legs and held in place with wooden pegs or "keys". Small tables were designed to be used as card tables, center tables or dining tables and were available with optional drop-leaves or shelves. Larger tables were used as library tables or dining tables.

"Turn-of-the-Century Furniture"

There are some pieces of furniture which were very popular at the beginning of the 1900s, but do not really fall into a style catagory. Never-the-less, they were popularly embraced by middle-class America and filled their homes and gardens for many years. For lack of a better place to put them, I have included a catch-all catagory to try to cover some of them.

Oak was the most popular wood during the "turn of the century". It was available stained a dark "antique" color, in a more natural "golden oak" color which was often enhanced with yellow pigments and coats of varnish, and "fumed" which gave the wood an aged grayish patina.

A new trend in furniture first appearing during the turn of the century was furniture available for purchase "unfinished". Unfinished furniture was referred to at the time as "in white" and was sold to individuals who wanted to stain, paint and finish their own furniture. A wide variety of hardware was also available (both metal and wooden) and a buyer could choose what type of hinges they wanted, whether or not they wanted escutcheons and often whether they wanted the furniture to have a marble or wooden top. This was like buying furniture a la carte. If you had money, you could buy the furniture finished the way you wanted. If you had talent, or needed to save money, you could buy only what you needed.

Another introduction to the turn of the century household was "buying on time" or, as we know it today – credit. For a few dollars down and a few dollars a month (plus "a small interest fee") homeowners were able to own pieces of furniture they would not have otherwise been able to buy.

Iron wire furniture - Iron wire furniture was patented around the beginning of the 1900s. It was created in an effort to make sturdy, functional, and inexpensive furniture. Iron wire furniture appeared to be graceful and delicate but was durable enough to be used outdoors and in public places like cafés, restaurants, pool halls and ice cream parlors. The chairs became known as "ice cream parlor chairs". They were mass-produced by a number of different manufacturers and sold in large quantities all over the country.

Looped metal wire was used to construct the backs and legs of chairs and the base of tables. Table tops and chair seats were made from metal or wood. Arm chairs often had wooden arm rests mounted on wire supports. The wood used for the chair components varied by manufacturer and could be oak or plywood.

Many of the chairs were left unpainted and had the natural gray metal of the iron and natural color of the wood showing on the seats and arms. Other chairs were originally available painted a variety of colors and have had numerous coats of paint applied since.

Tubular-iron beds - Iron beds were first introduced in Europe and did not become popular in the United States until the late 1800s. Once introduced, they remained popular throughout the 1930s. During the 19th century, it was a common belief that excessively decorated bedrooms were a health hazard. All of the yardage used to create the elaborate bed drapings of previous furniture styles would have been difficult if not impossible to keep clean, and the over-sized, abundantly carved headboards and footboards probably trapped dust, dirt, mold and a host of other things in their decorations. This could have been the basis for the belief that simple lines and limited decorations were a healthier alternative.

Iron beds had simple lines and were easier to clean and maintain than traditional wooden beds. These beds were referred to as "iron beds" but they got their strength and durability from steel rods. The headboard and footboard were often decorated with brass rods, finials and other decorations.

The iron was painted various colors which made a nice decorative contrast with the shiney brass decorations. White was the standard color for most iron beds because it harmonized well with golden oak and other light colored wood furniture which was popular at the time, and with other painted furnishings. Black paint was usually reserved for beds purchased for servant's use. The enamel paint (called "Japanning" in the Montgomery Ward and Sears and Roebuck's catalogs of the late 1800s) was also available in blue and maroon.

Bed designs ranged from elaborately decorated to very plain and utilitarian. Iron beds were by nature quite sturdy, but old metal can crack from rust or abuse, and once repaired may break again in the same spot. Rust hidden underneath coats of paint can cause the metal to deteriorate and create more damage. Rust needs to be neutralized and removed, not just covered up with another coat of paint, in order to prevent further damage to the metal.

* Iron beds remain popular today and reproductions have been manufactured for years. Newer beds are coated with an electrostatically applied baked on "powder-coat" finish which is chip resistant and fade resisant. This is a special finish and can not be repaired or removed like a regular painted finish.

Tubular-brass beds - Brass beds were a staple piece of furniture in middle-class homes during the late 1800s and early 1900s. Most beds were conservatively designed and their shiney surfaces were thought to be the perfect complement to dark walnut and mahogany furniture. They were also easy to keep clean which added to their popularity because of the common belief that excessive decorations or clutter in the bedroom could be hazardous to one's health. Brass beds were easy to manufacture and inexpensive to produce. Many of the models remained in production for years with few changes.

The shiney brass surface was meant to make up for the lack of decoration. The brass used in the construction of many beds was not solid brass, but rather brass tubing fitted over cords of steel. The steel added extra strength to the bed and reduced the price. Cast-iron was usually used for the bedrails.

A coat of lacquer was often applied to the brass to prolong the shine and prevent the brass from tarnishing. Lacquered brass should never be polished, soaked or washed with hot water. The solvents in the polish or the rubbing action will damage the lacquer finish or remove it.

Reproduction brass beds have been made for years. Reproductions will not show wear marks on the casters or on the brass like an old brass bed will. Newer beds are not as sturdy as older beds and the brass is usually thinner. Older brass usually had a higher copper content than modern brass and is often (but not always) a different color than new brass.

Brass beds are durable, but the tubing is hollow and susceptible to dents. I bought an antique bed a few years ago which seemed extremely heavy for its size. Upon closer examination I discovered someone had filled the brass tubing with cement in what I can only guess was a misguided effort to make the bed durable. I can only imagine how much time it must have taken and how difficlult a task it must have been. It goes without saying the "alteration" on this bed is nonreversable. Such extremes are not really necessary. Brass beds will last for generations with moderate care. No cement required.

* Some daybeds and regular beds have what appears to be a loosened rail on the footboard which spins freely in its socket. It is not broken. This was a feature called a *blanket rail* which allowed extra covers to be wrapped around the rail and then unrolled if additional covers were needed. Extra covers were stored on the rail and did not take up space folded at the foot of the bed.

Wooden beds -Turn of the century oak furniture was mass-produced in large factories all across the United States, but Grand Rapids, Michigan became the oak furniture center. Furniture was designed to be easily manufactured on a large scale and to appeal to the greatest number of people. Most of this furniture does not fit into any specific furniture style. Furniture designers borrowed freely from a variety of styles and adapted them to produce furniture as quickly and inexpensively as possible. Wooden headboards and footboards ranged from plain utilitarian examples to extravagantly decorated ones.

Incised decorations were created with a metal die which stamped the pattern into the wood to imitate carving. Hand carving was added if a more deeply carved look was desired. Veneer was often added to accentuate the stamped patterns. Relief decorations like scrolls, shells or other motifs were carved separately by machine and then applied to the surface of the furniture with small tacks or glue. Side rails which attached the headboard and footboard together could be made of either wood or iron.

Dressers - The words "dresser" and "bureau" were used interchangeably by Victorians to describe the same piece of furniture. The French considered a "bureau" to be a desk or a table used for studying or storing writing supplies. But Americans used the term to describe a chest of drawers, with or without a mirror.

Victorian dressers from the turn of the century often do not fit into one particular furniture style. They were often the result of a combination of styles. Furniture manufacturers throughout the East and Midwest mass-produced furniture for the working class without regard to any real defined alligiance to a particular style. They gave the people what they wanted.

Dressers were constructed of pine or another softwood and veneered with walnut, burl walnut or mahogany veneer. The wood could be decorated with saw-fretwork and incised carving. Marble-top dressers were more expensive than wooden topped ones, partly because the marble was often imported from Europe. In spite of the extra cost, they were extremely popular. The popularity was due in part to the obvious beauty of the marble, but also to the fact marble was easy to keep clean.

Bowfront dressers were mass-produced by manufacturers in the East and Midwest between 1880 and 1920 and sold through mail-order catalogues. They were then shipped by rail through out the United States. Bowfront, serpentine and oxbow fronts were more expensive to produce than straight fronts and were made in more limited quantities. Consequently the shaped dressers are more rare and valuable today.

Late Victorian bowfront dressers were constructed differently than other bowfront dressers. Colonial Revival bowfront dressers were made by gluing several pieces of wood together to build up the bowed area. In the 18th century, shaped fronts were formed by carving them from a single piece of wood. Late Victorian bowfront dressers were made by steaming and bending a solid piece of oak or quarter-sawn oak. The case was often made from an inexpensive secondary wood like pine, and then covered with veneer. They often had paneled sides and were held together with glue, nails and screws. Late Victorian pieces were often fumed or darkened with stain. They had iron or iron and wood casters attached to the bottom of the feet to make the piece easy to move.

Tall chests were made of oak or quarter-sawn oak, with paneled sides and a varying arrangement of drawer shapes and sizes. They usually featured a small swivel-mounted oak framed mirror on the top of the chest and had a bonnet cupboard intended as a storage area for large fashionable bonnets which were popular at that time. Gentlemen could also use them to store their silk or beaverskin hats. One of these tall chests would have been called a *chiffonier*. Chest of drawers were used to store "unmentionable garments" which would not have been proper to hang in an armoire or on a hook on the wall of a room. A *chifforobe* had a chest of drawers on one side and a narrow space with a door on the other side where a small amount of clothing could be hung. Chifforobes often had a full length mirror on the front of the wardrobe door.

* Some dressers have a concealed drawer at the bottom which is made to look like part of the front of the dresser. Occassionally dealers and collectors today will tell you these drawers were "secret hiding places" where our ancestors stored their valuables. While it is quite possible some of them did indeed hide their valuables in there, the drawers were designed with another purpose in mind. These drawers were called "slipper drawers" and were used as a place to store slippers.

Armoires - Victorian homes did not have built in closets so a piece of furniture was needed to store clothing and accessories. Tall wooden wardrobes or "armoires" were the answer. Armoires got their name from the French cabinets used to store armor. These large pieces of furniture had a combination of shelves, rods and drawers hidden behind locking doors. The *clothes press*, the area of the armoire where garments could be hung, was usually behind one of the doors and the other side consisted of a variety of storage areas. Armoires are not as imposing as they may seem. The back, sides, doors and shelves are held together with pegs. They can be disassembled for easy transport and then reassembled in their new location.

Commodes - Commodes were manufactured with wooden tops and with marble tops. Marble topped commodes were more expensive to manufacture and may have cost as much as a dollar extra at the time to purchase them. But marble was more practical than wood because the top of the commode was subjected to water and toiletries during use and marble would not be damaged like a wooden surface. The top of the commode often had small shelves which could be used to hold soap or an oil lamp. Commodes were often part of a bedroom suite consisting of a bed, tables and bureaus. If the commode has a marble top, the matching tables and bureau would also have generally had matching marble tops. Marble tops should show signs of wear. Commodes were subjected to water and ceramic water pitchers and bowls dragged across them. They should have small scratches and stains in the marble.

Commodes were considered more genteel than washstands and contained cabinets and drawers to hold toiletries and personal items. They also may have had a cabinet in which to discretely put the chamber pot. Lift-top commodes had tops which could be raised to reveal a bowl and a pitcher.

A scaled- down version known as a *half commode* or a *somnoe* contained one drawer and one cabinet and was used for smaller areas or more modest budgets.

* Some commodes have marble tops which are not original to the piece. Check under the marble for signs of wear to make sure the marks match the base of the commode. A replaced top can decrease the value of the piece as much as 40%.

Small cabinets, hanging shelves, open shelves and "whatnots" - Small hanging corner cabinets, often with mirrors on the doors, were used in bathrooms and bedrooms and other private areas of the home. They were designed for storing medicine and toilet and shaving articles and often had shelves inside the cabinet. Corner cabinets had more angles than a regular cabinet and were more difficult to construct than flat cabinets. Some more decorative cabinets had carved molding, scalloped edges or fret-carving. Cabinets made during the first half of the 19th century were made with dovetail construction. Later cabinets were nailed together.

Mirrored hanging shelves were not only used as wall decorations, but also served as portable dressing tables. They usually contained one or more drawers which could be used to store toilet articles. An upper shelf above the mirror could also be used for storage of additional toiletries, personal articles or pictures. Small round storage units were often attached to the sides of the mirror and were used to hold hatpins, hairpins, collar stays and other small articles. The broad shelf formed by the top of the drawer was used as a work surface.

These small shelves often have incised geometric carving, saw-cut fretwork and decorative edging. Walnut and chestnut were used on earlier pieces, but oak was more commonly used after the turn of the century.

Open wall shelves are the most common hanging storage pieces. They were produced in great quantity and in a variety of shapes and sizes. The sides and backboards could be elaborately shaped or plain and the wood used to produce them could be anything from inexpensive pine or poplar, to oak or other hardwoods. Some shelves contain a combination of hardwoods and softwoods. The quality of the construction also varied from dove-tail construction to pieces which were nailed together or glued.

"Whatnots" were multipurpose shelf units commonly found in Victorian parlors and sitting rooms. Originally, they were designed to hold sheet music and books, but the Victorians found other uses for them. Small ones could be placed on a tabletop, hung on a wall or in a corner and were used to display personal objects and knicknacks. Large floor models were often five feet tall and could be used to hold a variety of items including books and dishes. Larger whatnots may have had drawers in the base, and almost all larger whatnots were on casters so they could be moved easily. Some whatnots had adjustable tops which could be raised on a ratchet so it could be used as a reading desk. Whatnots could have shelves which were of similar dimensions or have graduated shelves. Some Victorian whatnots had mirrored backs so the objects on display could be seen from all angles.

Ètagéres are similar to large whatnots but they were generally larger, more elaborately decorated (sometimes with a marble top), may have contained a mirror or a drawer and were more expensive. Some whatnots were corner units and others were meant to fit on a flat wall. They were constructed of varnished cherry, walnut and pine and mass-produced by furniture manufacturers throughout the East and Midwest. Whatnots were often decorated with paint or gilding.

> * Reproduction whatnots will generally have a newer finish and obvious lack of use and age. The wood on a reproduction is usually inferior to the originals and the turnings and moldings will generally be less elaborate.

Open storage shelves or display shelves were available in a variety of sizes and were produced in enormous quantities. They were inexpensive and available to almost everyone. The quality of these pieces varies from well-made examples to poorly constructed junk. Even the well made pieces were constructed with glue, screws and nails construction. The molding, decorations and feet varied from very plain to decorative and well carved. Check under the shelf to ensure the molding and decorations are original to the piece and have not be added after production to increase the value.

A small portable stand or rack originally used to hold magazines or sheet music was called a *canterbury*. The name supposedly came from a clergyman who wanted a portable stand he could use for his sheet music and other items. Since Canterbury was a religious site in England, the name was chosen and it stuck. When pianos and pump organs no longer graced parlors the small stands were used to hold thin books and magazines.

China cabinets and sideboards - The china cabinet was a late 19th century invention and became popular at about the same time oak was reaching its peak in popularity. Consequently, most "late Victorian" china cabinets were manufactured from oak or quartersawn oak. The sides of the cabinets often had curved glass so the contents could be easily seen from all sides, and the doors were also made of curved glass. The top of the cabinet frequently had an oak framed mirror attached. Some cabinets had adjustable wooden shelves, others had shelves which were glued in place. A unique style of china cabinet consisted of two complete units connected by a small shelf.

Cornices, molding, veneering and decorative hardware embellished Victorian china cabinets and carving was used in abundance. Wooden columns were used to support the massive front of the cabinets and Greek architectural designs were often used as inspiration for the carving. Mythical beasts and human

245

figures could often be found carved on the fronts and sides. Female figures were called *caryatides* and male figures were called *atlantes*. Scroll feet were commonly found on china cabinets, but glass ball and claw feet were added to many cabinets. Cabinets without ball and claw feet had casters on the bottom of the feet to make the massive piece of furniture easier to move.

Glass mirrors and doors were a novelty only the rich could afford, until around 1825 when a carpenter named Enoch Robinson experimented with pouring hot liquid glass into wooden molds and then pressing it into shape with a plunger. His idea worked and with some refinements and improvements, glass began to be mass-produced and became inexpensive enough for the the middle-class to afford for their homes.

China cabinets were manufactured with both flat glass and convex glass fronts. The convex ones were more expensive then and remain so today. A few cabinets were even manufactured with concave glass. These pieces are very rare and unusual and extremely expensive. Some repairers will attempt to replace expensive convex glass with a piece of straight glass. The result is seldom successful or unnoticeable.

Convex glass front china cabinets have been popular almost since their introduction, and reproductions have been made for many years. Straight glass panels often had wooden grill work applied on the face of the glass as a decoration. Thin pieces of wood were glued together to form the pattern. The glass doors provided a safe, dustfree storage area for china and glassware and yet allowed it to be viewed and appreciated from most angles.

A sideboard or *buffet* was found in almost every Victorian dining room. The family linens, silverware, glassware and serving pieces were stored in and on this often massive piece of furniture. Sideboards had a varying numbers of drawers and shelves and could be topped with a high gloss piece of wood or a beautiful slab of marble.

Dining tables - Until the advent of extension tables, housewives had to make do with multiple tables of similar heighth which would be stored against the dining room walls until needed. They were then opened up to their full length and lined up next to each other in the middle of the dining room and covered with a table cloth to make them appear as one table. Sarah Josepha Hale, who published *Godey's Magazine and Lady's Book* told her readers in 1876 about an oval extension table which used a rope and small windlass mechanism under the rim to permit the table to expand and accept additional leaves. She assured her readers they would be delighted with the convenience of the table.

The idea was developed further and resulted in the "Fall Leaf Patent Extension Frame". On some tables, a thick pedestal base supported a top which had an extension mechanism to accept leaves. On some models the pedestal itself would also open to allow for even more leaves. Some standard four-legged tables had extension mechanisms where leaves could be placed in between the two halves to achieve the desired length. A *gate-leg table* had an extra gate-like leg which swung out to support a drop leaf when it was extended. In other types of drop leaf tables a type of wooden or metal bracket pulled out to support the leaves.

Hoosier cabinets, pie safes and ice boxes - Hoosier cabinets were designed to simplify a woman's job in the kitchen and were staples in American kitchens for nearly seventy years. The kitchen work table evolved into a domestic work station which held bins of flour or other meal, and kept necessary kitchen tools close at hand. A pull out metal, wood, zinc or porcelain enamel top pulled out to provide additional work space that was washable and easy to clean.

J.S. McQuinn founded the Hoosier Manufacturing Company in 1899 in New Castle, Indiana and the company continued to produce hoosier cabinets until 1942. During the heighth of their popularity more than 40 companies produced Hoosier cabinets - most of them based in Indiana - including The Sellers Company of Elwood, Indiana, Ingram Richardson Manufacturing Company or Frankfort, Indiana, Wasmuth Endicott Company of Andrews, Indiana and Boone and Greencastle. The company name is often embossed on a brass tag or a metal handle on the cabinet, or printed on the bottom of the attached instruction cards often found inside cabinet doors.

These cabinets were originally called "comprehensive kitchen cabinets". Many of them were manufactured in Indiana and one company is said to have called their product a "Hoosier cabinet" in homage to the state's nickname, and the name stuck and has been applied ever since to all of these cabinets regardless of where they were made or by whom.

Hoosier cabinets were made in a variety of styles and sizes, but they all contained the same basic components. The freestanding cabinets consisted of two pieces – a base section with drawers for flatware and utensils and cabinets for pots and pans and other kitchenware, and a top section that offered a variety of storage areas, gadgets and a pull out work surface. The top section was usually enclosed behind a dust proof rolltop door. The two sections were connected together with brackets designed to allow the table top to slide forward and back.

Hoosier cabinets featured a variety of "worksaving" devices which varied with the price of the cabinet. In addition to the drawers and cabinets, the standard Hoosier came with a flour bin and a flour sifter, a glass canister set, a spice set and a bread drawer. Deluxe models could include a swing-out ironing board, a meat grinder, a cake box drawer, an alarm clock, useful gadgets such as menu planners and bill and coin or grocery list holders or a desk along with many other options.

The average Hoosier measured 40" to 48" wide and was 69" to 72" tall. Narrower "junior size" cabinets were available for smaller kitchens. These juniors measured approximately 36" in width. If space was really a problem, there were also models available that fit under a kitchen window. Deluxe models could be 56" in width or more and were advertised as "almost kitchens in themselves".

Standard cabinets had glass or wooden panels inserted in the upper cabinet doors. Deluxe models often had frosted glass or slag glass inserts. Some more decorative models had colored glass panels on the cabinet doors.

The most common Hoosier cabinets were made from oak or from a combination of fruitwoods with a painted enamel finish. The most popular colors were ivory, gold, gray and green. Some Hoosiers were originally manufactured in a golden oak finish but the "natural look" was not as popular then as it is today, and many cabinets sporting a natural finish today were originally finished with a coat of enamel. The interiors of all cabinets were painted white or off white to give the impression of cleanliness. Some Art Deco-style Hoosiers made during the late 20s and 30s had the exteriors stencilled with geometric designs in bright orange and blue or red and black.

If you want to check to see if the current finish on the the cabinet is the original, pull out a drawer and look underneath in the corners and seams or use a flashlight to check the seams inside the cabinets. Also check the groove between the slats on the rolling tambour top. You should see evidence of previous coats of paint or early finish if there was one. The paint used on Hoosier cabinets was very difficult to remove, and because of its prominent grain pattern, oak is one of the most difficult woods to remove paint from even under ideal circumstances. Hoosier cabinets were often placed close to hot stoves in small kitchens and the heat from the stove had a tempering affect on the paint which made it even more difficult to remove. If the cabinet has been painted it will be virtually impossible for all of the previous paint to be removed.

The edges of the pull out porcelain shelf were subjected to a lot of wear and you will often find that repairs have been made to the edges or flat work surface. The damage can be easily touched up with DEVCON Appliance Touch-Up Paint or Duro White Appliance Touch-Up or a similar product. Before attempting a repair, wipe the area with white paper towels dampened with mineral spirits to thoroughly degrease the area. Use the brush in the cap of the product bottle or for best results use a thinner artist's brush. The thinner brush will give you greater control and will make the repair less noticeable. Dip the brush into the paint and use thin, even strokes over the scratches or chips. Then feather the edges of the repair to blend with the rest of the finish. Allow sufficient drying time before attempting to use the work surface.

If the scratches or chips are deep you will need to apply several thin coats of paint allowing at least 10 minutes drying time between coats. Any excess paint can be cleaned up with lacquer thinner.

Pie safes were used in Victorian kitchens to store food and protect it from insects and mice. The wooden framed cabinets had tin panels in the sides which were decoratively pierced into stars, hearts, or geometric patterns. The panels allowed air to circulate through the cabinet to prevent food from molding.

Pie safes have been reproduced over the years and are often made from old pieces of wood and tin to make them look like originals. Check the construction for evidence of age.

Old tin may develop rusted areas. These can be safely removed by lightly rubbing a 4/0 steel wool pad dipped in mineral oil or vegetable oil over the rusted areas. Buff off the oil with a soft cloth once the rust is removed.

An *ice box* was, of course, the predecessor of today's refrigerator. It was a metal-lined wooden box with a compartment that contained a block of ice and was used to keep food cold so it wouldn't perish prematurely.

It is a common belief that ice boxes were originally made of oak, and reproduction ice boxes almost always are. But original ice boxes were more often made from ash or elm wood and were just stained to look like oak. Some ice boxes have had their metal lining removed so they could be refinished or so they could be used for another purpose other than an ice box. But the small holes from the tacks used to hold the sheets of metal in place will usually remain on the interior of the cabinet.

Reproduction metal labels and hardware are available from woodworking supply stores and catalogs. Some unscrupulous people will use this hardware to add an identity or some additional "value" to an old ice box. Plain hardware may also be replaced with fancy embossed hardware in an attempt to make the piece appear to be a more deluxe model. "Aging" techniques can be used on reproduction hardware to make it blend in with the old look of the wood.

Desks - Even the most modest Victorian home had a desk or a piece of furniture which was used to hold writing supplies, books and magazines. Desks were important pieces of furniture and were often given prominence in a room. There were a variety of desks for the Victorians to choose from. The *fall leaf desk* (which we would call a *slant front desk* today) had a front which opened to reveal the writing surface and a small storage area. The fall leaf is supported by a chain attached to the body of the desk or a bracket to keep the lid open while in use.

Secretary desks had glass fronted storage cases above the desk and drawers beneath. The front dropped open like the fall leaf desk revealing a series of cubbyholes, and usually a small cabinet, for storage. The *Lincoln desk* was a fall-front desk with a table base and a full length drawer underneath. The desk was named, of course, after President Abraham Lincoln.

Cylinder desks have a quarter-round front which rolls down to conceal the writing surface when not in use. Inside the desk are cubbyholes or pigeonholes used to contain writing accessories. If glass cabinets were added to the top of the cylinder desk it was called a *cylinder secretary desk.* Cylinder desks are different than *rolltop desks* (otherwise known as *tambour desks*) because the cylinder is a solid piece of wood and the tambour is made up of narrow horizontal strips of wood attached to a canvas backing.

Wooten desks were invented by William S. Wooten and were probably the most compact and organized desk ever invented. The two half-barrel shaped sides swung open to expose a writing surface and compartments for books, letters, book keeping and a multitude of other writing accessories.

A combination desk-bookcase-display cabinet became popular during the "Golden Oak Era". Different manufacturers varied the designs, but the basic requirements were a slant front desk portion opening to reveal cubbyholes and storage areas for writing supplies, several drawers below the desk area, and a tall bookcase which comprised the other side of the unit. Convex glass was frequently used in the door to keep books free from dust but straight glass was also used depending on the manufacturer. Some units had mirrors and shelves above the desk lid, others may have been embellished with carving and fancy-shaped feet.

Most of these units were designed with the desk portion on the right side and the bookcase on the left. A right-handed person could use the desk and reach conveniently to their left to retrieve a book. Some left-handed combination desks were made with the cabinets and desk in the reverse order for left-handed people, but very few of these cabinets were manufactured as there seemed to be little demand for them. A few larger desks were manufactured with full-length bookcases on both sides of the desk area, but these too were rarities.

Rolltop desks were popular during the turn of the century, especially those made from oak. These massive pieces of furniture provided lots of storage for books and writing supplies and more than an adequate amount of room to work. When the work was done, the tambour top could be rolled down to conceal the contents and locked to secure them. Some rolltops were made in what is known as a double ripple which looks like an "S" when the top is closed. A standard rolltop only rounds out once.

Bookcases - Bookcases often had glass doors on the front to protect books from dust and moisture and locks on the doors to keep the contents secure. The standard bookcase had two glass doors parallel to each other. A *breakfront* has at least three sections with the center section sticking out farther than the cabinets on either side.

The most common bookcase during the turn of the century consisted of individual rectangular sections which could be stacked together. The apron and legs served as the bottom section and a separate top piece, often decorated with leaded glass or some type of decorative wood carving served as the top. What went in between these two pieces was up to the purchaser. Sections with glass doors which pulled up and then slid in and disappeared could be stacked to any desired heighth. The units fastened together on the back to secure them to each other. These bookcases are sometimes called "lawyer's bookcases".

Chairs - Victorian chairs were often decorated with carving. But in many cases the "carving" was not really carved – it was created by machines. *Press back chairs* had decorative back panels which were created with metal dies which pressed against the wood and forced the design into the wood fibers. Furniture catalogs from that time period describe these chairs as "carved" but mass-produced furniture was pressed not carved.

Hundreds of thousands of these chairs were produced between the middle to late 1800s. They were sturdy and inexpensive and could be used in almost any room of the house. Dining room chairs (or "diners" as they were called) were often more decoratively carved than other chairs and were made in matching sets, often containing twelve or more chairs. Diners were frequently decorated with small brass plates cut into decorative designs. These brass plates were tacked on to the back chair rail. David W. Kendall of the Grand Rapids Phoenix Furniture Company first introduced such decorations in 1879 and his competitors were quick to follow suit.

Many of these chairs had seats which were woven with cane, rush, reed or splint or had machine woven cane pounded into a groove on the top of the seat. Factories farmed out seat weaving on a piecework basis to women and children who could not work away from home. There were few child labor laws and children were an available work force. Trucks from the factory would deliver chairs and supplies and then pick up the finished products. In this way the factory was able to use cheap labor and workers who otherwise would not have wages were able to earn some money.

Upholstered chairs - Upholstery fabric wears out, and the older a piece of furniture the less likely you will find original upholstery fabric. Obviously, because of its rarity, original fabric will increase the value of a piece of furniture. But properly reupholstered furniture is not necessarily devalued because of the repair. Part of the value of furniture is based upon whether or not it is functional. If an upholstered piece is no longer functional then the reupholstering is necessary to retain its value. How the piece is reupholstered may cause the value to fluctuate. The *underupholstery* should be saved whenever possible. The more original components which remain the better. Furniture should be reupholstered in a similar fabric using similar techniques to the original in order to retain the value.

If you are lucky enough to find a piece of furniture which has been stripped of its fabric you can see detailed evidence left from former upholstery jobs: the types of tacks or nails used, the holes in the wood will tell you the number of tacks used, you can see if there have been repairs to the frame, you can often see evidence of previous refinishing done to the wooden arms and legs, and you can get an inside look at the construction of the chair. If you have an upholstered piece, and are able to remove the fabric you will often see remnants of previous fabrics used in earlier reupholstery jobs.

While you are examining the stripped chair frame, take a look at the corner supports. *Corner blocks* should be found in all of the corners of a chair or sofa and above the legs where the seat frame comes together. Corner blocks stabilize the chair and help provide additional support to the seat.

The corner blocks should be constructed of wood which is at least as old as the chair. Newer wood is a dead give-away there has been a repair. Antique corner blocks were always unfinished and unstained. If the corner blocks on the chair are either stained or have a clear finish you will know there have been some modifications. Fakers do not usually go to the trouble of faking the inside of an upholstered chair. They will spend their time and talents faking areas which will show. Repairs are often necessary and corner blocks break and need to be replaced. But occasionally, you will come across a chair where all of the corner blocks are inconsistent with the age of the chair.

Craftsmen in different areas of the country have been known to use different shaped corner blocks at different time periods, and the shape of the corner block should be consistent with the style of the chair and the region in which it was manufactured. Triangular blocks of wood which have been horizontally cut and are glued and nailed into place are typical to chairs made in Boston and some parts of New York during the 18th century. Corner blocks of vertical cut softwood, two pieces wide, which have been cut to a quarter round and glued are characteristic of chairs made in Connecticut, Philadelphia and parts of New York. Cleats which cross the corner of the chair are typical of those from Portsmouth, New Hampshire and some pieces made in England.

Platform rockers - Rocking chairs have remained popular since their invention, but even after the rockers were widened and stopped cutting up carpets they continued to damage wooden floors. The solution to this problem was the *platform rocker*. Platform rockers were quite innovative for their time and were designed to rock only within a fixed area defined by their bases.

Most platform rockers had an upholstered seat and back (some had a wooden back with an upholstered seat) with a rounded wooden bottom which sat on an elevated trestle-like base. The base usually had casters to make the chair easier to move around. The seat portion of the chair was attached to large spring mechanisms mounted on each side of the interior of the base. The springs rocked the chair on the platform and the rocking parts never touched the floor.

Many manufacturers received patents for their variations on the platform rocker design. Some rockers had a "non-rocking feature". A small piece of wood attached to the trestle base could be rotated to lock the chair in an up-right and non-moving position. (See the photograph below.)

Once introduced, platform rockers could be found in just about every Victorian parlor, regardless of the economic level of the home.

The arrow points to the non-rocking mechanism underneath a platform rocker. In the center of the picture you can see one of the two springs which allow the chair to rock.

Horn chairs - Chairs made from horns were a Victorian invention. Steer horns and elk antlers were used in place of wood to create unique frames for upholstered chairs. This fad for using exotic animal parts to create furniture lasted from the 1860s until the beginning of the 1900s. Furniture was created from elephant tusks and other animal horns and antlers, and umbrella stands were made from elephant feet. Horn furniture was primarily a western invention, but was manufactured in small quanties throughout the United States. It was popular with people who had a taste for both the exotic and the eclectic.

* Horns are a gelatinous substance and can become dry and brittle with age. The edges can become rough and may chip. Lightly chipped edges can be smoothed by buffing with very fine sandpaper or an emery board. Broken pieces of horn can be reattached with epoxy resin glue. If the broken horn is part of the structural frame, it is unlikely the furniture can be successfully repaired or will be durable enough to withstand use after a repair. Horn furniture is still manufactured in Mexico and by some craftsmen in this country. Carefully check all of the components of the piece of furniture for evidence of age.

* Antler furniture is often held together with screws and very strong glue. The furniture is extremely durable and requires no special care except an occassional dusting and a periodic coat of wax if desired. Antler furniture is still manufactured today. Older pieces can be identified by the patina on the antlers and from the styles and designs of the furniture.

Umbrella stands - Umbrella stands were a popular fixture in Victorian homes from the end of the 1800s through the 1920s. They were used for the obvious purpose of holding umbrellas, but also contained canes and walking sticks used by gentlemen around the turn of the century and could even be used to hold the parasol of the lady of the house. Umbrella stands were mass-produced out of oak wood in large factories throughout the United States. They were constructed entirely of machine cut and turned pieces which could be assembled in the factory or at the point of sale. The drip pans in the bottom of the stand were made from brass, copper or painted tin.

* Reproduction umbrella stands are usually made from lighter colored oak than period pieces and the wood is smaller in diameter. Originals stands were usually 1-1/2 to 1-3/4 inch thick. Reproductions can be 1/4 inch to 1/2 inch smaller. The wood used on reproductions is often a lighter weight than the originals.

Old umbrella stands should show water damage to the finish or the wood on the base of the stand, around the drip pan and on the legs. Drip pans were subject to rust and many have been repainted, replaced or lost over the years. A new or new looking pan does not necessarily mean the umbrella stand is new.

Bentwood furniture - Bentwood furniture first became popular in the United States in the early 19th century, but there is little proof it was made here at that time. Thonet Brothers and Kohn were two of the major manufacturers with factories in Austria and Hungry. Many other pieces were imported from Czechoslovakia.

Ash and beech were the most commonly used woods for bentwood furniture and they were steamed and bent into a variety of shapes. The seats on bentwood chairs were often made of plywood. Some bentwood chairs have contoured plywood seats. Bentwood furniture was not considered to be very decorative, but it was sturdy, functional and inexpensive. It was often used for high chairs and children's furniture. Older bentwood furniture is generally constructed of wood which is more rounded or circular as opposed to newer pieces which appear more oval or flat.

Paper labels were commonly applied to the bottom of bentwood furiture but many of them have not survived today. A label can be used to identify the manufacturer and to accurately date a piece of furniture.

A label under the seat of a bentwood chair.

Wicker furniture - Wicker furniture became extremely popular in the United States between 1850 and 1900 and was created by many different manufacturers throughout the country. *Wicker* is not a material. It is a generic term referring to furniture woven from a variety of materials such as *rattan, willow, reed* and *seagrass*. The term "wicker" is believed to be Swedish in origin (*wika*, to bend and *vikker*, meaning willow). The popularity of wicker furniture in the United States was sparked by a Massachusetts grocer named Cyrus Wakefield.

Ships bringing goods from Asia often used rattan as ballast. Once reaching port, the rattan was either dumped into the harbor or left to rot on the docks. Cyrus Wakefield became intrigued by the abundance of this product and experiemented until he discovered a way to recycle it. He found that rattan could be woven to produce useful and inexpensive furniture, and in 1855, the Wakefield Rattan Company (which was later renamed Heywood-Wakefield) introduced wicker to the masses.

A Heywood-Wakefield brand found under a chair seat.

Early wicker pieces were often plain and had little detailing, but by the 1890s natural wicker furniture was more fanciful and was elaborately designed and decorated with latticework, beaded rails, scrolls, lacy brackets and beaded edging called "rat-tail". They often had wooden seats or caned seats framed with wood. Wicker furniture was originally available with a choice of a natural finish or painted finish, but a lot of wicker furniture has multiple coats of paint today which are not original.

Wicker furniture was a standard fixture on porches and in sun rooms, but also was used as accent pieces in parlors, bedrooms and throughout the house. Manufacturer's catalogues, home decorating magazines and "lady's magazines" from the turn of the century can often help identify manufacturers and give some idea as to what the original finish may have been on a particular piece of furniture.

> * The value of a piece of furniture can be affected if the wicker is seriously damaged, but will generally not be affected if the caned seat has been replaced or repaired since few original seats have survived today. Repairs to the wickerwork itself may or may not affect the value depending upon the rarity of the piece and the quality and extensiveness of the repairwork. The price of wicker furniture is often based upon the design and condition of the furniture not its age.

Victorians enjoyed having Boston ferns and flowering plants in and around their homes and wicker planters and plant stands were popular additions to parlors, sitting rooms, sun porches and patios. It was not unusual for a large house to have as many as two dozen planters and plant stands.

Plant stands and planters were not generally designed in any particular furniture style and were produced in great quantities over a long period of time. Hardwoods (usually birch or maple) were used for the frame and wicker was woven over it. Plant stands varied in heighth and often had multiple shelves. The wicker was left in its natural unfinished state or was painted using bright greens, reds or whites.

Wicker smoking stands resemble plants stands and are often mistaken for them, but they are smaller in heighth and diameter. They usually contain a small round upper shelf with an indention for an ashtray, a larger lower shelf and have an arched handle used to carry them from room to room. Smoking stands were often made as an accessory for a set of wicker porch or patio furniture. They were almost always painted and are seldom found in an unfinished state.

The weaving on older pieces of wicker furniture differs from modern wicker and the furniture should show signs of age. However, years of exposure to water and moisture can weaken wicker and permanently damage it. Carefully check the furniture for repairs or damage. Repainting will generally not decrease the value of a piece of wickerwork. But repairs which have been improperly done and camoflauged under a coat of paint will.

The process of weaving and constructing furniture from wicker remained virtually unchanged until 1917 when an American named Marshall Burns Lloyd patented a method of weaving together strong strands of paper fiber with wire to produce durable furniture. The fiber was woven to form flat sheets of wickerwork which were then wrapped and fitted around pre-assembled wooden furniture frames. The process eliminated much of the labor involved in producing and weaving wicker from reed, and enabled manufacturers to use less expensive materials for the weaving. In 1912 only 15% of all wicker furniture was made of fiber. By 1920 that number had jumped to about 50%. Furniture is still made today using this technique, often using original designs.

This new machine-made furniture was durable, strong, lightweight and easy to move around. It was also comfortable, affordable and required little maintenance. The low price made machine-made wicker furniture available to middle-class and lower-class families. Unfortunately, along with the low price came a loss of intricate detailing which could only be produced by skilled craftsmen. Machine-made wicker was not as weather-resistant as its natural counter-part and was designed for indoor use and sun porches. It was quite often finished with one or more coats of paint to increase its durability. Factory paint choices were often bright colors such as blue, green or red, but white and brown furniture was also available.

Bamboo furniture - Bamboo is strong and very durable, and has been used as a furnituremaking material for many years around the world. It did not come into common usage in the United States until the Victorian period when it was used to create hall racks, étagères, shelves and planters, and was used as the framework for wicker furniture. Earlier pieces (made before 1925) are generally considered to have more interesting designs and be better constructed.

Pieces of bamboo were wrapped with rattan and held together with nails. This simple furniture was not designed in any particular furniture style. Furniture shops specializing in manufacturing bamboo and rattan work were scattered throughout the United States, between the 1920s and the 1940s but furniture was also imported from Southeast Asia.

Bamboo was usually left in its natural state, but occassionally it was decorated with bands of paint or burned (pyrographic) areas. Some "bamboo furniture" is not made of bamboo at all, but is maple or a hardwood stained to look like bamboo.

Check bamboo furniture carefully for evidence of damage or repairs. Use and constant exposure to moisture and water can cause permanent damage.

* New pieces of bamboo will not have the aged look of an older piece. Bamboo mellows with age and new bamboo is much lighter in color and will not have the same

patina. Earlier pieces of bamboo furniture have joints wound with wicker, chamfered corners and often have brass finials. Mass-produced newer pieces will be lacking these details. They will also be more lightweight than antique pieces and are usually poorly made.

Bamboo magazine racks were factory-produced in the United States between the end of the 1800s and the beginning of the 1900s. Similar racks have often been reproduced since, but they lack the patina of age and the detailing found on older pieces. Bamboo planters were usually inexpensive and could be purchased at department stores or flower shops. They were also sold as part of a set of parlor or porch furniture.

Accessories - Victorian homes were filled with a variety of decorating accessories. Picture frames, slipper wall pockets, hat racks, comb cases, shadow boxes, and mirrors were but a few of the more common items. The first plastic items manufactured in the United States were made during the Victorian era. *Gutta-percha* is made from the gutta-percha tree which grows in Southeast Asia and was used to make the boxlike cases which displayed daguerreotypes. A patent for the process was issued in 1854. After the patent date, gutta-perch was used to create other types of boxes, wall frames and other decorative items.

Art Deco Furniture

The American Art Deco period, which was popular from about 1925 to 1945, was based upon a postwar French movement seeking a return to fine craftsmanship and luxury. It took its name from *L'Exposition Internationale de Arts Décoratifs et*

Industriels Modernes which was held in 1925. The Art Deco look consisted of simple, streamlined traditional forms. The French Art Deco style featured fine craftsmanship, decorative techniques such as inlays and veneers and lavishly applied costly materials. The American Art Deco style, on the other hand, was less elaborate and was focused more on form than expensive materials. It used ordinary materials like paint and lacquer, and the wood and shape of the furniture created the decorative effect.

American designs copied the sleek geometric shapes made popular by the French but created them using modern materials like tubular steel. The use of tubular steel was considered revolutionary in the 1920s and early furniture designs which incorporated it were considered avant-garde. Brass and aluminum were used for simple, inexpensive mass-produced furniture from the end of the 1920s until World War II.

French furnituremakers used sophisticated decorative techniques, while Americans placed their emphasis on techniques which were easy to do and could be mass-produced. But the resulting mass-produced furniture was seldom well made. Inexpensive, mass-produced wooden furniture was made from pine or other local wood, covered with thin coats of veneer, then painted to imitate ebony or ivory inlay in imitation of the French pieces, or "false-grained" to make plain wood look like expensive figured wood. Veneer was applied on some Art Deco pieces with the grain running alternately horizontally on one section and then vertically on another section to achieve a decorative contrast. Inlay and ebonized wood were used to accentuate the veneered patterns. Many pieces of American Art Deco furniture appear to have a Chinese influence which is reflected in the styling, color schemes, hardware and lacquerwork.

Art Deco furniture was often false-grained to make an inexpensive local wood appear to be a more expensive figured wood. These pieces should be carefully inspected for damage on a regular basis. Once damaged, they are very difficult to repair properly without ruining the effect of the piece. Some false graining is so convincing many people do not realize it is not real wood until they attempt to strip it or refinish it and it starts to dissolve off of the furniture.

Many pieces of Art Deco furniture were designed for the modest size of rooms in apartments and small homes. Drop-leaf dining tables were popular because they could be pushed against the wall if space was at a premium or used as a center table. Some drop-leaf tables had one leaf (instead of the traditional two) which could be used to expand the size of the table.

The most advanced Art Deco designs were developed by leading architects, and interior designers who produced unique one-of-a-kind pieces. Many of their designs were adaptions of traditional forms which were streamlined and modernized to fit the period. The better quality Art Deco pieces were made of solid wood instead of veneers, had paneled rather than plywood backs, German silver rather than plastic drawer knobs, and inlaid decorations instead of false-grained imitations. Herman Miller, Jules Bouy, Eugene Schoen and Paul T. Frankl are some of the Art Deco designers of the period whose furniture is highly sought after today, and the prices can be substantial.

For the most part, Art Deco furniture was moderately priced and quite affordable for the average homeowner. Unfortunately, except for designer pieces, most Art Deco furniture was not very well made.

Department stores and large manufacturers offered modern, streamlined pieces for every room in the house – from sofas and armchairs to bedroom sets. The coffee table or cocktail table made its appearance during the Art Deco period. These rectangular or circular shaped tables were made of wood, usually finished with clear lacquer and often had a blue mirrored glass top set into a simple wooden frame.

During the 1930s and 1940s American furniture manufacturers simplified the Art Deco designs and mass-produced simple furniture which had very restrained designs and minimal decoration. Many experts call these later adaptions of the Art Deco style *Art Moderne.*

Donald Deskey was considered by many to be the leading Art Deco or Art Moderne designer. Unlike other designers of the time, he did not rely on transforming traditional designs into modern interpretations. His pieces were uniquely American, featuring streamlined designs made with modern materials and were simple yet elegant.

Liquor cabinets first appeared in the late 19th century, but became more common by the 1920s to 1930s. They evolved from the wine storage area of the traditional sideboard. Many Art Deco pieces were painted with lacquer and were originally white, black or gray. Additional coats of paint may have been added since the original coats were applied and the colors today may not be original.

Humidors were another piece of "vice furniture" which became popular during the 20th century. They were small wooden cupboards with a metal-lined cabinet used to keep pipe tobacco fresh and moist. They were often designed to be part of a parlor or living room set which would have included several chairs, a sofa and some occassional tables of various sizes. These cabinets are small enough to be used as bedside tables or end tables today and may be found with the metal lining removed. Look inside the cabinet for evidence of the small tack holes which would show where the metal was once attached.

The "blonde look" in furniture became popular during the 1930s and 1940s and was sold either by the piece or by the set in both high-end and inexpensive price ranges. To achieve the "blonde look" ash, pine, oak and maple were left unstained and given a clear finish of lacquer to accentuate the wood grain. Some woods were bleached to remove the natural wood color and make them more blonde and then finished with a clear coat. Other woods were painted or stained with pigments to make them resemble "blonde wood".

Glass and lucite were used as tops on many Art Deco

tables and even used to create legs and other structural supports. Glass was a new material for furniture construction and incorporating glass into the design gave the furniture a very modern look. Unfortunately, glass tops were breakable and made the furniture less functional.

> * Glass table tops can be easily removed from most pieces of Art Deco furniture and it may be difficult to tell whether the piece of glass is original to that particular piece of furniture, if it has been taken from another piece of furniture or replaced outright with a new piece of glass.

Art Deco furniture was often flamboyant and more than a little "over the top" and some pieces appear quite odd by today's standards. Tables contained built-in lamps, ash trays, storage areas – even fish tanks! Many pieces seemed to have been designed with shock value in mind. Some furniture buyers seemed to feel they had to go 180° in the opposite direction from the traditional furniture of the past in order to be in style.

Large round mirrors on dressers and vanities are almost synonymous with the Art Deco style. Original mirrors were quite large and often have been broken or lost over the years. Check the back of the mirror for screw holes and new support brackets. Check the mirror to see if it is original to the piece.

Wall mirror frames were made of plastic, aluminum, steel, brass and other industrial materials during the Art Deco period. These frames were usually more durable than wooden frames but still may have been repaired over the years. Check the backs of the frame for evidence of repairs.

Small dressing tables with matching stools were also popular during the 1930s and were used in bedrooms, bathrooms and theater dressing rooms. They often had fold out side shelves for additional space and basically served the purpose of a portable makeup case on legs.

Wicker furniture made a comeback during the Art Deco period. Tables, chairs, plant stands and shelves were manufactured from reeds, rattan and willow branches. Bamboo was used to create some bentwood Art Deco furniture. It was moderately priced, sturdy and very utilitarian. Wicker and bamboo furniture was mass-produced in factories all over the United States but the two largest centers of production were New York and New England. It was designed to be used inside the house or outside on the patio or porch. Bamboo furniture often had a wooden frame for added support and upholstered cushions for added comfort.

The process for creating bentwood furniture was developed in Austria during the early part of the 19th century by a German named Michael Thonet, and the technique is still in use today. As a matter of fact, the company is still in business today and has never stopped making the furniture designs which made them popular in the mid-19th century. Wood was steamed and then slowly bent into different shapes while being held with quick-release metal clamps. The resulting bent wood was used to make a variety of furniture components which were used to create unusual and distinctive Art Deco furniture.

Bentwood furniture was produced in large quantities during the middle of the 19th century. Some of it was made in the United States and some was imported from out of the country. Many of these pieces of furniture are still quite serviceable today. Paper labels were comonly applied to the underside of chair seats, under table tops and on the back of case pieces of furniture. Labels can help identify the origin of the furniture and the date it was manufactured.

Heywood-Wakefield was one of the largest American furniture manufacturers. They produced quality furniture at affordable prices. Their designs were restrained and had minimal ornamentation. The Heywood-Wakefield name and logo was stamped or branded inside a drawer or under a chair seat as a way of identifying their pieces. Other companies put labels or brands on the back or bottom of the furniture. Many companies had catalogues illustrating the various lines of furniture they produced. You can check these catalogues today to see how the furniture originally looked and also to help date a piece of furniture.

Upholstered furniture from the Art Deco period was frequently overstuffed and the frame was often designed in a geometric shape. Art Deco furniture was frequently made to look "built-in" or was used as a room divider. Fabrics tended to be solids rather than prints, and contrasting fabric was often used to accent details. The upholstery was tufted on earlier pieces, often in complex patterns, but this was eliminated later in the period in an effort to emphasize the angularity of the furniture.

Daybeds or chaise longues had upholstered wooden frames and metal springs for comfort and support. They often had fabric skirts which covered all sides of the chair or fringe covering the legs. Chaise longues were mounted on casters so they could be easily moved. Chaise longues made later in the 19th century had thinner arms than the earlier examples and were covered with more ornately tufted fabrics.

Art Deco stools were often made of chromed tubular steel or aluminum and had upholstered seats, often made of leather. Stools could be backless or have low metal backs. Many Art Deco stools were based on traditional designs but interpreted with modern materials. Other Art Deco stools were more like over-stuffed ottomans and had wooden frames which were completely covered in upholstery fabric.

* Many dealers will rechrome, relacquer or otherwise refurbish Art Deco furniture before selling it because, unlike wood furniture, use and wear do not make furniture manufactured from modern materials more attractive.

Skyscraper furniture - Skyscraper bookcases, desks and chests of drawers consisted of blocks of various sizes fastened together in immitation of the architectural skylines which were quickly developing in major American cities after World War I. Tall skyscrapers like the angular Empire State building represented the bold, new mechanical age. Skyscraper furniture was uniquely modern and sophisticated, and in bold contrast to all of the furniture that came before it. It was considered a symbol of sopisticated tastes during the 1930s.

Modern Furniture

Art Deco furniture is considered by some to be the beginning of *Modern Furniture*. Others consider furniture based on the designs of the *Bauhaus* (a school of art and design in Germany) to be the beginning of the style. Bauhaus designs, also known as the *International Style*, were focused on new materials, functional forms and machine production.

Marcel Breuer and Ludwig Mies van der Rohe moved to the United States when Hitler shut down the Bauhaus and their unique designs were very influential on American Modern furniture. The tubular steel chair with cantilevered seat which has become almost synonomous with the modern age was one of their designs. Bauhaus designs also affected furniture designs in Denmark, Sweden and Finland. Traditional craftsmanship and peasant designs were combined with the Bauhaus designs and the resulting *Scandanavian Modern style* was copied by some American furniture designers and commercial furniture manufacturers.

Designers took ideas from the Bauhaus as a point of departure for their own unique designs and created a variety of interpretations of the modern style for more than twenty years. Charles Eames created plywood or plastic chairs which were molded to the shape of the human body. Modern Age (a prominent New York retailer who specialized in advanced furniture

designs) commissioned custom-designed furniture for their
trendy clientele. Some designer pieces were based on
conservative, traditional furniture styles while other pieces were
radical and almost impractical for use as furniture.

Paul Frankl was an Austrian-born architect and furniture
designer who played a major role in the American Modern
furniture movement from the 1920s until his death in 1958.
His geometric lines and curvilinear shapes were quite distinctive
and differed from the functional Bauhaus designs. Russell Wright
was one of the most successful and famous industrial designers
from the 1930s to the 1970s. He designed ceramics, flatware
and furniture. His furniture was often constructed of "blonde
wood" or bleached wood and was very plain and simple in its
design and construction. His more popular designs were
produced and sold in quantity even though he was considered
"too commercial" by some of his peers.

Wendell Castle was an artist and craftsman who created
contemporary furniture out of rare woods. His designs bore more
resemblance to sculptures than furniture. He created beautiful
pieces of art with fluid carving accentuating the grain of the
chosen woods. Today his pieces can be found in galleries
specializing in contemporary furnishings – usually with a hefty
price tag attached.

Herman Miller Company, Inc. of Zeeland, Michigan
was one of the first American furniture manufacturers to
specialize in Modern furniture. The company started out as a
traditional furniture manufacturer and changed at the beginning
of the Depression to producing exclusively Modern furniture.
Designers and architects from around the country worked with
Gilbert Rohde, their head designer, to create the company's distinctive furniture designs. The Herman Miller Company had a
reputation for well-balanced designs and simple construction.
Labels were generally placed under tops or on legs as proof of
identification.

Tubular-steel was introduced as a furniture material in

the 1920s by European designers, but by the 1930s Americans were using it for furniture for their kitchens, play rooms, and other rooms of the house and even outside on the patio. Tubular-steel side chairs and arm chairs designed by the Bauhaus inspired American designers to create their own interpretations of the originals. American manufacturers modified the Bauhaus ideas and began mass-producing similar designs during the 1930s. Mass-produced pieces were moderately priced but still retained much of the character of the original Bauhaus models. Tubular-steel, chrome-plating and imitation leather were all exciting new modern materials at the time and the combination created a daring avant garde piece of furniture for the average homeowner who wanted to appear modern and up-to-date.

Tubular-steel was used to create Modern style beds which were simplified interpretations of traditional brass beds. Steel beds were less expensive to produce and to buy than brass beds, and required less maintainance.

In 1950, Hans Knoll (one of the leading modern furniture manufacturers in the United States) commissioned Harry Bertoia (a prominent American metalsmith and sculptor) to design several chairs. The resulting steel wire chairs became masterpieces of American furniture design and similar chairs are still manufactured today. An original Hans Knoll chair will have a label under the seat or under the upholstery.

Steel wire was welded together to form a grid pattern and combined with metal tubing to form the furniture components. The furniture was either chrome-plated or vinyl-coated in a variety of colors. The backs were concave and the sides were straight-edged and angled inward. The seats were concave with straight sides, curved fronts and hollowed centers. The chairs were comfortable and inexpensive and vinyl-coated ones were often used as outdoor furniture.

Fiberglass and iron armchairs are classic examples of Modern furniture which are recognized by almost everyone. The molded fiberglass body of the chair was contoured to fit the human body. The back was arched and curved into the project-ing arms. All of the edges of the chair were smooth and curved outward. The legs and base could be simple or a complex arrangement of ironwork.

Fiberglass can be easily scratched, chipped or damaged and is very difficult to repair. The older the fiberglass the more susceptible it is to damage. Use care when handling old or designer pieces.

Several designers used laminated plywood pressed into various shapes to create modern furniture including the American designer Charles Eames. He was known for furniture which was shaped to the contours of the human body. His designs were simple and understated but very recognizable, and imitations were, at the time and still to this day, considered as counterfeits and not reproductions. His pieces originally had labels to identify them but labels can be damaged or removed over time. Manufacturer catalogs and period decorating magazines can be used to help identify unlabeled pieces.

Modern lacquered furniture was mass-produced from the 1920s until after World War II. Pine or hardwood was shaped into a variety of geometric shapes and painted with neutral colored lacquer to resemble bleached wood. Bright colors were sometimes used to accentuate and emphasize the geometric shapes. Geometric table designs usually combined circular and square shapes in various combinations with glass or metal accents. The furniture consisted of over-simplified designs which seem to emphasize the fact they were machine-made. Many companies sacrificed quality for quantity and the craftsmanship varied greatly from one manufacturer to the next. The result was a lot of poorly-constructed mass-produced furniture.

Studio furniture - After 1945, another furniture design was developed called "studio furniture". The furniture was handmade, in small quantities, in artist's studios and the small quantities produced and high prices limited its commercial appeal. Although the number of "studio furniture" pieces were limited, they varied in appearance from practical and traditional to fanciful and inventive. The common features were a return to fine handcraftsmanship and an appreciation of wooden surfaces. Furniture had come full circle and had returned from whence it came.

Tramp Art

American *Tramp Art* is a type of folk art generally considered to date from the time of the Civil War through the 1930s. Most Tramp Art consists of smaller pieces such as mirrors, decorative boxes and picture frames, but larger pieces of furniture were also created.

The Tramp Art style is said to have originated in Germany or Scandinavia but there appears to be no conclusive evidence to document the claim. Tramp Art pieces can be found in practically every industrialized nation of the early 1900s.

Legend has it hobos and tramps were responsible for the majority of Tramp Art. Some have gone so far as to point out that hobos whittled the wood and tramps carved the wood. While an interesting discussion could result in trying to explain the difference between whittling and carving, I am not sure what differentiates a hobo from a tramp. Regardless of what you call the carvers, they were usually untrained craftsmen who used a simple penknife and lots of time and imagination to notch-carve wood into various geometric patterns, and then layered the many small pieces of wood into three-dimensional stacks to create their art.

Before the days of cardboard cigar boxes and packing boxes these items were made from wood. Once used, they were considered "disposable items". Tramp Art craftsmen salvaged the free wood from these boxes and also used crates, pallets and plywood for their projects. Used wood was the most common medium, but linoleum, sheet metal and even corrugated cardboard and whale bone have been used to create Tramp Art.

Squares, triangles and circular patterns were crafted with thin strips of wood to create inlaid decorations for the project. Hearts and stars were also popular shapes. The successive layers were held together solely by notching the wood – no glue or tacks were used. The wood was layered until it formed a recognizable object. Each layer was smaller than the previous layer creating a pyramid-like effect. If the piece had an applied finish, it was usually lacquer or stain, although paint and even gilding was used on some pieces.

Crown of Thorns - Crown of Thorns is another type of Tramp Art. This technique uses interlocking wooden sticks, which have been notched to intersect at right angles to each other, to form joints and self-supporting objects. It is usually used to create small items like mirror frames and picture frames. The technique got its name because the finished items resemble the "crown of thorns" Jesus Christ was said to have worn.

Because of the primitive nature of Tramp Art, pieces can easily be recreated and passed off as original. Check the wood or other materials to help verify the age. The finish and other materials used should correspond with the purported age of the piece.

Section Three
Faking It

Furniture will develop signs of age and wear on several different levels. The wood, the finish, the hardware and even the upholstery or seating will become modified from time and use. This is normal and is to be expected. When a piece of furniture shows no signs of wear or use, it is either a prime specimen which has been remarkably cared for, or has been repaired, refinished or is a fake.

Fortunately, outright fakes are not that common which is why they receive the publicity they do when they are discovered. Every few years a large private collection or a famous museum discovers a questionable piece of furniture in their collection. Most of the furniture the average homeowner will come to own and appreciate in their lifetime is nowhere near the priceless catagory and is more likely to be functional old furniture which possibly contains some sentimental value.

This does not mean these pieces of furniture do not deserve to be well cared for or should not be repaired if necessary. But there is no reason why repairs have to be glaringly obvious. A trip to the crafts store or home improvement center will reveal a myriad of products which can be used to promote rust on metal to make it look older, duplicate patina on brass or copper to take away the "new" look and make it look "aged", and products which will crackle paint, dull finishes and generally add years to a piece of furniture in anywhere from a few minutes to a few hours.

The following pages contain step by step instructions to help you blend furniture repairs and make them relatively unnoticeable. You will learn how to "age" hardware and fasteners so they blend with the originals, "age" a finish, distress wood, create a fake grain pattern, create marbling, ebonizing and generally take the "new" out of repairs on a variety of surfaces.

This book and the information it contains are not intended to be used to create "new antiques" nor is it a textbook for a new generation of con artists. The information is presented with the hope it will be used to preserve family heirlooms so they can be appreciated by future generations.

Fake Facts

Some pieces of furniture are ingeniously crafted and the materials and techniques used are so convincing it is difficult to determine the difference between the furniture in question and a genuine antique. Other pieces, regardless of the craftsmanship and materials involved, can be quickly dismissed just by using some simple logic. A close examination can often be quite enlightening.

Age does not necessarily equate to value. There has always been junk furniture which is poorly constructed of inferior materials. In most cases you would be better off buying a newer piece in good condition rather than an older piece in poor condition. Condition is a large factor when trying to determine value. Repairing a genuine antique can be quite costly and you will not necessarily regain the money spent on repairs with an increase in the value of the furniture.

Beds

• Antique beds frames are generally not as wide or as long as modern beds. This is easily explained when you realize people have grown taller over the years. A modern double (full size) mattress and box spring are made to standard measurements: 54" wide by 75" long. Twin sizes are 39" wide by 74" long. Antique mattress can be costume made to your dimensions by some mattress manufacturersAn antique full-sized bed frame (or double bed) is often only a few inches wider than today's standard twin size bed. A double bed (or full size bed) used to be the largest size available unless you had a one custom-made. A bed marked "king size" or "queen size" can sometimes be found at antique stores. If you check carefully, you will find the siderails have been extended or the headboard and footboard have been modified. Unless the piece was an expensive "one-of-a-kind" custom creation it is probably not an un-modified antique and the price should reflect that.

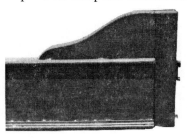

This antique bed was made longer by adding a piece of wood to the end of each siderail and then replacing the hardware.

Early beds were often numbered with Roman numerals on the rails, inside the tenons and the posts, just under the mortises. The bed could be assembled correctly by matching up the pairs of Roman numerals ("I" to "I", "II" to "II", etc.) If the numbers do not seem to run in a logical sequence, or if the numbers appear to have been carved or branded differently, all of the pieces may not have originally belonged to the same bed.

Desks

• *Pedestal desks* are made up of three parts: the top and two side sections. Parts from different desks can be "married" to make a desk. Close examination will often turn up evidence of a different veneer pattern, varying wood colors or different wear marks which are inconsistent with the rest of the piece. Some larger desks are reduced in size to make them more saleable. Remove the drawers and look under the top for evidence of saw marks or patches on the inside. Both incised carving and relief carving can be added to furniture "after production" in an attempt to increase value.

• *Kneehole desks* were originally designed to be used as dressing tables, *not* desks and the small drawers were designed to hold brushes, combs and other personal grooming articles. The backboard was made from a secondary wood because it was not intended to show. Early desks were made from walnut, then during the middle of the 18th century mahogany became the wood of choice. Pine and other less expensive woods were only used on reproductions which were made at a much later.

• Bureau style desks are relatively inexpensive and readily available compared to other styles of desks, and they are really not worth faking. Some of the examples which have surfaced over the years were created by covering an old oak bureau with walnut veneer which was stripped from another piece of furniture.

Chests
• Chest-of-drawers can be converted into a kneehole desk. Check the veneer on the sides and on the recessed cupboard door. The veneer should perfectly match the veneer on the rest of the piece. The construction of the inner sides of the small side drawers should match the outer sides. The dovetails should all look the same, have the same spacing and look as if they were made by the same person. The runners from the drawers should have made wearmarks on the carcass of the desk.

• Chests-on-chests are one of the more commonly faked pieces. To make sure you have an original and not a marriage you will need to check the details on both the top and bottom pieces to make sure they match. The dovetails on both pieces should be the same size, have the same spacing and there should be similar carving on all drawers.

The top piece alone may have canted corners or both the top and the bottom may have them. But you will never find a piece where only the bottom has canted corners. The wood on both pieces should match exactly. Decorative details such as crossbanding should be identical on both pieces. Look for evidence of changed hardware. If the hardware has been changed on one piece it should be consistently changed on the other. If one piece has filled holes from previous hardware (or exposed holes) and the other does not, you probably have a marriage on your hands.

Bookcases
• Large bookcases and display cabinets (some of which were intended to be built-in to the room of a home and were built to individual specifcations) may be cut down or altered to make them more saleable today. The cabinet may be reduced in depth by cutting through the sides and shelves and then replacing the backboard. Look for evidence of freshly cut wood which will appear lighter than the surrounding wood. Check the measurements of the piece and compare them to pieces of similar age and style. Some slight variations in the size of furniture can be expected, but for the most part, unless the piece was custom-made, bookcases, tables, chairs, etc. from a particular period should bear a strong similarity to other

pieces like them. Pediments are often removed to reduce the heighth of a piece of furniture. Look at the top of the bookcase for small holes which would have held the pegs of the pediment to keep it in place. If the carcass has been adjusted to reduce the heighth, the slots for the adjustable shelves may appear too close to the top or bottom. Shelves always allowed a minimum of eight inches of clearance between shelves to allow for the heighth of books.

• Bookcases and side cabinets often had wooden doors or "blind doors". The problem with a solid wooden door was the contents of the cabinet had to be removed in order to be seen and admired. These panels can be removed and replaced with glass, brass grilles or pleated silk fabric to give the furniture a lighter and more open look. Researching similar pieces to see what kind of doors they had may help determine whether the doors are original or replacements.

• Cabinetmakers would usually line up the horizontal muntins on glass doors so the edges of the shelves would not show. If the muntins and shelves do not line up, you may be looking at a piece of furniture which has been altered or had the doors replaced.

Cabinets
• In the early 20th century cabinets were often created from wardrobes. To check for this modification, look at the proportion of the top and the base. If the base appears low in proportion to the top there is a good chance it is a modified wardrobe. If there are drawers instead of

cupboards, the shelving adjustments are toothed ladders on each side of the cabinet with removable rungs forming the shelf supports, and modern glass in the doors, it is probably a modified wardrobe not an original cabinet.

Commodes
• Commodes or "night tables" were used to conceal chamber pots. Some commodes had "dummy" drawers which did not open and had hinged tops which would be lifted up for use. Some of these pieces have been converted into small chests, and the dummy drawers have been replaced with real drawers with new linings. This modification involves the use of a lot of new wood and should be quite obvious to spot without too much investigation.

Tables
• Early writing tables are usually worth more than later ones. The earlier tables had slender tapered legs. The legs generally got thicker and heavier as time progressed. Some writing tables have had the thick legs removed and replaced with slender square ones to give the piece the illusion of age. The original legs may be cut off and completely removed, but evidence of the thick leg should still be visible on the underside of the table top near where the new legs are connected. It is difficult to match old and new wood and the wood will be a different color on the legs and the base of the table. All of the components of an original table should be of a similar color and grain pattern.

• The coffee table as we know it today is a fairly modern American invention. There are no true antique coffee tables. Many library tables have had their legs shortened to convert them into coffee tables, and other antique tables have sacrificed parts to make them conform to the proper dimensions. But while the table may be an antique, and may well be serving a useful purpose, it does not change the fact the value has been diminished and that it did not start out its life as a coffee table.

• Fake farmhouse or refectory tables can be made from old floorboards or other old timber. Look under the table top for evidence of saw marks. Circular saw marks will be evidence the wood has been cut since the early 20th century. Hand saws were used on earlier pieces and they will leave straight cut marks. Newly cut wood will have a pale color unless it has been stained in an effort to "age" it. Original tables were one or two planks wide, never three, and the tops were seldom fastened to the table. Reproduction tables all have sawn tops not split, and are fastened with machine-made pegs which are uniform in size and shape. The top will often be fastened to the legs. If you remove the table top, there should be a distinct outline of the base of the table on the underside of the top if it is truly old.

• Center tables and drum tables were used as decorative pieces in hallways, parlors, and drawing rooms. They could be quite large and were often more than four feet in diameter. Many early center tables were originally used as writing tables and they had leather tops. Some of these tops have been removed and the table top has been refinished as a plain wooden top or has been veneered.

These tables were frequently made from rosewood or mahogany. Rosewood is a very oily wood, is difficult to work with and finish, and was expensive, so the bulbous stems and bases were often carved from beech or a similar wood and then stained dark to resemble rosewood. If rosewood is improperly stripped and re-finished it will turn very dark and the grain will be all but obliterated. Once rosewood has turned dark, the process is irreversible.

• Drop leaf tables have a tendency to warp. The top of the table may be secured to a frame, but the leaves are attached with hinges and generally have nothing but a wooden bracket or a gateleg to hold them in place. Mahogany tops were often one inch thick and will generally not warp unless they have been exposed to extreme conditions. Thinner tops could indicate the piece is a Victorian copy. Softer woods like pine, however, can warp and twist to the point where the table becomes unusable.

Always extend both leaves on a drop leaf table, then stand back and examine the table from a distance to see how the top really looks. Then, take a good look underneath the table. If there is a gateleg or a support bracket, there should be an arc in the wood from where the leg has rubbed the underside of the table as it was pulled out for support. If there is no noticeable arc, or if there is more than one arc, the top may have been repaired or replaced.

• Gate-leg tables were made in all sizes and some were so large they needed two gates to support the flap. Most antique gate-leg tables were made from oak, but walnut and other woods were occassionally used. The central section of the table or "bed" of the table was made up of anywhere from one to three planks. The feet on the bottom of the gate should show more signs of wear than the other feet and there should be a noticeable arc on the underside of the table from the gate rubbing as it was moved back and forth. The bed of the table maybe lighter than one or both of the flaps depending on how the table was used. If the flaps were both opened at the same time they will usually be equally faded and aged. If the table normally sat with one or more flaps down the bed will have received more exposure and wear and will be a slightly different color.

• Dished top tripod tables have a top which is carved lower than the surrounding edges. These tables can have either pie-crust or plain edges. Some dish top tables started their life as a flat top table. The top may have been hollowed out in an attempt to make the table more desirable or valuable. To determine whether the table has been hollowed out after it was manufactured, look underneath the table. A plain top table will have bearers underneath which are attached to the top with screws. The table tops are generally made from thin pieces of wood and the screws are generally just below the surface of the top. If the top is "dished out", the screws will appear through the surface leaving holes which will need to be filled or plugged. Shine a light at an angle on the top of the table and the plugged holes will become obvious, no matter how good a job the woodworker may have done to conceal them.

• Pembroke tables are small occassional tables which are usually veneered, have leaves attached by hinges that can be opened for additional table space and have one or more shallow drawer underneath the top. The drop leaves can be round, square or oval in shape and are supported on wooden brackets. The name supposedly came from the Countess of Pembroke who was the first person to order a table meeting this description. Pembroke tables were popular because they could be easily moved around, extended to gain more table space, and provided additional table space for drawing, writing, needlework or dining.

The sofa table evolved from the Pembroke table. They are usually longer and narrower than a Pembroke table and the leaves are usually on the short ends of the table not the long sides. Table tops are subjected to a lot of wear and when severely damaged are occassionally re-placed. Check the direction of the grain on an original table. The grain will run across the width of the table instead of along the length of the table. Many replaced tops will have the grain running the wrong direction and will have the grain running along the length of the table.

Some sofa tables from the 1820s and 1830s are made to look older by using the end-supports from cheval mirrors as replacement legs. Check the wood carefully to make sure the grain is consistent throughout the table. Look for screwholes which do not line up with an existing screw, or where the screw would not be needed to hold two pieces of wood together on the furniture.

• Bedside tables have been made since about 1750 and most of them vary very little from the original designs. They usually have a cupboard area with two small doors, or a tambour sliding door. Below the doors you'll find one or possibly two drawers. Individual fake bedside tables are not generally a problem. But, since many people would like to have a set of two tables – one for each side of the bed – dealers or restorers may be tempt-ed to make two tables appear to be a matched pair. A matched pair of tables can often sell for ten times the price of a single table. That kind of profit could be good motivation. To make sure a pair of bedside tables are truly an original pair, check the construction of both tables. It should be similar both inside and out. The underside of the tables and the backboards should be made from similar wood. The quality of the wood and the figuring of the grain should be similar. Locks, hinges and any other hardware should match. Signs of wear may differ on the tables but look for uneven signs of aging which can be artificially created.

Chairs
• A stretcher rail on a chair which appears too close to the ground may be a sign of a chair which has had its feet or legs cut down. A standard chair seat is 18 inches from the ground.

• Before the 19th century, corner braces were rectangular blocks of wood placed into the seat frame from the top creating an open triangle in each corner. These blocks were glued in place. Solid corner blocks fixed with screws are used on later furniture. The type of corner blocks used on the chair will tell you if the chair has had replacements or if it is a copy.

Sideboards
• Sideboards were a standard fixture in most homes from the end of the 18th century until well into the 20th century. Square tapering legs were generally considered more desirable than the round turned legs found on sideboards from the beginning of the 19th century. Because of this, some round legs have been removed and replaced. If the leg is original, it will extend to the top of the sideboard and be constructed from one piece of wood. If the leg was altered, it would have been necess-

ary to cut off the turned section at the base of the drawer. If you look carefully, you should see where the two pieces of wood have been joined. The joint may have been partially covered with veneer or camoflauged with stain or finish, but there should be a definite seam and a noticeable difference in the color and type of wood between the two sections.

Nails, screws and fasteners
• Old nails and screws can be added to a piece of furniture in an effort to make a repair seem more authentic or to make a piece of furniture appear older than it is. Do not date a piece of furniture based upon a few fasteners. If a nail or screw is rusty, the wood surrounding it should also show signs of rust. If the screw or nail has darkened and oxidized with age, the wood around it should also be discolored. Be suspicious of inconsistencies. If new screws are used on an antique, the screw holes will often have to be modified to accept the new screws. Holes in the furniture will often have to be lengthened or widened to accomodate a new screw. New screws will generally not fit into the screw holes on old hinges. Thehinges may have to have the holes enlarged to accomodate new screws, or the hinges may have to be replaced.

Pro Tip: When removing more than one screw at a time label them so you know where they came from and can return them to their correct holes. Old screws can cause permanent damage to a piece of furniture if returned to the wrong hole because many were hand-made and can vary in length and width. Place your hand on the wood surface opposite the screw hole as you start to turn the screwdriver. Stop turning before then screw breaks through the wood and mars the surface.

• The most commonly faked fastener is the "five clout nail" or "rosehead". Rusted mis-shapened upholstery tacks are almost indestinguishable from the real thing without removal from the furniture and close examination.

Miscellaneous
• Arms and legs are the two most commonly replaced components of furniture. Carefully check to make sure the wood of the legs and arms matches the wood on the rest of the piece of furniture.

• Some tea caddies and small pieces of furniture were decorated with shagreen (the skin from certain species of sharks). An imitation that simulates the graining of genuine shagreen can be created by pressing tiny seeds into the outside of moist horse skins.

• Plain veneer panels applied to an otherwise decorative piece of furniture are a sign the veneer may not be original to the piece and may have been replaced.

• If there is not an accumulation of dirt, grime and wear marks surrounding the hinges on doors the veneer may have been steamed off and replaced.

• Furniture from the Queen Anne period is the most frequently faked type of furniture. It has classic lines, has remained popular for a long period of time and is very expensive. An old oak carcass can be covered with old walnut veneer, fitted with old hardware and then lacquered and "aged". The result is almost identical to an authentic Queen Anne piece. Check veneered areas carefully for patches. If the veneer was removed from another piece of furniture it may have had marks in the wood from previous wear around handles or keyholes. These wear marks are often cut out of the veneer and plugged with an undamaged piece of veneer. The inside of the drawers will show evidence of previous hardware. If there are holes on the inside which do not show on the outside, the front of the drawer has probably been reveneered. Plugged holes can also be found inside a drawer which has been reveneered.

• Advertisements are sometimes cut from old newspapers and glued on a piece of furniture in an attempt to simulate a furniture label. Check resources to see what authentic labels looked like, and compare the label on the piece to see how it measures up.

• Overly large pieces of furniture do not sell well because homes are smaller today and these gargantuans from the past do not fit in modern rooms. The most popular size of bureau today is 36-38" in width. The most popular sideboards are 48" wide or less. If the furniture has been reduced in depth there will be evidence of new wood showing at the back where the cut was made.

To reduce the depth of a drawer, the drawer backs are removed, then the drawer sides are shortened and the drawer backs are replaced. This is difficult to do without leaving some trace of evidence. If you suspect depth reduction, use a chisel or a screwdriver to slightly pry the drawer back from the sides. If you see new wood, the drawer has been shortened. Another clue can be attained by removing the drawers and looking at the wear on the carcass caused by the runners. If the piece is unaltered, the wear marks should stop about 1/2" away from the backboard. If the wear marks continue all the way up to the backboard the piece has been reduced.

If a piece has been reduced in width, the central locks on the drawers will generally be relocated and their original location will be patched. The hardware on a large drawer will need to be repositioned if the drawer is reduced in width. The old holes may be filled or may still be visible on the inside or on the edge of the drawer. At least one side of the drawer will require some reconstruction if the drawer is reduced in width. Check both sides for uniformity in color, age of the wood and signs of wear.

If a piece of furniture has been reduced in heighth, the doors will need to be reconstructed. Check the wood on the ends for saw marks and uneven color. If the doors have glass fronts with glazing bars, the glazing bars will need to be adjusted to the new heighth.

• Make sure any piece of furniture with a top, a base and legs is constructed of pieces which all started out together and belong on the same piece of furniture. Many tops have been married with a new base or a new set of legs. Check the underside of the table top. You should see a shadowy area where the wood has been exposed to air over the years. Exposure will cause the wood to lose some of its oil and will change the color of the wood. If the shape of the shadow does not match the underside of the table, thenthe piece is not all original. There should be similar marks on the base or the legs. If the table has a leaf support there should be evidence of wear from where the support has been moved back and forth over the years.

• Many inexpensively made 19th century mirror frames

were not made from carved wood but were instead, made from a molded composition called "compo". The putty-like substance was applied over a wirework frame and then gilded. When new it resembled carved wood. But with age it tends to shrink and crack and the gilded surface may begin to show damage.

Surface Preparation

Regardless of the surface, before beginning any repair it is necessary to thoroughly clean the area and make sure it is free from grease, wax, dirt and other contaminates. A clean surface will allow you to analyze the condition of the furniture and can help you determine how much repair work may be required. A thorough cleaning may reveal a beautiful finish which is still intact and requires no further work, or it may expose flaws and problems you did not even know existed. A complete and thorough cleaning is especially important if you suspect any type of spray polish has been used on the furniture during its lifetime.

Many spray polishes contain silicones and they will resist any type of finish you try to apply over them. Silicones are formulated to repel water and resist staining. Unfortunately, silicones also resist traditional cleaning and removal methods. The only way to remove silicones is with turpentine. Moisten a clean soft cloth (or white paper towels) with turpentine and lightly rub a small area of the surface. Start in an inconspicuous spot and use light pressure. Moisten but do not over-saturate the cloth with the turpentine. You should see the dirt and grime start to come off the furniture and appear on the cloth. Turn the cloth as necessary to prevent redepositing dirt on the furniture and remoisten the cloth as needed. Dry the furniture after it is cleaned with a clean cloth. Work on a small area at a time and continue in this manner until you have cleaned the entire piece of furniture. Then, using clean cloths, repeat the procedure to make sure the surface is no longer contaminated with silcones.

If a finish is applied over a silicone contaminated surface the finish will pull away from those areas and create "fish eyes" or "crawling". Some strippers contain wax which can also affect the application of a finish coat if it is not properly neutralized and removed. The best way to deal with fish eyes and crawling is to prevent them in the first place. Thoroughly clean and degrease the finish to remove any trace of grease or silicones. If you have applied a finish coat and notice fish eyes appearing, dampen a cloth with paint thinner and wipe off as much of the finish as possible. Then, wipe the surface with a cloth dampened with turpentine to decontaminate it.

If you allow the finish to dry, and then attempt to sand out the indentions, you will create a bigger problem by wearing off the finish and possibly the color surrounding the fish eye, and will not remove the contamination in the process. There are some chemical compounds called "fish eye retarders" which can be added to finishes to reduce the risk of fish eyes, but they do not work well with all finishes. It is easier to decontaminate the surface and eliminate the problem before it starts.

If you do not suspect silicone contamination, and just want to thoroughly clean your furniture, the best and safest way to clean off many year's worth of dirt, wax and polish is with mineral spirits. Moisten a soft cloth or white paper towels with mineral spirits and lightly rub the surface. Turn the dirty area under as you go so you do not redeposit loosened dirt on the furniture. Follow up by buffing the furniture dry with a clean dry cloth. Work on a small area at a time, slightly overlapping the cleaned areas with the next area you are going to do. Take your time and be careful. Do not catch the cloths on loose veneer or trim as they can be easily ripped from the basewood.

When the furniture is finally completely clean, you may think the finish has deteriorated or the mineral spirits has damaged the finish. Mineral spirits can not damage any normal finish which is in good condition. Mineral spirits is a degreaser and acts as a lubricant and dirt carrier not as a solvent or a stripper. The finish may appear deteriorated because small cracks and imperfections in the finish become filled with dirt and wax over years of use and when the dirt and wax are removed you can see the finish for what it really is.

If the furniture is particularly dirty or has been exposed to an excessive amount of smoke or grime, you may need to use a solution of 20% household ammonia and 80% water to remove it. Use the solution carefully and sparingly. Ammonia can darken some woods and can damage some finishes. Test the solution in an inconspicuous area to see how it is going to affect the finish and the wood. Do not use excessive liquid as water can dissolve old glues and loosen joints or veneers. Moisten a rag or a sponge with the solution and wring it out so it is damp but not wet. Work on a small area at a time rubbing gently to soften the dirt, then follow up with a clean rag lightly moistened with clean water. Buff with another cloth to dry. Work as quickly as possible, on small areas, and dry thoroughly.

"Weathering" or "Aging Wood"

Old wood, especially wood which has been left outside, often develops a silvery-gray color. This aged color can be duplicated by applying a wash of iron sulfate or iron chloride to the wood. Or, if you would rather not buy expensive and potentially dangerous chemicals, you can fill a large glass container with iron nails or iron filings and then cover them with full strength white vinegar. Allow the mixture to sit for several days. If you used iron filings, you will need to strain the mixture through some coffee filters before using so you do not end up with sharp metal shards in the wood grain on your furniture.

Apply the vinegar mixture to the furniture with a natural bristle brush and allow it to penetrate and dry. The mixture will accentuate the grain patterns of the wood and the coloring effect will vary from a light gray to a blackish color depending on the type of wood the solution is applied on.

Iron mixtures seem to work best on woods which are high in tannic acid. If the furniture you are trying to "age" is made from a wood naturally low in tannic acid, you can improve the results of this process by applying a coat or two of strong tea to the furniture first and allowing it to dry before applying the iron mixture. Tannic acid can be purchased at some hardware stores and diluted to a strength of five parts tannic acid to ninety five parts water and applied to the furniture instead of using strong tea. But it is toxic if eaten or inhaled and is suspected of being a cancer-causing agent, so strong tea is a much safer alternative and is highly recommended.

> * **IMPORTANT:** If you choose to use tannic acid, always remember to add the acid to the water a little at a time. If water is poured into the acid a chemical reaction may occur which could cause the mixture to violently and unexpectedly spray out of the container.

Another method to achieve a "weathered wood" look almost instantly is to combine one or two cups of baking soda with one gallon of water. Mix together until the baking soda is completely dissolved. Then scrub the solution into the wood surface and follow with a rinse of clear water. Allow the furniture to dry away from direct sunlight. The degree of "weathering" achieved will depend on the type of wood, its porosity and the actual age of the wood.

Pro Tip: Always remove hardware from the furniture before attempting to "weather" or "age" wood. The chemical reaction involved in the "aging" process could cause a reaction with the metal on the hardware and create permanent dark stains in the wood. The chemicals could also potentially damage the hardware.

Some books recommend using lye to "age" wood and give it a distressed look. This is a very bad idea! Lye will raise the grain of the wood, remove the color from some woods and will darken other woods, and will generally leave the wood looking dead and lifeless. Lye will need to be neutralized after use to stop the burning action and will continue to be active until it is neautralized. Lye solutions penetrate so deeply into the wood they can even adversely affect a new finish once it is applied.

* **IMPORTANT:** Lye will burn your skin if you should accidentally come in contact with it, can cause permanent blindness if it gets in your eyes, and can cause respiratory problems if the fumes are inhaled.

Natural Stains

Modern commercial stains provide a variety of colors to choose from, are readily available, and are easy to apply. But if you want to duplicate the look of an antique you will have to use stains similar to what was originally used on furniture at the time it was made. Most antiques were finished with either *vegetable stains* or *chemical stains.*

Vegetable stains - Vegetable stains were made from natural substances acquired from various plants, roots, berries, nuts, leaves, etc. The resulting stains are quite similar to modern *analine dye water stains*.

Early cabinetmakers mixed up vegetable stains in their shops and every craftsman had their own "secret recipes" for achieving the desired wood tones. Most of these stains are *water-based stains* and when they are applied to wood they will swell the wood and the grain will raise. The wood will need to be lightly sanded or lightly rubbed down with steel wool after the stain has dried to remove the rough texture. You can prevent the stain from raising the grain quite as much, by moistening the wood with clear water *before* you stain the piece of furniture and letting it dry. This will raise the grain, of course. Use sandpaper or steel wool to smooth down the grain. Repeat the process of moistening the furniture, allowing it to dry and smoothing the wood. *Then* apply the water-based stain. If the wood is prepped in this manner the stain will not cause the grain to raise noticeably.

Berry juices were commonly used in early vegetable stains to achieve a red color and the pigments usually penetrated very deeply into the wood. These old red stains are almost impossible to bleach out. The best way to deal with them is to use commercial stain or a darker natural stain and stain over them.

Chewing tobacco stain: Chewing tobacco can be used to make an inexpensive stain which can be used to give an "antique look" to walnut, oak and pine furniture. To make the stain, shred some chewing tobacco into a pot and add 4 cups of water. Simmer over low heat for 15 to 30 minute. Dip a piece of scrap wood into the stain to check the color. Add more tobacco if necessary to darken the color. When you achieve the desired color, allow the stain to cool, strain it through several layers of cheesecloth or a coffee filter to remove the tobacco particles then store the stain in a jar with a tight-fitting lid.

If you want a stain which can be used on cherry or brown mahogany, use the recipe above, but add some beet juice. Test the color on a scrap piece of wood or in an inconspicuous place on the furniture. To apply the stain: brush on the furniture, allow to penetrate the wood and then wipe off the excess. Allow to completely dry before applying a finish coat. If the wood is not the desired color reapply another coat of stain.

Remember wood will appear darker when wet. Always allow the stain to completely dry before determining whether or not you have acheived the desired color.

Walnut husk stain: Walnut husks can be used to make a dark brown colored stain. Walnuts are covered in a soft green husk as they grow and develop. When the nuts mature, the husk turns a dark brown color. When the nuts are harvested the husk is removed revealing the walnut shell beneath.

To make a stain from the husks, place a bunch of walnut husks in a pot that has no exposed metal. You will need to use an enameled pot or one with a nonstick coating or an earthenware container. Be forewarned the pot may become discolored during the stainmaking process. Add enough water to cover the husks and about a tablespoon of caustic soda to a gallon of water. Simmer the mixture over low heat for several days. Or, if you do not wish to have it on the stove that long, simmer it for a few hours and then put it into a clear, tightly covered container and allow it to sit in the sunlight for about a week.

When the mixture has achieved a dark brown color, allow it to cool, then strain the liquid through several layers of cheesecloth or a coffee filter to remove the husk particles. Store the stain in a jar with a tightfitting lid. Dilute the stain with aditional water if a lighter stain color is required. If the stain is not dark enough, you will need to apply several applications.

Brazil-wood shavings stain: Use a wood plane to shave a piece of Brazil-wood. Place the shavings and enough water to cover them in an enameled pot or one with a nonstick coating and simmer the mixture over low heat for several hours. Allow the mixture to cool, then strain it through several layers of cheesecloth or a coffee filter to remove the shaving particles. The stain can be diluted with water if a lighter color is required. Store the stain in a jar with a tightfitting lid. This stain produces a reddish-brownish color.

Chicory root stain: Place roasted chicory roots in an enameled pot or one with a nonstick coating. Add enough water to cover the roots and simmer for about an hour. Allow the stain to cool, then strain it through several layers of cheesecloth or a coffe filter to remove the root particles. Store the stain in a jar with a tightfitting lid. This stain produces a yellowish-brown color.

Coffee stain: Make a pot of very strong coffee. Strain through several layers of cheesecloth or a coffee filter to prevent coffee grounds from getting on the furniture. Coffee will color most woods a medium brown color. There is no point in saving the excess stain when you are done with it. Just make another pot of coffee for the next project.

Tea stain: Use loose tea and make a very strong pot of tea. Strain the tea through several layers of cheesecloth or a coffee filter to prevent tea leaves from contacting the furniture. Tea will color most woods a golden brown color. Like coffee stain, there is little purpose in storing excess stain as it is easy to make another pot of tea for the next project.

Chemical stains - Early cabinetmakers used chemical stains alone and also applied them before or after an application of vegetable stain. Chemical stains will penetrate deeper into the wood than any other type of stain and are the most permanent type of stain available. Chemical stains do not add color to the wood, they alter the existing natural color of the wood. All wood contains hundreds of chemicals and the natural color of the wood is determined by the chemical content. The chemical composition of wood depends on the species of tree, the soil it grew in and the climate at the time it was growing among many other variables.

Tannin is one of the most common chemicals found in wood and is in almost all woods to some degree. The chemicals in the wood will react with other chemicals mixed together as a stain and can be used to create a new color. Early cabinetmakers discovered certain chemicals could be used to alter the color of different species of wood. Chemical stains will work best on woods with a high tannin content. Walnut, oak, chestnut and mahogany are all high in tannin content.

Chemical stains can be difficult to work with and the results are often unpredictable because the chemical content can vary from board to board within the same piece of furniture. Always do a spot test on a small area in an inconspicuous place to see how the stain will look on your particular piece of furniture.

The chemicals used to create chemical stains are often poisonous, caustic, harmful or irritating. Many of the chemicals are hard to find except through a chemical supplier or chemical wholesaler because they have no household use. Chemical stains can cause a poisonous gas if they are applied to wood that has been previously bleached. If you are unsure if the wood has been bleached, do not use a chemical stain.

Use chemical resistant brushes, such as nylon or polyester to apply chemical stains. It should go without saying that gloves, goggles for eye protection and a respirator mask should be used for protection when working with chemicals.

If the chemical stain uses an acid, always remember to add acid to water a little at a time. If water is poured into acid a reaction could occur which would cause the acid to spray out of the container.

Chemical stains will react with metal hardware and will create dark stains in the wood around the hardware. It is critically important to remove any metal hardware from the furniture before staining. Even nails and screws can present a problem unless they are set below the surface of the wood.

Wood putty and wood filler will not be affected by chemical stains. If the furniture has previously been filled with wood filler or wood putty do not attempt to apply a chemical stain. If you plan on using wood putty or wood filler, wait until after the wood has been stained before applying them.

Most chemical stains are dissolved in water and applied in liquid form. One major exception is *ammonia fuming* where the chemical is applied to the wood as a vapor.

To help prevent raised wood grain, wet the wood and then allow it to dry. Then lightly sand it or rub it down with steel wool. Then, rewet the wood, allow it to dry and rub it down again. Prepping the wood in this manner will result in a more even color when the stain is applied and will help prevent raised wood grain. The stain will need to be evenly applied or the wood will become streaky and the final color will be uneven. You can achieve a more even application by wetting the surface first and then applying the stain while the wood is still wet. Always apply the stain in daylight but not in direct sun. Daylight will give you the most accurate color representation.

Tannic acid is usually used as a primer coat for woods which are naturally low in tannic acid, but it can also be used as a stain to darken woods which have a substantial amount of their own natural tannic acid.

Ammonia will darken most woods and can be used to give a grayish "aged" look to wood. An application of caustic soda will give most woods a grayish tone similar to what can be achieved with ammonia.

Potassium permanganate will produce a wide range of brown tones depending on the wood it is applied on. Potassium dichromate creates yellowish brown tones on most woods. Copper sulfate will give wood a grayish-black color and will accentuate grain patterns. Iron compounds will result in grayish or blackish tones. All of the chemicals listed above will need to be dissolved in water prior to use. The proportions of chemical s and water vary depending on the type of wood being stained and the desired final color you are trying to achieve.

Green copperas (also called sulphate of iron) will give a blueish-gray tone to oak wood, a grayish tone to sycamore wood and will mute the redness of mahogany. Green copperas is poisonous so use care during application. Dissolve the crystals in warm water and mix thoroughly until the water turns a muddy green color. Apply the stain evenly to the wood with a natural bristle brush. Remember wood will look darker when wet than it will once the stain has dried.

Mahogany can be darkened and oak can be given a greenish-brown tone by applying a stain made from bichromate of potash. Dissolve the crystals in water and stir to make sure the solution is well mixed. The resulting stain will be a deep orange color, but the color of the wood once stained will depend on the type of wood. Test the stain in an inconspicious place and allow it to dry completely before checking the color. Adjust the amount of water if the stain needs to be lightened. Apply the stain evenly with a natural bristle brush.

Oak can be "weathered" by applying a stain made from American potash (also called crude caustic potash). The wood will turn a dark brown color and the grain will blacken and become highlighted. Dissolve the potash in water and stir to mix thoroughly. The amount of water needed will vary depending on the intensity of the desired wood color.

Burning

Burning will obviously darken wood and can make the it looked somewhat aged, if the procedure is done properly. Unfortunately, when it is not properly done it makes the wood looked ... burned, and of course it damages the furniture. The technique involves moving a blowtorch back and forth across the wood, fast enough to prevent the wood from catching fire, to create irregular darkening of the wood. Softer areas of the wood will get darker faster than harder areas. Corners will darken more than flat open areas because the corner will contain the heat. Edges of the furniture where the cross grain comes together tend to burn quickly and can burst into flames if you are not careful. A brass bristle brush is rubbed on the wood in the direction of the grain after the wood is burned in order to remove loose charred wood. You may also need to sand the wood or rub it out with 2/0 steel wool. Practice the technique on a scrap piece of wood before you try it on a piece of furniture.

Burning is often followed up with a coat of stain to blend the burned wood and make it look more natural. An application of clear finish or a coat or two of wax can also be applied to protect the burned finish.

Burning is dangerous and the results are unpredictable and I personally don't think the results are worth the risk. It should go without saying this technique should never be done to a true antique.

Distressing

Distressing is a method of adding artificial wear marks to a piece of furniture to make it appear as if it has been exposed to more wear and use than it actually has. The two biggest problems with artificial distressing are: marks applied to an area where you would not normally find signs of wear, and overdoing it to the point where the marks are not believeable. Wear and damage can be expected on chair rungs, legs and arms, the edges of tables, desks and chests, the edges of drawers, anywhere that would normally be banged or bumped during use. Excessive distressing applied to the side of a chest or the back splat on a chair would immediately draw attention and one would have to wonder what would have naturally caused distressing in a place like that? If you are going to distress wood, think about how the wood would have been damaged through normal use, and then plan your attack accordingly.

There is almost no limit as to what can be used to distress wood. Other antique repair books seem to like to recommend using tire chains. They suggest hitting the furniture with chains to create signs of wear. Unfortunately, most furniture does not get that beaten up during "normal use" and this results in furniture that looks like it has been beaten with a tire chain. Soup bones broken to a sharp point can be used to scratch or dent wood and duplicate animal scratches or teeth marks. Desk tops can be distressed by using some of the same objects which would have distressed it through normal use. Drop letter openers, metal scissors or hole punches, drag bookends and staplers across the top, place a piece of paper on the wood and write on it so your writing leaves impressions in the wood.

Table tops can be distressed by dropping dishes or rolling pins on them. Table edges can be dented by bumping them with a piece of wood to duplicate the damage done by a chair. Chairs rungs can be distressed by rubbing them with the sole of a pair of work boots.

A key ring can be a great distressing tool. Drop the keys on the furniture with some force from a few feet above the surface. The variety of shapes on the keys will produce a series of indestinguishable marks. While all this may not be as much fun as covering a hammer with a sock or using rocks and chains to bang away at the furniture, and it will take longer, it will produce more natural and authentic-looking signs of wear.

Not all distressing involves scratching, gouging or denting the wood. Other signs of distressing can be ink stains, burns, water marks, candle wax and wear around the pulls and hardware.

Ink stains - Ink stains are often found on desk tops and in desk drawers. Old-fashioned ink formulas were different from the ones in use today. The tannin-based liquids were strong enough to rot the nibs of pens and easily penetrated through old finishes. Many of these old stains were then sealed in under multiple applications of wax and today they have mellowed into a greenish-purple color which is almost impossible to duplicate.

Liquid ink and India ink can be purchased by the bottle or in small cartridges. These can be both be used to simulate an ink spill or small ink droplets.

Burns - Cigarettes and cigars can create terribly ugly burns which penetrate deep into the wood on a piece of furniture. These can be duplicated in the same way they would have originally happened: place a lit cigarette or cigar on the furniture and let it burn. Cigarettes and cigars have a filler added which keeps the tobacco burning and makes it burn hotter. Surprisingly enough though, when you are actually trying to create a burn you may need to relight the cigarette as they have a tendency to snuff themselves out. Obviously, you will want to stay nearby while the burn is taking place and have some water handy in case things get out of control.

More burns were caused on antique furniture by clay or wooden pipes than by cigarettes. These can also be duplicated in the same manner as they would have originally occurred.

Burns are not confined to damage from smoking materials. They can also be made by hot pans and dishes can be found on kitchen tables and dining tables, burn marks from candles can be found on tables and dressers, even hot pokers could have damaged the legs of tables or chairs kept close to a fireplace.

Water marks - Water marks can either be white marks, which are damage to the finish, or black marks, which are damage to the wood. White water marks can be created by placing wet glasses, clay pots or cups of hot liquid directly on the furniture surface and allowing them to sit there. Some finishes will develop a water mark more quickly than others, and the longer the offending article remains on the finish, the deeper the stain will become.

Black water marks will usually take some time to create naturally because the water has to penetrate through the finish and into the wood. A wet glass or a clay pot or other container left to sit on the finish should start to create a black mark within a few days. How dark you want the mark to be will determine how long you should leave the container on the wood.

If you want to fake a black water mark instead of waiting for a real one to form, find an empty can the diameter of the desired ring, and lightly coat the rim of the can with dark walnut wood stain, then press the can rim on to the wood surface. You may want to practice a few "water marks" before applying one on the furniture surface. If you are unhappy with the results, you can usually wipe off most of the stain if you immediately wipe the area with a piece of 3/0 steel wool dipped in mineral spirits.

Another type of water mark can be applied to the feet of tables and chairs to simulate damage which would have occurred from sitting on damp dirt floors. Fill several small plastic containers with a mixture of dirt and water then place the legs in them. Allow the legs to stay in the mixture for at least 24 hours. The wood will absorb the dirty water which will swell the wood grain and may cause the leg to split. The finish may dissolve or be discolored and dirt will be soaked deep into the wood pores. When it is time to remove the legs, wipe off the excess dirt and buff lightly with a small piece of 3/0 steel wool if desired.

Wax - Wax on an antique is most believeable if you use a creamy colored beeswax candle instead of modern colored candles. Let the wax drip on the furniture, then allow it to set. Once the wax has hardened, use a plastic credit card to remove most of the wax, then buff with a soft cloth or the palm of your hand to smooth the wax and work it into the wood.

Signs of wear around hardware - If you look at antique furniture there will almost always be signs of wear around the hardware from generations of hands rubbing on the finish. Remove the hardware, and use a piece of 2/0 steel wool to rub the wood and the finish in the area surrounding the hardware. A coat of "antiquing wax" can be applied after the area is rubbed down to give it a more authentic look.

On lighter woods, mix some dirt and water together until you have a thick paste. Wipe the paste on the wood, making sure to work it deep into the wood grain. Wipe off the surface film. A coat of wax or "antiquing" wax can be applied over the dirt to seal it in. Then re-apply the hardware. If you also want to "age" the hardware see the instructions for *"Aging" Hardware*.

Worm holes - No discussion about distressing wood would be complete without including *worm holes*. They are probably one of the most commonly used distressing techniques, and usually one of the most obvious fakes because they are so poorly done. Most books on antique repair will, at some point, present what they consider "the best way to make worm holes". Since they are so obviously fake, I do not believe there *is* a best way to make them. But if you should decide to give it a try, a nail with the point slightly flattened or an ice pick which has been slightly flattened are probably the best tools to use.

Natural worm holes are the exit holes used by wood-boring beetles to escape the wood. Under the surface of the wood are a series of tunnels which run through the wood. If you are going to try to duplicate worm holes you will need to make the holes at an angle to the wood and not straight in to the wood. Also remember the holes are not round. They are off-round. "Antiquing" wax applied to the area and then wiped off will fill the holes with "aged dust" and make them look less newly made.

Keep in mind all wood still looks new under the surface because it has not been exposed to air and contaminates. Holes made into the wood will reveal new wood. A thin coat of stain can be brushed over the worm holes to darken the wood inside the hole. Natural "worm holes" are usually clustered together in groups not scattered helter-skelter across the furniture. It also helps to remember how wood worms get into and out of furniture so you can place the holes properly. (Read the section on "Woodworm" for more details.)

A myth has been perpetuated for several decades that you can duplicate worm holes in wood by shooting a shotgun loaded with birdshot at a piece of furniture. What you will end up with is a piece of furniture that looks like you shot it full of birdshot (and probably some very concerned neighbors!). The holes created by birdshot will be too big to be believeable, and will be spaced wrong, and you may end up ruining a perfectly good piece of furniture.

The Finish

If you are going to attempt to repair or replace the finish on a piece of furniture, you will need to know what the finish is. Most finishes can not be successfully applied over another finish and they will either not adhere at all or will flake off after the finish is dried.

Wax was most likely the very first protective coating ever applied to furniture and continued to be popular well into the late 1800s. It is not technically considered a finish since it is rubbed into the wood and does not coat the wood. If you want to duplicate the look of a coat of wax on an antique, use a kitchen grater or a wood shaver to cut a block of beeswax into fine pieces. Pour turpentine over the shredded wax and allow to soak until the wax is completely dissolved. Stir to mix thoroughly. The mixture should be the consistency of thick paint. If the consistemcy isn't right, adjust the amount of wax or turpentine.

Use a soft cloth to rub a small amount of the mixture onto the wood surface. Allow the wax to dry, then buff with a soft lint-free cloth. Do a small area at a time and do not apply too much wax. Thin coats will dry quicker than thick ones and will result in a better finish. You may want to apply several coats of wax to build up the finish, but completely buff out the previous coat before applying a new one.

Wax finishes work best on close-grained woods. Open-grained woods can trap wax in the large wood pores, and the wax will eventually turn white and become quite noticeable. To prevent wax from ending up in the pores and becoming an eyesore, early cabinetmakers would tint the wax with lamp black or burnt umber. Any wax trapped in the pores would then accentuate the grain instead of accentuating the wax. Today you can use Universal colorants (available in any paint department) to tint the wax to duplicate this effect. Black tinted wax was often used by early cabinetmakers on fumed furniture to accent the grain of the wood. Wax in the pores can also trap dirt and other contaminates and cause the finish to deteriorate prematurely.

There are six types of furniture finishes: *shellac, lacquer, paint and enamel, penetrating finishes* and *oil finishes.* Of these, only shellac, lacquer, paint and some oil finishes will be found as original finishes on antiques. Few antiques will be finished in a varnish as their original finish. Varnish will almost never be found on mass-produced furniture because it is very slow drying and was not a cost-effective coating. Varnish is technically not really a product, but rather a generic name for clear finishes consisting of synthetic resins. Penetrating finishes are a relatively modern finish and will only be found on antiques which have been refinished.

Shellac - Shellac is the only survivor of the alcohol-based varnishes which were used throughout the 18th century to create high gloss finishes on furniture. These finishes used to be called spirit varnishes. Shellac is made from natural resins secreted by a type of beetle called a *lac bug* (tachardia lacca) found in India and its neighboring countries. The bug eats tree leaves and then deposits a secretion on the tree bark. The secretion is scraped off by hand, cleaned and refined, and then dissolved in alcohol. Before it is applied to furniture it is usually diluted further with denatured alcohol to make it flow out smooth and dry quickly. This is called "cutting shellac".

When talking about shellac, a "pound cut" describes how many pounds of shellac will be dissolved in one gallon of denatured alcohol to prepare the shellac for application. A medium thick shellac would be a called a two pound cut. This means two pounds of dry shellac would have to be dissolved in one gallon of denatured alcohol. Do not use common wood alcohol (methanol) in place of denatured alcohol as this could make the shellac brittle. Also, be aware some products labeled "Shellac Solvent" often have a high methanol and water content which may prevent the shellac from drying properly.

Shellac was the most popular furniture finish in the beginning of the 1800s, and for the next fifty years, just about every piece of commercially manufactured furniture with a clear finish was finished with shellac. Other pieces of pre-Victorian furniture were either painted or simply given a coat of wax and sent out the door. If you know a piece of furniture with a clear finish was made between 1800 and 1850 you can be pretty sure the original finish would have been shellac.

Shellac is available in two colors: white and orange. White shellac is just orange shellac which has been processed to bleach out the color. Most refinishers use orange shellac on dark woods or reddish woods (like walnut or mahogany) because it accentuates the grain patterns and white shellac on lighter colored woods like oak and pine. The darker the color of the shellac, the less refined it is. Refining will not only remove the color, but also decreases the shelf life and makes the shellac less durable.

Other types of shellac which more closely resemble the earlier more primitive finishes used on authentic antiques are available at some woodworking supply stores. These specialized shellacs are: *seedlac, button-lac, garnetlac* and *blonde shellac*. All of these specialized shellacs will need to be diluted with denatured alcohol or a combination of denatured alcohol and isobutinal before use.

Seedlac is the lowest grade of shellac. All other refinements of shellac flakes are made from seedlac. Seedlac will need to be strained prior to use because of its low grade of refinement.

Button-lac gets its name from the fact the flakes look like little dark brown buttons. Button-lac is a very low grade, dark brown shellac which was commonly used during the 17th and 18th centuries. It can be used to patch or repair an old finish on a nice antique, but can also be used on newer woods to "mellow" them and give them an aged look. Because button-lac is is not as refined as other more commonly available grades of shellac, it will need to be strained prior to use.

Garnetlac is more refined than button-lac but is still less refined than most commercial brands of shellac. It will need to be strained prior to use. Garnetlac is not as dark as button-lac and has a more amber color, similar to orange shellac.

Blonde shellac is the highest grade of shellac available. It is extremely clear and very thoroughly refined. Blonde shellac can be used on light colored woods without changing the color of the wood.

Some older furniture has a special transparent black finish on it. This finish is *black shellac*, and it consists of shellac with lampblack added to it. Early phonograph records (the ones made before "unbreakable" records came along) were also made from shellac with lampblack added. You can mix up a small batch of black shellac by crumbling broken records into a jar and then adding enough denatured alcohol to dissolve them. The jar will need to be covered with a tight-fitting lid to keep the mixture from evaporating. Store the mixture in a warm place for several weeks while the recor pieces are dissolving. Add additional denatured alcohol if necessary after the records have completely dissolved to obtain the proper spreading consistency. The resulting finish can be used to touch up an old finish or can be used to apply a new finish coat.

To repair an existing black shellac finish, first, thoroughly clean the surface to remove all surface dirt and old wax or polish. Then, use a small artist's brush to apply the black shellac, taking care to feather the edges to help blend the repair into the existing finish.

To apply a new finish coat, use the black shellac as you would normal shellac, applying thin coats and allowing sufficient drying time in between coats.

Lacquer - True lacquer was discovered in China about 3000 B.C. The natural sap of the Asiatic sumac was used as a wood finish, undiluted except for the addition of a coloring agent. The word "lacquer" has been in use for many years – long before lacquer as we know it was developed. The word was used to describe a variety of finishes which bear no relationship or resemblence to today's lacquer.

Lacquer is often found as the original finish on furniture made after World War I. Furniture assembly lines were developed before the war, but after the war the process was speeded-up to make it more profitable. Lacquer finishes could be sprayed on and had short drying times, so lacquer became a popular and profitable finish. Most of the furniture made after the middle 1920s was finished in lacquer.

Old lacquer dried to a dull finish and had to be "rubbed out" to a obtain a high gloss. Modern lacquers are available in a variety of sheens from matte to glossy and it is no longer necessary to rub out the finish to get a high gloss shine.

Lacquer is not a good choice if you are refinishing an antique because it has a solvent effect on most stains and paints. Lacquer requires a special filler coat over either water stains or spirit stains (powdered stains which have been mixed with lacquer thinner), and it should be applied over a sealer coat of shellac. Since it is generally unknown what the underlayers are on an antique, using lacquer as a top coat could jeopardize the whole piece if the lacquer turns out to be incompatible with a stain or filler already on the furniture. Lacquer also results in a very high gloss finish when it is properly applied. Most antiques have a softer sheen and the high gloss finish is inappropriate.

Paint - More antiques were originally finished with a coat of paint than most people would ever imagine. Many pieces of furniture with a clear finish today were originally painted. Turned chairs, Windsor chairs, tavern tables, and quite a few beds, chests, stands and dining tables were originally finished with a coat of paint. Evidence of the original paint can often be found hiding in the corners, under drawers, inside the case of a chest, or underneath the hardware. It is almost impossible to remove every trace of original paint from a piece of furniture. In many cases, you only have to look in the wood grain to find small flecks of the original color.

Wood with an attractive color, nice figuring and pretty grain would have normally been finished with a clear finish. Other woods may have been stained to imitate grained wood, given a wash of red paint to make them look like "poor man's mahogany" or painted with several coats of paint to completely hide the grain. Red was a popular color because it could be used to "imitate" mahogany wood, but black, yellow, gray and white were also popular paint colors.

Milk paint - Milk paint, is a flat-finished paint predominately found on country furniture and primitive antiques. Milk paint is more transparent than conventional paints and has a tendency to vary in hue across the painted surface. The colors are more muted than traditional paint and it has a very distinctive characteristic look.

Early milk paint was made from rancid milk or buttermilk and clay, berries, blood and other natural ingredients were used as colorants. Lime was added to the paint to increase its durability. The chemical reaction between the lactic acid in the milk and the lime gave milk paint a very durable finish. Most milk paint has a flat, lustreless sheen. If a higher sheen was desired, egg whites were added to the paint to give it a semi-gloss finish.

Once it has completely cured, milk paint dries to a very durable, long lasting finish. The natural stains and deep penetration of the paint will often stain the wood beneath the paint layer and the wood can retain color long after the surface coating has powdered away.

Milk paint is very difficult to remove and will resist most paint removers and commercial strippers. The only known solvent for milk paint is undiluted full strength ammonia used right from the bottle. But even full strength ammonia can be no match for a fully cured coat of aged milk paint. Most furniture finished with milk paint was constructed from open-grained wood and had numerous layers of paint applied to help fill in the grain. The wood grain is often so completely filled with paint that removal is virtually impossible.

Determining an existing finish - To identify the existing finish on a piece of furniture you will need to perform a few spot tests in an inconspicuous area. Wax finishes and oil finishes are rather easy to identify by their feel and appearance. But how can you tell the difference between a lacquer finish, a shellac finish and a varnish finish?

Moisten a small piece of lint-free cloth with denatured alcohol and lightly rub the finish in an inconspicuous area. If the finish is shellac, denatured alcohol will start to dissolve it and you will see a softened area on the furniture and traces of shellac on your cloth. Denatured alcohol is the solvent for shellac.

If you notice no change in the finish after the first test, moisten another small piece of lint-free cloth with lacquer thinner and lightly rub the finish in a different inconspicuous area. If the finish is lacquer, lacquer thinner will start to dissolve the finish. Lacquer thinner is the solvent for lacquer. If neither denatured alcohol nor lacquer thinner has any affect on the finish, then the finish is probably varnish.

Furniture "revivers" - Most people who have dabbled in antiques have learned how to take a few short-cuts along the way in order to save time and money. One of these short cuts involves using "furniture revivers" which are said to spruce up the existing finish without having to remove the old finish and apply a new one. This is pretty much a case of "if it sounds too good to be true, it probably is" because most "revivers", whether commercial or homemade, can potentially cause more harm than good.

"Revivers" often contain linseed oil as a main ingredient. Linseed oil will darken wood over time and can create an uneven, blotchy finish if it is applied over a cracked or damaged finish. Some "revivers" contain pumice which can leave a maze of fine scratches on a delicate finish. Others contain ammonia which will darken wood and damage some woods and finishes. Another type of "reviver" contains a large amount of alcohol and some colored resins. The alcohol evaporates leaving the resin deposits to color the wood and fill in scratches and cracks. Unfortunately, alcohol can damage furniture finishes and repeated use of these products will dry out the finish more and more with each application causing additional damage, which will then require additional coats of the reviver to fix them. A vicious damaging cycle. If you choose to try a reviver, test it on a small area in an inconspicuous place. Better advice would be to avoid them all together.

Fuming - Household ammonia can be used to give an "aged" look to a clear finish or a coat of paint and can also be used to "age" bare wood. The fumes will darken and "age" wood especially woods like oak with a high tannic acid content. Gustav Stickley used "fuming" to achieve the distinctive color on his furniture in the early 1900s and many other furniture manufacturers quickly followed suit. It is said Stickley got the idea of using ammonia to "age" oak from looking at the oak flooring in stables and seeing how the natural ammonia from horse urine and manure darkened the white oak and gave it the appearance of age. Oak wood was plentiful, inexpensive and had a very high tannic acid content. Oak furniture with a fumed finish was very popular for many years. Chestnut, mahogany and walnut are also high in tannic acid and can be successfully fumed.

Fuming creates an even color throughout the piece of furniture and leaves no lap marks or brush marks because the ammonia is not applied to the wood, the ammonia vapors change the natural color of the wood. Fuming will stain the entire piece of furniture in one operation and can be used in conjunction with other finishes without having to remove the other finish first. Ammonia vapors penetrate deep into the wood and produce a color change which is more than just a surface coating. No liquid comes in contact with the furniture so there is nothing to raise the wood grain, or dissolve or dilute glue used in the construction of the furniture or holding veneer on to the base wood.

RCA Victor used the fuming process on some of their more popular Victrola cases and in a notice to their dealers and distributors they described the fumed oak finish as "one of the most difficult to repair of all the art finishes". Scratches and other damage to the finish can be difficult to repair because the fuming effect is achieved by a chemical reaction. Some small damaged areas can be successfully repaired and blended with the rest of the piece by using a small artist's brush to apply full strength ammonia straight from the bottle to the damaged area. Make sure the work area has adequate ventilation and wear a protective respirator mask to protect yourself from the fumes. Several applications may be necessary to achieve the desired results. Wrap the area with clear plastic wrap after the ammonia application to help prevent evaporation and speed up the fuming process.

Fuming requires an airtight container large enough to contain the entire piece of furniture (usually a fuming tent or a fuming box). The furniture should be placed in the container so the fumes have access to all sides of the furniture, and the container must be completely filled with ammonia fumes. Then the furniture needs to be exposed to the fumes long enough to achieve the desired color or effect. A wooden box or crate can be used for smaller pieces of furniture. All of the cracks and joints of the box will have to be completely sealed with caulking to prevent the fumes from escaping. Duct tape can be applied on the outside of the joints and seams for additional sealing.

Remove any hardware from the furniture prior to fuming. The chemical reaction involved in the fuming process may adversely affect hardware and the metal could create permanent dark stains on the furniture.

Industrial ammonia is stronger than household ammonia and will produce optimum rusults. If you can not locate 26% industrial ammonia you can use household ammonia for the fuming process, but because it contains a weaker solution the fuming process will take longer.

> * **IMPORTANT:** Breathing concentrated ammonia fumes can be extremely dangerous or fatal. Be sure to work in an area with good ventilation and wear a respirator mask.

Pour ammonia into glass or ceramic dishes and place the dishes on the bottom of the crate, then put the piece of furniture into the crate. Seal up the container and allow the ammonia fumes to work for a minimum of 24 hours. Household ammonia should be given at least two days.

Smaller pieces of furniture can be successfully fumed by placing the furniture in a large plastic trash bag with a container of ammonia. Seal up the bag and check frequently to see how the color is coming along. Be careful of fumes when opening the bag! Remove the furniture when you achieve the desired color.

The fuming process contains a lot of variables – the amount of ammonia and time needed to achieve the desired color will depend on the type of wood, the temperature of the room where the fuming is being done, the amount of finish on the wood, the amount of tannin in the wood and also on the strength of the ammonia. Check the furniture after 24 hours to see if it is getting close to the desired color. Then check every eight hours or so after that. Wear a respirator mask when opening the crate and make sure you are working in an area with good ventilation.

If you are not satisfied with the results and want a deeper color, add more ammonia to the dishes and reseal the container. Repeat the process until you achieve the desired color. If some parts of the fuirniture seem to be getting darker than others, you can apply a coat of paste wax to those areas and then re-expose the furniture to the fuming process. The wax will help prevent the darker areas from getting darker while giving the other areas a chance to catch-up.

Fuming will continue to darken the wood even after the furniture has been removed from the fuming box and allowed to air out. It is a good idea to stop when you think you are getting close to the color you want. Ammonia is different than other alkalis in that it will completely evaporate and not leave a residue on the wood which needs to be neutralized.

Once the color is achieved, the furniture can be left as is, or given a light coat of paste wax to help seal in and protect the fumed finish.

Liming - Liming is another method of adding a distinctive whitish-gray aged look to furniture and it is done almost exclusively on oak furniture. To begin, the furniture will need to be wire brushed to open the wood pores. Next, make a creamy paste of lime solution (approximately one half pound of lime to 1-1/2 cups of water) and force it into the wood pores with a brush. Wipe off any excess solution and allow the wood to dry. Use steel wool to buff down the raised grain and then apply a coat of wax or a shellac or lacquer finish.

Ebonizing (imitating ebony wood) - Natural ebony wood is very dense, has a very close, even grain and a distinctive dark black color. Ebonizing was done as a detailing effect on many antiques, especially those with an Oriental influence. To duplicate ebony, you will need a suitable wood (beech is traditionally used to imitate ebony), water-soluble analine dyes (because they have good penetration and are able to sink deep into the wood) and you will need to create a black wood filler to rub deep into the grain of the wood. To create the black filler, use a small amount of plaster of Paris powder and a small amount of black analine dye. Add a few drops of water if necessary until you have a thick paste consistency. Rub the filler into the grain of the wood by wiping with the grain and then across the grain. Push and work the filler into the grain. Wipe off the excess with a cloth dampened with linseed oil.

Use analine dye to stain the wood, adding a drop or two of ammonia to the dye to make it sink in more deeply. If the color is not dark enough add a bit more dye. If the black seems too "flat" add a few drops of laundry bluing to make the color come to life. Use several thin coats of shellac as the finish coat, lightly rubbing out the shellac with 3/0 steel wool between coats and allowing sufficient drying time between coats. Use a small piece of 3/0 steel wool to lightly soften the final coat to duplicate the soft sheen of ebony wood.

This technique can be used to duplicate Oriental furniture and the old Japanned finishes. The more coats of shellac you apply the deeper the final finish will appear. It is critically important to allow each coat of finish to completely dry before applying the next coat and to carefully rub down the finish between coats. Use a tack rag to wipe off the surface between applications of shellac to remove all traces of dust.

False graining - False graining is an ancient art form dating back several hundred years. It reached its peak during the 19th century when false graining, or *faux bois*, was used on doors, paneling and furniture to transform plain, commonly available local woods into rare and exotic specialty woods. False graining is a specialized skill requiring experience, patience and a very steady hand. When properly done it can be difficult to differentiate between false graining and the real thing. Many people are not aware a piece of furniture has false graining on it until they attempt to strip the furniture and the "wood" starts to dissolve before their eyes.

The tools for false graining are simple: a few good brushes in a variety of small sizes, some feathers (to apply some of the graining effects), a wine cork (if you want to make knots in the wood), some turpentine and paint, some rags and a piece of the wood you would like to fake or a very clear color picture. It is critically important to have a good idea of what the wood you are trying to imitate looks like so you can reproduce it as closely as possible.

Special rubber graining tools can be purchased to help create grain patterns, but for the most part they produce a very fake look with no natural variation. The tool is dragged downward in a curving line through an applied glaze, while moving the curved head of the tool backwards and forwards in a rocking motion. Unfortunately, the tool can only make one pattern, so you will need to have a variety of different tools in order to create a natural look.

The following will give you some general instructions on how to apply false graining to duplicate walnut or fully grained oak. The techniques will need to be varied depending on what type of wood you are duplicating. False graining will look more natural and real if the graining colors are applied to a wet surface. This will cause the colors to bleed which gives a closer representation of real wood.

The two basic motifs of false graining are *straight grain* and *heartgrain.* These two motifs can be combined into as many pattern variations as there are types of wood.

You will need to apply a base coat which is as close as possible to the main background color of your wood sample. Most woods will look best if an eggshell colored paint with a flat sheen is applied as a base coat. The paint can be tinted with a dab of yellow ochre to simulate pine, with ochre and raw umber for ash and oak, a dab of gray or some black and white added to for weathered oak, brown madder for mahogany and cherry, burnt sienna for brown mahogany and flesh colored oil paint for the lighter "blonde look" furniture. Choose an acrylic oil paint in a color close to the background color of the wood (usually burnt umber, raw umber or burnt sienna). Apply a dab of the paint into a small bowl and add enough water to make a thin wash. Use a fine brush to stroke the wash over the paint. While the wash is still wet, lightly drum the paint brush across the surface to create a speckled surface. This will create the background grain of the "wood".

Use another small dish and mix a medium brown colored tint. Use a very fine paint brush or a feather to paint a heart grain (the part of the grain which resembles a series of stacked chevrons). Use your picture or sample as your guide. Dilute the remaining tint with some more water and brush it on the rest of the surface around the heart grain to create the finer grain of the wood. You may want to try dragging a dry brush across the grain to soften the lines and make the grain lines less distinct. Allow the finish to dry at least four hours.

When the graining is dry, use another dish to mix up a glaze consisting of linseed oil, oil colors and enough turpentine to make a glaze consistency. Apply the glaze to the entire surface. Then, hold a piece of linen cloth taut between both hands and gently dab the glaze to create the effect of crossgraining. Do the entire surface including the heart grain area. Use a fine brush to blend any areas which may appear too distinct. Allow the finish to dry at least two or three days.

> *** IMPORTANT:** Do not leave cloths with linseed oil laying around as they are very flammable and subject to spontaneous combustion. Thoroughly rinse the cloths and then lay them out flat to dry before disposing.

Once the finish is dry, a spray coating of shellac will seal in the false graining without disturbing it. Do not attempt to brush on a finish coat. When the shellac is dry, you can apply a coat of varnish, or a coat of wax, if desired, or leave the finish "as is".

Equal quantities of water and vinegar can be tinted with powdered pigments to make a quick-drying color glaze. This would be used in place of the oil-based glazes in the previous instructions. Water glazes will not form an even film over an oil paint base. The glaze will pull apart and separate into droplets. This separation is technically called *crissing*. Rub the surface with a damp sponge which has been dipped in powdered chalk and brush off any excess. This will allow the graining color to adhere properly.

* Some other techniques which can be used to vary the finished look: After you have applied the graining, flick a feather across the grain to remove some of the wet glaze to simulate lighter areas of the grain pattern. Different sizes and types of feathers will produce different results. A small comb can be dragged across the glaze to simulate straight grain. Vary the pattern by alternating pulling the comb straight down and in a wavy motion.

Bird's eye maple: Bird's eye maple was often used as a decorative accent on frames, small pieces of furniture and on panels on larger pieces of furniture. Bird's eye maple is expensive and, because of all of the small knots, can be difficult to stain and finish. Consequently, not all of the bird's eye maple you see on antique furniture is real bird's eye maple - some of it is false grained wood.

To simulate bird's eye maple, tint the base coat with yellow ochre and use a combination of raw sienna and burnt umber for the glaze. Apply the glaze over the base coat, then drag a dry natural bristle brush downwards through the glaze alternating the pressure on the brush and moving the brush from right to left to produce a ribbon-like pattern. Cover the entire surface with bands of this ribbon pattern, slightly over-lapping them as you go. Use the knuckle of your little finger to dab the glaze to form the dots for the "eyes" of the maple. Allow the finish to dry for about 15 minutes and then use a dry brush to slightly soften the edges. While the glaze is still wet, use a crayon closely matching the burnt sienna color to draw the graining of the wood. Use a color picture or a piece of real bird's eye maple as a guide.

Knots: To duplicate knots, dip a wine cork into the color you are using for the graining and press it vertically into the glaze and twist it on the spot where you want the knot. Use a very fine artist's brush to paint a few small cracks radiating out from the center of the knot. Soften the lines and the edges of the knot with a very small dry paint brush.

Pro Tip: Some Victorian chairs with light finishes and caned seats have deep black streaks on them which can not be removed with either bleach or strippers. These marks were caused by lampblack which was brushed on the chairs and rubbed into the grain as the first step in a false graining process during the Victorian period. Since the chairs were not intended to have a light finish, the only successful way to deal with these marks is to stain the chairs a darker color or re-apply false graining and return the chairs to their original appearance.

Marbling - Real marble was created by disturbances in the earth's crust thousands of years ago. Molten limestone fused with mineral deposits and when the mixture cooled and crystalized an infinite variety of shapes and colors were formed.

Marbling is a type of false graining, but instead of simulating wood grain you are simulating marble or another type of stone. A similar technique can be used to simulate tortoiseshell. Marbling is a type of trompe l'oeil which can be done well enough to fool the eye, but obviously will not fool the hand. It may *look* like marble, but it will not *feel* like marble. If you are trying to restore a dresser or a dry sink with a missing top, it can be an economical alternative to finding another piece of marble. The cost of a marble top can be prohibitive for quite a few budgets and the weight of marble can be dangerous to dry antique joints. A piece of wood cut to fit the top, and then marbled can provide a beautiful top for an otherwise useless piece of furniture.

Marbling can be divided into two techniques: *dispersion*, which uses solvents (usually alcohol, water, or mineral spirits) to mottle the painted surface and carefully drawing the *veining* which adds detailing..

It is important to have a piece of real marble or a large, clear color photograph for use as a reference when drawing the veining and pebbly shapes in the stone. Always practice on a sample piece before attempting to work on the furniture.

There are numerous marbling techniques and you can use both water and oil colors. The surface to be marbled needs to be clean and smooth and free from any grease or wax. You may wish to fill the wood grain with gesso before begining the marbling process to achieve a smoother finish. (*See Duplicating an Aged Paint Finish for instructions.*)

Cream-colored Carrara marble: Apply a coat of egghell colored paint in a flat or low gloss finish as the base coat. Allow the paint to dry for 24 hours and then lightly sand the surface to smooth. Use a tack rag to remove any traces of dust. Apply a second coat of eggshell paint, and allow to dry for two days, then sand again and use a tack rag on the surface again to remove any accumulated dust.

To make the glaze, apply a dab or two of yellow ochre and white oil paint in a small dish and add some linseed oil (about 1 teaspoonful) and a few drops of Japan drier (which will speed up the drying time of the glaze). Mix together until it is the consistency of light cream. Use a brush to apply an even coat of glaze to the painted surface. The application of the glaze coat is technically called "rubbing-in". Take a plastic bag and scrunch it up in your hand to form a loose ball, then press it against the wet glaze to create a broken pattern all over the surface. You are aiming for a random uneven pattern. Use a dry brush to lightly blend the pattern and feather the edges.

To create the veining, mix together zinc white and Payne's gray with a small amount of linseed oil to make them flow easier. Use a sable brush and holding it at a 90° to the surface draw in the veining, twisting the brush from time to time to create natural variations. Or use a feather to form the veins. The tip will produce fine lines. Used sideways it will create wider veins. The barb of the feather can be split and then drawn through the glaze for a ridged effect. Conte pencils and crayons can also be used to create veins in the marble.

Varying the pressure and the direction of the veining tool will give a more natural appearance to the veins. Use your sample as your guide for the veining. Natural veins are angular rather than wavy, and even curving veins are made up of tiny straight lines. The veins should diverge, rejoin and diverge again as they flow across the piece. Do not over-do it and add too many lines. Carefully blend the veins so they appear natural and look like something *in* the marble not *on* the marble. Always work towards yourself for best results. Allow the veining to dry at least two or three days.

Apply a thin coat of spray shellac to seal in the graining. Then apply several coats of spray lacquer if desired. Varnish has a yellowish color and if you apply coats of varnish it will add a yellow tint to your work. The yellow tint will also darken with time as it ages. When the final coat is dry, use a piece of 3/0 steel wool to buff down and flatten the sheen.

> * **IMPORTANT:** Do not leave cloths or brushes with linseed oil on them laying around after use. Linseed oil is flammable and is subject to spontaneous combustion. Rinse cloths with water and lay out flat to dry before disposing. Rinse brushes thoroughly before disposal.

Black and green marble: Apply a base coat with flat black paint. Allow to dry for 24 hours, then lightly sand to smooth the surface. Use a tack rag to remove all traces of dust from the surface. Apply a second coat of paint and allow it to dry for two days, then lightly sand again, and wipe off with a tack rag to remove any accumulated dust.

Apply a very thin green glaze made of Prussian blue and raw sienna. Then dab the glaze with a small piece of cloth to allow some of the base coat to show through.

Create the veins with a mixture of white and a lighter green (which can be created by mixing Prussian blue and a chrome or cadium yellow). Use the spattering technique *(see instructions for spattering on page 329)* to spatter the green glaze. Then use a very fine artist's brush or a feather to add very fine white veins. Allow the surface to dry a minimum of two or three days.

Apply a thin coat of spray shellac to seal in the graining. Then apply several coats of spray lacquer if desired. When the final coat is dry, use a piece of 3/0 steel wool to buff down the sheen.

Pink marble: Apply a base coat of off-white flat paint. Allow to dry for 24 hours, then lightly sand to smooth the surface. Apply a second coat of paint and allow it to dry for two days, then lightly sand again, and wipe off with a tack rag to remove any accumulated dust.

Apply a glaze made from cadmium red, Alizarin crimson, orange and white. Scrunch up a piece of plastic wrap in your hand and use it to dab at the glaze to create a random broken pattern. Mix together another glaze of violet, Thalo blue, raw umber and white and drizzle the glaze over the surface with a wooden craft stick. Use a paint brush or a piece of plastic wrap to dab the glaze blending some areas and leaving other areas undisturbed. Allow the surface to dry a minimum of two or three days.

Apply a thin coat of spray shellac to seal in the graining. Then apply several coats of spray lacquer if desired. When the final coat is dry, use a piece of 3/0 steel wool to buff down the sheen.

Spattered finish - Marble can be *spattered* to help break up the glaze and add interest to the graining. To spatter the surface, you will need a thin glaze and a thick brush (the brush does not have to be wide just thick so it will hold more glaze) and a stick or another brush you can use to tap against the loaded brush. Dip the thick brush into the glaze and then hold it over the surface and tap it hard with the stick or the paint brush handle. Droplets of paint will spatter across the surface. A fine spatter can be achieved by dipping the brush into the glaze and then holding it over the surface while you tickle the brush bristles with your fingers.

Another method is to hold a fine piece of screening over the surface and wipe a paint brush dipped in glaze across the screen. Allow the paint to completely dry. Then apply a thin coat of spray shellac to seal in the spattering.

Stippling - Stippling is another technique which can be used to add variety to your marbling. Stippling creates a freck-led, speckled look. The base coat should be several tones lighter than the glaze or a totally different color to get the most benefit from stippling.

The final texture you achieve will vary depending on the brush you use. You can buy a professional *stippling brush* which has very fine bristles and will produce a very subtle effect. But they are quite expensive and are not necessary as you can get good results using any flat brush.

Apply a base coat, then apply a glaze coat as evenly as possible. When the whole surface has been glazed, dab the glaze with the brush, making sure to keep your movements similar and the pressure firm. You may want to prime the brush with a little glaze before you begin because the clean dry bristles may remove too much glaze. Do not dab too hard or the brush may slip and leave a skid-mark. Work quickly so the glaze does not become too dry to work. If the glaze dries to a tacky state it will become impossible to blend the colors and will result in heavy streaks. If this should happen, wipe off the glaze from that area and start again. As you work, wipe the brush bristles with a cloth to remove excess paint. Any uneven patches can be touched-up later by stippling *on* a little color instead of stippling it *off.*

Stippling can also be created by dabbing the surface with a small piece of towel, a sponge or a crumpled piece of tissue paper.

Some different graining effects can be achieved by slapping a small rag on the wet glazed surface. Or by pressing a piece of clear plastic wrap onto the wet glaze then lifting it off. Repeat across the surface. This will remove the glaze in irregular patterns remarkably similar to genuine marble. Allow to completely dry.

Apply a thin coat of spray shellac to seal in the stippling. Then apply several coats of spray lacquer if desired. Use 3/0 steel wool to dull the sheen if necessary.

Tortoiseshell - It is very important to have a piece of tortoiseshell or a good clear picture of tortoiseshell to use as a guide so you can duplicate the look accurately.

Apply a pale gold base coat. Allow to dry for 24 hours, then lightly sand the surface to smooth. Use a tack rag to remove all traces of dust from the surface. Apply a second coat of paint and allow it to dry for a minimum of two days, then lightly sand again, and wipe off with a tack rag to remove any accumulated dust.

Mix a fairly thick glaze tinted with raw sienna and apply over the base coat in diagonal streaks. Next, mix some raw sienna oil paint and a little mineral spirits (paint thinner) to make a thick glaze and apply some blobs and streaks. Then mix some burnt umber with a little mineral sprits and apply some more blobs and streaks. Splattering can be done with both the burnt umber glaze and the raw sienna glaze. (See instructions for

Spattered finish on page 329.) Use a dry brush to soften and blend the streaks and blobs and make them look more natural.

Allow the surface to dry a minimum of two or three days. Apply a thin coat of spray shellac to seal in the graining. Then apply several coats of spray lacquer if desired. When the final coat is dry, use a piece of 3/0 steel wool to buff down the sheen.

Crinkled, crazed or cracked finishes - As discussed earlier, most finishes expand and contract with variations in the temperature and humidity. Wood will also expand and contract for the same reasons. Problems can occur when the finish and the wood do not expand and contract at the same rate. This results in a variety of finish problems including "alligatoring" which generally occurs with shellac or lacquer and leaves the finish with a bumpy texture resembling an alligator's skin, and cracking and crazing which mottles the finish with a series of broken lines. These textured finishes are often associated with signs of age.

 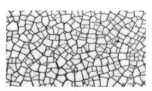

The secret to intentionally creating a cracked or crazed finish is to use two different finishes with incompatible drying times. A slow drying base coat is applied, and while it is stretching and hardening, a fast drying top coat is applied over it. The dry top coat will lose its flexibility and will crack as the base coat continues to shrink and dry.

Clear finishes can be brushed on for the base coat, but the top coat will need to be sprayed on in order to have it dry quickly enough to not disturb the film of the base layer. The finishes may need to be thinned to get the right consistency. It is important to experiment with this technique prior to using it on a project. The top coat has to be applied to the base coat at just the right stage of drying in order to get the best affect. The base coat should be skinned over but not tacky. If the base coat is too wet, the top coat will just blend in and make a thick mess. If the base coat is too dry, the stretching and cracking will not occur. It is also important the two finishes be compatible. Unfortunately this is not an exact technique, and results can vary and be unpredictable.

This technique can also be used on a painted surface. A quick drying enamel or colored varnish can be used as the base coat and a water-based or latex paint can be used for the top coat. If the base coat is too wet, the top paint will disperse. If the base coat is too dry the top coat will not adhere.

Another variation is to use colored paint for the base coat and then apply varnish as the top coat. It will create cracks in the finish without adding color.

A thin glaze can also be applied over the cracked finish to emphasize the cracks. (See *Glazes and "dirty varnish"* below.)

Pictured above is a packaged "Antiquing Kit". The kits contained a base paint, a glaze and often a metallic accent and were quite popular for refinishing furniture and giving it an "antiqued look".

Glazes and "dirty varnish" - A glaze is a thin transparent film usually applied over another finish. The "antique white finish" commonly found on French Provincial furniture and the

"Southwest Look" is achieved by mixing a couple of tablespoons of varnish with a couple of tablespoons of mineral spirits and some white or off-white oil paint mixed in to achieve the desired color. Do not use acrylic oil paint. It will not mix properly with the varnish. The glaze is brushed on the furniture and then wiped off with a rag to remove excess finish, leaving a slight film on the surface and color in the carving and joints of the furniture.

Other colors of oil paint can be mixed with varnish and mineral spirits and used over a clear finished piece of furniture to add coloring into the carving and crevices and add an "aged" look to the piece. I have always referred to this concoction as "dirty varnish" because that is what it looks like when you mix it up. It comes in handy for taking the "new" look out of a repaired sections of wood.

The color can be custom matched depending upon the amount of oil paint used and the color of paint chosen. A small dab of black oil paint can be used to darken the color. White, off-white, buff or flesh-colored oil paint can be used to lighten the color. Brown Madder is a perfect color match for red mahogany or cherry furniture, Burnt Sienna will match brown mahogany, reddish mahogany and some walnuts, Burnt Umber will match walnut and dark oak, Flesh can be used for some maple woods and for many "blonde look" pieces, Yellow Ochre can be used for light oak, but may need to be toned a bit with some Burnt Sienna. Gray oil paint mixed with varnish and mineral spirits can give a piece of furniture a grayish "aged" look.

A water-based glaze can be made by thinning latex paint with water until it creates a thin film or "wash" on the wood surface. You may find the proportions may be as high as 80% water to 20% paint to achieve this consistency. The idea is to have a very thin glaze with a hint of color. White or off-white paint can be used as described above to create a French Provincial look. Brown paint can be used to accent details and carving on walnut or oak furniture.

After the glaze is completely dry, you may want to protect it with a light spray coating of shellac or lacquer.

Pickled finish - A pickled finish is similar to the white-washed look previously described, except paint is used instead of a glaze. The paint is applied with a folded up rag and rubbed into the wood grain - both with the grain and against the grain of the wood. Do not over-saturate the cloth with paint. Remove any excess by wiping the rag on the edges of the paint can and apply only enough paint to fill the grain. Allow the paint to dry, then rub the wood across the grain with fine steel wool until all of the paint has been removed from the surface. The only paint remaining should be in the grain.

Apply several coats of clear finish to seal in the pickled finish. Then buff the final coat of clear finish to remove the gloss and give the piece a matte finish. This special effect will work best, of course, on woods with an open grain pattern.

Duplicating an aged paint finish - Pale painted furniture was popular during the 18th century. French and Swedish furniture of the Louis XV and Louis XVI periods are known for their smooth painted surfaces and the distinctive depth to the creamy whites, soft blueish-grays and other subtle colors. The difference between these painted finishes and painted furniture from other periods was the smooth base coat provided by layers of gesso which were rubbed into the wood to fill the grain and provide a perfectly smooth surface on which to apply the paint.

Craftsmen have been using gesso to create smooth resilient surfaces which could be finished with paint or gold leaf for thousands of years. Thicker layers of gesso can be worked to simulate carved wood, and many "carved" wooden picture frames are not carved or wood.

If you need to repair a traditionally painted piece of

furniture or want to duplicate a period piece, prime the wood with a gesso base before painting. After the gesso base is complete, apply the coats of paint and then a coat of glaze or an application of "antiquing wax" to give the piece a patinaed look.

Gesso needs to be applied in an unheated area such as a garage or a basement to prevent it from drying too quickly. Artificial heat of any kind will cause the gesso to dry on the surface while remaining moist underneath and the gesso will crack and break off. Metal nails and fasteners which come in contact with gesso will cause it to discolor and breakdown.

Traditionally, gesso was made with rabbit skin glue, plaster of Paris and enough water to create the proper consistency. Water-soluble white glue can be used instead of rabbit skin glue. The proportions are not exact and it depends on how much gesso is required for a particular project. Too much water will make the gesso too runny. Too much glue will make the gesso too glossy. The ideal gesso consistency is that of light cream.

Use a natural bristle brush to apply an even coat of gesso to the furniture. Watch out for bubbles which may form on the surface, and rub them out as soon as possible. Even a tiny bubble will ruin the smooth surface you are trying to achieve.

When the first coat of gesso has dried to the touch (which should take between one and two hours) apply the second coat by brushing it on at right angles to the first coat. Do not allow brush marks to build up. Corners, carved detailing and other difficult areas can be done by holding the brush vertically and dabbing the gesso on.

When the surface is just dry, smooth it off by wiping the entire surface with a slightly dampened cloth. Use light pressure and stop occassionally to rinse out the cloth. Make sure you wring any excess moisture from the cloth so it does not become too wet. When the surface has been completely wiped down allow it to dry, then apply another set of coats like the first and second ones. Repeat the steps until you have a total of six to eight coats of gesso.

After the last gesso coat is applied, smooth the surface off again with a slightly dampened cloth as before. Then allow the surface to harden for at least a week before applying the first coat of paint.

Gesso can be used to patch a damaged area on a piece of furniture and a new coat of gesso will usually amalgamate itself with old gesso. Apply layers of gesso on the damaged area following the instructions above. The final coat of gesso should be slightly higher than the surrounding areas. Then, use a slightly dampened cloth to smooth the patched area down and blend it to the surrounding edges. After the patched area is completely dry, coats of paint can be applied and blended to match.

When the gesso has completely dried, mix eggshell colored oil-based paint with a few drops of Universal Colorants to tint the paint the desired shade. Thin the paint with a little mineral spirits so it is more of a "wash" than a paint. Apply a coat of paint and allow it to dry. Apply a second coat of paint and then use a clean cloth to wipe across any carved areas or other places which would normally be thinner from years of use. Allow the paint to dry completely.

If desired, a glaze can be brushed over the dried paint and then wiped off to add detail to the carving and to give it the illusion of age. Or you can apply a coat of "antiquing wax" to give the illusion of age. For directions see pages 338-339.

Vinegar painting - Vinegar painting was used by country craftsmen to imitate false graining which was so popular during the 19th century. Prepare the surface with a base coat of flat paint in the desired shade. Allow the paint to dry at least 24 hours, then lightly rub the surface with 3/0 steel wool and wipe with a tack rag to remove any accumulated dust. Apply another coat of paint if desired and allow it to dry for at least 48 hours. Then use a tack rag to remove sanding dust.

Mix the graining medium by combining 1/2 cup of

white vinegar, 1 teaspoon of sugar and a squeeze of liquid detergent in a glass jar with a tight-fitting lid. Shake the mixture to combine all the ingredients. Pour about 1/2 to 1/4 of the mixture into another jar with a tight-fitting lid and add powdered pigment to color the mixture. Mix together until it becomes a paste consistency. Then add enough vinegar so the mixture just starts to run when a sample is applied to a piece of cardboard and held vertically.

Wipe the furniture surface with white vinegar then use feathers, brushes, fingers, crumpled paper, and a variety of other items to apply the graining motif with the vinegar paint. If you do not like the look, simply wipe off and start again. When the vinegar painting is completely dry apply a coat of shellac or two for protection.

"Aging" a painted surface - A painted surface can also be aged by applying paint remover to edges, carvings and any place else which would normally show signs of wear. Wear gloves to protect your hands and goggles to prevent stripper from getting in your eyes. Use a wooden skewer or toothpicks to get the paint remover into cracks, crevices and grooves. Allow the paint remover to start to wrinkle the paint, then use paper towels and a dabbing motion to remove the paint from the area and lift off the paint and remover. This will stop the action of the paint remover before it goes any further. Rinse off any remaining paint remover with paper towels or cloths dipped in water. When dry, apply a coat of clear finish or a coat of wax if desired.

Two other methods which can be used to prematurely age a painted surface involve manure and lighter fluid. For the first, horse manure or steer manure is mixed with a bit of water to form a paste consistency and is then applied to the furniture and allowed to sit for anywhere from a few days to a year or more. Be careful not to oversaturate the furniture with water as it could dissolve any water-soluble glue used in the furniture construction. When it is time to remove the coating, wash it off using clear water and the dry the furniture thoroughly.

A light coat of paste wax or "antiquing" wax can be applied as a final coat if desired. Manure contains ammonia and its own natural coloring and will add a darkened "aged" look to furniture.

The other method is much more dangerous, to both the furniture and the person performing the technique. Obviously this procedure will need to be done outside if you decide to try it and a fire extinguisher and a garden hose should be close by at all times. Douse the painted surface with lighter fluid and then ignite it. When done properly, the lighter fluid will flash and burn off leaving behind a honey-colored crackled finish that resembles mellowed old paint. Unfortunately this method can be unpredictable, and it is worth repeating that *it is dangerous.* The other methods of "aging" paint are strongly recommended over this method because they are safer and produce better and more predictable results.

Asphaltum - You may occassionally come across an antique finished with a unique transparent black paint called "asphaltum". It was used on furniture from the early 1800s until after the turn of the century. Asphaltum was made by dissolving asphalt (as it came from the earth) in turpentine and then boiling the mixture with shellac and resin to improve its drying qualities. Asphaltum produced a distinctive transparent black finish with a brownish cast which is almost impossible to duplicate.

"Antiquing" wax - Mix equal parts of pumice and a soft paste wax. Beeswax has a light color and a nice fragrance but any furniture wax that does not contain silicones will do. Make sure the wax specifically says it is "for use on furniture" – do not use car wax or floor wax. The pumice and wax will be easier to blend if the wax is warmed first. *Do not heat wax on a stove or microwave oven. Wax is flammable!* Allow wax to sit in the sun or place the container in a pan of hot water for a few minutes until it is softened.

After the mixture is combined, apply a thin coat of wax to a small section of the furniture using a piece of soft cloth. Thin coats of wax will dry harder and faster than thick ones. Allow each coat to completely dry before applying another one. Make sure to work the wax into the carving and crevices. Allow the wax to dry for about ten minutes, then buff out with a lint-free cloth rubbing in all directions. Finish by rubbing with the grain. Work on one small area at a time, and then move to another area.

When you are done waxing the furniture there will be a light dust in the corners and crevices of the furniture and it will have a slightly worn buffed look which makes the piece look instantly old. If desired use a piece of 3/0 steel wool to remove some of the sheen from the wax on the rungs, stretchers, arms or other areas which would normally be subjected to wear. If you want to add more signs of wear, the furniture can also be "distressed". For instructions, see *Distressing* pages 304 to 309.

Refrigerator dust - The dust that accumulates on the coils on the back or underneath a refrigerator can be brushed off and saved in a jar and applied to furniture or mixed into "antiquing" wax. Push the dust into cracks and crevices on the furniture and into carvings. Lightly brush over it with a fine paint brush to eliminate any excess. This dust is usually a combination of dirt, dust, hair and a variety of other materials and creates the illusion of age.

Worn gold finish - To achieve a worn gold finish, stain the wood with a dark wood stain and allow it to dry thoroughly. Then mix up a glaze made of thinned down off-white paint colored with metallic gold artist's oils. Apply the glaze to the base coat, then wipe it off with a soft cloth to simulate wear. Allow the glaze to dry for a day or two until completely dry to the touch. Then apply a second glaze made of pale cream paint (use water to thin latex paint, mineral spirits to thin acrylic paint) to which approximately 1-1/2 oz. of rottenstone has been added. Mix thoroughly to combine the ingredients. Wipe the glaze over the undercoat and gold glaze. Use a soft cloth to wipe off some of the glaze on the edges and carving if desired to simulate wear. Allow to dry completely. Then apply a thin coat of spray shellac to seal. Another coat of spray shellac or a coat of spray lacquer can be used as a top coat if desired. Use 3/0 steel wool to rub down the gloss to achieve an even dull sheen.

Streaked gold effect - A streaked gold effect can be achieved by applying a base coat of off-white paint. Allow to dry for at least one day. Next, apply a glaze made of thinned off-white paint colored with gold metallic artist's oils. Apply the glaze to the base coat, then wipe off with a soft cloth to simulate wear. Allow to dry for a day or two until completely dry to the touch.

Next, apply a second glaze consisting of raw umber or raw sienna thinned with mineral spirits. Wipe over the gold with a soft piece of cloth dipped in the glaze to highlight, leaving dark pigment in the cracks and crevices and gold showing through on the raised areas. Allow to dry completely.

Seal with a coat of spray shellac. Apply another coat of shellac or a coat of spray lacquer if desired. Use 3/0 steel wool to rub down the gloss to achieve an even sheen.

Striping - Striping brushes can be purchased at auto supply stores and crafts stores and special striping tools which have a little wheel that rolls along the surface to keep the stripe consistent are also available. These tools are not really necessary because striping is really rather simple once you get the hang of it. An inexpensive striping brush can be made by pulling about ten bristles from a 3" paint brush and tying them together with a piece of thread. Use your third and little finger to steady your hand on the project and slowly pull the brush towards you to make the stripe. Remember, antique striping was done by hand. It had variations and was not perfect.

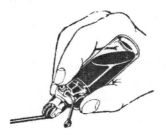

This striping tool has a small wheel which rolls along the furniture surface to ensure the stripe remains consistent.

Striping is traditionally applied in grooves and crevices of moldings and beveled edges but can also be applied in other areas to accent the furniture. It is usually done in gold or silver but can also be done in any color that contrasts with the furniture. Practice on a piece of furniture to familiarize yourself with the brush stroke. With practice, you will find you can change the size and shape of the lines with just a turn of your wrist or a slight change in the amount of pressure you use.

Apply a thin sealer coat of shellac to the area you are going to stripe and allow it to dry completely. The shellac coating will make it easier to wipe off the paint if you should make a mistake. Do not be tempted to use masking tape to help make a straight striping line. Tape may damage the finish when it is removed, and paint can seep underneath the tape creating a jagged edge not a clean stripe.

Fly specks - Real fly specks are created by real flies and are deposits left behind after the fly has defecated on the finish. "Fly specks" on furniture are small flecks of paint commonly found on country furniture and on quite a bit of contemporary furniture. People who bought country furniture came to expect to see those "cute little spots" on furniture which had been stored

341

in barns, attics or porches, and reproductions started having spots added to them to duplicate the originals. Most people have no idea why the spots are there. They just know "that's how it's supposed to look".

Fly specks are easy to duplicate. Mix up a thin glaze (as described in *"Glazes and "dirty varnish"* on pages 332 and 334) then dip a paint brush in the glaze. Hold the paint brush over the surface to be "specked" and tap the handle with a stick or another paint brush to splatter droplets of glaze across the surface.

You can also dip the brush in the glaze and then, while holding the brush over the surface, "tickle" the ends of the brush with your fingers. This will cause a light spray of glaze.

Another method is to hold a small piece of screening over the surface and brush a paint brush which has been dipped into glaze over the screening.

If the fly specks appear too obvious, they can be softened by dipping a brush in turpentine and spattering the turpentine over the surface.

Removing fly specks - Real fly specks (not "created" ones) can usually be removed from furniture by brushing the affected area with a stiff brush. Stubborn spots can be removed individually by using the edge of a craft knife or single edge razor blade and carefully lifting the spot from the surface. Very stubborn spots, or large areas can be removed by covering the area with a piece of cheesecloth moistened with linseed oil. Allow to remain on the surface for about ten minutes. Then wipe off the spots and the excess linseed oil.

Shading - Shading is done in an effort to duplicate the uneven colors furniture achieves during its natural aging process. It is usually done around the edges of panels on doors or side panels. Shading can also be added to carved areas to emphasize the carving and to make carving look less "new". It is usually done with a thin glaze of color and looks best when applied with a sprayer. Spraying will prevent the shading from having hard definite edges and will more closely duplicate the misty effect of natural shading.

Do not be tempted to use brown spray paint or spray stain to apply shading. It will look very fake and unnatural. Commercial furniture manufacturers often use shading on contemporary furniture and then apply fly specking afterwards to give plain inexpensive wood more character.

Crazing Veneer

If you have made a repair to a veneered surface, it will quite often look obvious and new even if you have perfectly matched the grain and color, because the wood around it is crazed with a network of tiny lines all over the surface. You can duplicate this effect by wetting and then drying the new piece of veneer prior to application. Saturate the veneer by weighting it down under water for about 30 minutes. Remove the veneer from the water, place it between two pieces of thin paper and iron it with a very hot iron.

The iron will singe the wood and create tiny cracks. Use a very sharp blade to cut the veneer into the required shape then, when the veneer is dry, glue it in place.

Another method of crazing veneer is to heat some clean sand in a pan on the stove using low heat. Use tweezers to hold the veneer into the hot sand. Leave the veneer in the sand until a pattern of fine lines appears in the wood.

"Aging" a Leather Top

If a leather top is replaced, the leather will look too new next to the aged wood. Leather can be "aged" by rubbing on a coat of wax which has been lightly tinted with brown colorant. A small dab of burnt umber mixed in with the wax can do wonders to "age" the surface. A small dab of brown paste shoe polish can also be added to the wax. Mix thoroughly before applying to the leather. Buff the wax off with a soft cloth.

"Aging" Brass Hardware

There is a wide variety of reproduction brass hardware available. The only problem is most of it looks too "new". There are several ways of removing the "new" look. One of the easiest is to hold the hardware over a burning candle until the brass is all smoked and blackened. Use pliers to hold the hardware so you do not burn your fingers, but becareful not to mar the brass with the teeth of the pliers. Allow the hardware to cool, then use a soft cloth to gently wipe off some of the black soot, leaving enough to give the piece an old tarnished appearance.

Patination fluids (available at most craft stores) can also be used to add an "aged" look to brass hardware. You may need to remove a protective lacquer coating from the brass before it can be "aged". Use an old toothbrush to brush lacquer thinner on the hardware or pour some lacquer thinner into a bowl or a small tin can and soak the hardware for a few minutes. The coating should slip right off. Wipe the hardware with a soft cloth to dry. Then, wipe the hardware with a cloth dampened in mineral spirits to remove any traces of lacquer or other contaminates.

If lacquer thinner does not remove the coating it can be removed with paint stripper. Follow the directions on the can. After the finish is removed wipe the hardware with a cloth dampened with mineral spirits to remove any traces of coating or contaminates.

Wear gloves to protect your hands and use small pieces of cotton to dab the patination fluid onto the hardware. Apply it in a random pattern for the most natural effect. Stop as soon as you have achieved the desired effect. Rinse the hardware with water and then dry with a soft cloth. Lightly buff with a piece of 3/0 steel wool to give the hardware a more worn look. Apply a thin coat of light wax to protect the finish coat if desired.

Brass, copper or bronze can also be "aged" to have a verdigris finish. Craft stores sell patination fluids which will color the hardware the green or bluish color usually acquired only with time.

Do not use these products on hardware made from iron, tin or steel and do not use on plated copper or brass as this may result in an over-all rusted looking reddish brown instead of the intended greenish color. Before attempting to do the hardware do a spot test on a small area, in an inconspicuous area (on the back of the hardware for example) so you can see the affect the product will have on your particular hardware.

Brass hardware can also be patinaed by soaking it in pickle juice or a solution of white vinegar and salt. Lightly abrade the hardware with a piece of 2/0 steel wool then place it in the pickle juice to soak for an hour or more. Repeat the process until you achieve the desired color. Protect the "aging" with a spray coat of lacquer or spray shellac.

"Aging Screws

Old screws come in handy when you are working with antique furniture. New screws stand out and just scream "Re-placement!" for all the world to hear. If you don't happen to have any old screws laying around you can "age" some to use. Make extras so you will have them for other projects.

Old screw holes often become enlarged from age so you

may need to use a larger size screw than what was originally used on the piece. Put the screw into the hole and screw it in completely. Be careful when applying a new screw not to turn the screw in too tight, or use a screw that is just a tad too long. You may end up driving it through the piece of furniture and destroying the top or side panel of your furniture.

Quite often when the screw is fully in place, you may notice it doesn't sit properly in the hole and may not be completely countersunk. Mark the screw so you know where you will need to remove the excess from the screwhead, and then remove the screw. If there is more than one screw, mark them so you know which screw goes where. On old furniture it can make a big difference.

Use a file to size the screw down so it will sit properly in its screwhole. Filingthe screw will also remove the turning marks which are a dead giveaway it is a new screw and will reduce the depth of the slot on the top of the screwhead - another indication of a new screw.

If the slot seems to be reduced to the point where you will not be able to use a screwdriver to reinstall it, you will need to use a hacksaw blade to cut a new slot. Again, this will work to your benefit as original screws had their slots cut with hacksaw blades. Make your new slot slightly off-center and it will rival the originals in appearance.

Allow your modified screws to sit outside for anywhere from a few days to a few weeks and the metal should aquire a weathered look. Lightly rub some mineral oil onto the screws and reapply them to the furniture.

Another method of "aging" screws can be done by gripping the screw with a pair of pliers and then holding the screw into the flame of a cigarette lighter or the flame of a gas stove burner. It will take a minute or two for the protective coating to burn off. Remove the screw from the flame and drop it into a can of water. The combination of heat and water will "age" the screws within a few minutes. If the screw doesn't look old enough, repeat the process.

Most screws on exposed surfaces on furniture were countersunk and then covered with small plugs of wood. Some screwheads were covered with a plug of wax, but this is more common with modern refinishers than it was with original craftsmen. Unfortunately, with the passing of time, wooden plugs will shrink and fall out, and many have gotten lost and are missing.

Wooden plugs are available in several different styles including rounded button top (at the top of the illustration), domed top (on the bottom on the left) and flat top (on the bottom on the right). They are usually available in birch, cherry, mahogany, oak and walnut.

Wooden plugs can be purchased from lumber yards, woodworking supply stores and some craft stores. They are available in three different styles: flat head, domed head and button head (with a slight lip on it) and are usually available in several different species of wood. The flat plugs are used when you would like to camoflauge the screw in the wood and the rounded top plugs are more decorative and made for show.

Stain and finish the plugs to match the furniture. You may need to use some of the "aging" techniques so the new wood of the plugs blends more easily into the old wood surrounding them. Then apply woodworker's glue or hide glue to the plug and put it in the screwhole over the screwhead. You should be able to push the plugs in place with your thumb, but a small tack hammer may be necessary to get them settled in nice and tight. If you use a hammer, wrap the head with a few layers of cloth or attach the lid from a 35mm film container to the hammerhead with some putty to prevent damage to the wood. Make sure to use water soluble glue so you can easily remove the plugs should the need arise.

"Aging" Cement Furniture

Cement benches and other furniture pieces can be "aged" to take away the "new" look by applying a thick coating of plain yogurt to the furniture and allowing it to sit for several hours or overnight if possible. Use a garden hose to rinse off any remaining yogurt. Yogurt will give the furniture a slightly marbled, patinaed look.

The process can be repeated if you would like to increase the effect.

Glossary

American Empire style - A furniture style that became popular in the United States around 1815 and remained popular for almost 50 years. Based on the *Empire style* made popular in France around the beginning of the 19th century.

American Mission style - An adaption of the *Arts and Crafts style*. Simple flat boards were used in the construction, and decorations, stains and finishes were kept to a minimum.

Ammonia fuming - A method of coloring wood by placing it in an airtight container and exposing it to ammonia fumes. This produces a distinctive grayish color.

Anglo-Japanese style - A Victorian substyle that appeared in the United States between the late 1870s and 1900 following an Oriental trend in England and the display of Japanese objects at the Philadelphia Centennial Exhibition in 1876.

Art Deco - A furniture style that originated in France, and was popular in the United States during the 1920s and 1930s. The Art Deco look consisted of simple streamlined traditional forms and geometric shapes.

Art Moderne - A term often used to describe the later adaptions of the *Art Deco* period. Donald Deskey is considered to be the leading Art Moderne furniture designer.

Art Nouveau style - A furniture style which was well received in Europe but did not gain acceptance in the United States until the French brought an exhibit of furniture to the French Pavillion at the World's Fair in Saint Louis. The style was noted for tight "S" curves and elongated natural forms.

Arts and Crafts movement - A late 19th century movement in England based on William Morris's concept of rejecting mechanized designs. The style was popular in the United States from 1900 to 1920. *Mission style* furniture is usually considered part of the Arts and Crafts movement.

Asphaltum - A paint made by dissolving asphalt (as it came from the earth) in turpentine and then boiling it with shellac and resin to give it better drying qualities. The paint was transparent black and was used on furniture from the early 1800s until the turn of the century.

Base wood - Wood used for the *carcass* of a piece of furniture that is intended to have veneer placed on top of it.

Beauhaus - A school of art and design in Germany. Marcel Breuer and Ludwig Mies van Der Rohe left the Beauhaus when Hitler shut it down, and their designs were influential on American Modern furniture. The tubular steel chair with cantilevered seat, which was one of their designs, has become almost synonymous with the modern age.

Bedroom suit (or bedroom suite) - A set of furniture usually consisting of a bed, a dresser, a chest of drawers, possibly one or two nightstands and one or two chairs.

Belter, John Henry - A German immigrant who was credited for bringing the wood-bending techniques and carving style that defines *Rococo Revival* furniture to the United States. He is considered the most important American cabinetmaker during the *Rococo Revival* period.

Bentwood - Wood that is steamed and then bent into shape to be used in furniture construction. The technique was perfected by Michael Thonet.

Bird cage - A mechanism located under a table top and at the top of a pedestal that allows a tripod table to be rotated as well as tipped.

Black shellac - *Shellac* with lampblack added. The resulting finish is transparent black.

Blanket rail - A rail on the footboard of a daybed or regular bed that spins in its socket and appears loosened, but is in fact intended to roll freely so a blanket or extra cover can be wrapped around it and unrolled if the occupant of the bed required additional covers. This eliminated the necessity of storing extra covers folded at the foot of the bed.

Bole - A type of burnishing clay used to smooth out irregularities in *gessoed* surfaces. Also used to add a color base under *gilding*.

Bombé - A kettle-shaped piece of furniture with an over-hanging molded top. The bombé form was only used on three types of American furniture: chest of drawers, slant-front desks and for a brief time slant-front secretary desks.

Boston chairs - Leather upholstered chairs popular during the *William and*

Mary period. These chairs were made all over New England – not just in Boston in spite of the name.

Bow front - An outward curved front on a chest of drawers.

Burl - A protruding growth on a tree that reveals beautiful graining when sliced.

Button-lac - A very low grade dark brown *shellac* commonly used during the 17th and 18th centuries and sold today in small button form.

Cane (or **Caning**) - Strips of *rattan* that are tightly woven into patterns for chair seats.

Carcass - The main body of a piece of furniture.

Carpet cutter - Early rocking chairs earned this nickname because the thin wooden rockers used to wear out carpets and tear up wooden floors.

"Carved up" - A term describing furniture which has been decoratively carved after its original construction.

Carver - A term used for dining chairs with arms.

Carver chairs - Also called "*Great Chairs*". Named after John Carver the first governor of Massachusetts Bay Colony. Special chairs reserved for important guests and senior members of the household.

Chemical stain - Chemicals used alone or in combination with other chemicals to change the color of wood. Chemical stains will penetrate deeper into the wood than any other type of stain and are the most permanent type of stain.. They do not add color to the wood. They change the existing natural color of the wood. Most are applied to the wood in a liquid form. One popular exception is *ammonia fuming.*

Chest-on-drawers - A chest with a top that opened for storage and had a full sized drawer underneath. They were frequently painted in very bright colors.

Chest-on-frame - A paneled lift-top chest used by early Americans during the Colonial period to store their valuables.

Chest-on-stand - The English term for a *highboy*.

Chiffonrobe - A piece of furniture containing a chest of drawers on one side and a narrow space with a door on the other side where a small amount of clothes could be hung.

China Trade Furniture - Furniture made of bamboo, *cane* and exotic woods (like Oriental rosewood) manufactured in China expressly for export to the United States. It was usually made of a combination of Chinese and Western elements. The designs combined elements of the American Sheraton, American Empire and Oriental styles. China Trade Furniture was popular during the early part of the 18th century.

Chippendale, Thomas - An English cabinetmaker who published *The Gentleman and the Cabinet-Maker's Director* in 1754 and influenced furniture designs from the mid to late 18th century, and for many years after that.

Coffer - A joined and panelled low chest with a lid.

Colonial Revival style - A furniture style that lasted in the United States from 1876 until 1925. This style was a result of the wave of patriotism which resulted from the celebration of the United States Centennial.

Commode - A decorated cabinet or chest of drawers.

Compo - A putty-like substance which, when *gilded*, bears a resemblance to carved wood. Commonly used on mirror frames in the 19th century.

Console table - A small side table that originated in France. Console tables were supported by two legs at the front and were attached to the wall in the back. They were designed to be placed against a wall, not to be free standing.

Cottage furniture - Mass-produced furniture from the *Renaissance Revival* period made of inexpensive local woods *false-grained* to look like more expensive figured woods.

Country furniture - A style of plain primitive furniture with subtle if any decoration. It was not necessarily made in the country.

Cromwell chair - An over-sized chair named after Oliver Cromwell the 17th century English leader.

Crown of Thorns - A style of *Tramp Art* which uses interlocking wooden sticks, which have been notched and attached to intersect at right angles to each other, to form joints and self-supporting objects. The name comes from the fact these items resemble the "crown of thorns" which Jesus Christ is said to have worn. Mirror frames and picture frames are the most common items made with this technique.

Cylinder desk - A desk with a quarter-round front which rolls down to conceal the writing surface when not in use. Inside the desk are cubbyholes, used to contain writing accessories. If glass cabinets are added to the top of the cylinder desk it is called a cylinder secretary desk.

Cyma curve - A classic double curve that got its name from the Greek word for "wave form". The cyma curve became the dominant motif form of the *Queen Anne period.*

Distressing - A method of adding artificial wear marks to a piece of furniture to give it the appearance of having been exposed to more wear and use that it really has.

Dovetail joint - A joining of two boards at right angles to each other with interlocking flared tenons.

Eastlake, Charles Lock - A prominent English author who wrote *Hints on Household Taste*, and advocated a less mechanized society and a return to more simple furniture.

Eastlake style - Furniture made in the *Arts and Crafts style* named after *Charles Lock Eastlake.*

Ebonized - Wood filled and stained black to imitate ebony.

Egyptian Revival style - A sub-style of the *Renaissance Revival* period which lasted from 1870-1880 and was triggered by Napoleon III's resumption of the French archaeological excavations in Egypt.

Elbow chairs - A term used for dining chairs with arms.

Empire style - An early 19th century style of furniture inspired by Napoleon.

Escutcheon - A decorative plate made of metal or wood that surrounds a keyhole to protect the wood from damage from a key.

Étagére - A Victorian shelf unit used to display knick-nacks.

False graining - A wood finishing technique where plain inexpensive wood is painted to look like expensive figured wood. Also called faux bois.

Federal Style - An American style of furniture influenced by English Neo-classicism. Popular from 1780 to about 1830.

Fish glue - An animal glue similar to *Scotch glue* that is made from fish heads, skins, swimming bladders and bones.

Frass - A combination of fine wood particles and deposits from wood-boring beetles.

Fuming - A process of exposing wood to *ammonia fumes* to achieve a grayish aged color.

Gentleman's chair - A wide upholstered chair with upholstered arms or partially upholstered arms.

Gesso - A hard, plaster-like substance.

Gilding - The process of applying expensive sheets of *gold leaf* to a surface primed with *gesso*.

Glaze - A thin transparent film usually applied over another finish.

Gold leaf - A decorative wood finish made from 22 to 23-1/2 carat gold that has been beaten into very thin sheets.

Gothic Revival style - The first of the mid-19th century *Victorian Revival styles*.

Greene, Charles Sumner and Henry Mather - West Coast furniture designers who adapted the *Arts and Crafts style* with an Oriental influence.

Gutta-Pencha - A species of tree which grows in Southeast Asia and produces a substance which was used during the Victorian era to create the first plastic items manufactured in the United States. Gutta-pencha was used to create the boxlike cases which were used to display daguerreotypes and was also used for mirror frames and other small decorative accessories.

Hale, Sarah Josepha - Publisher of *Godey's Magazine and Lady's Book* a popular Victorian magazine.

Hall, John - Author of *The Cabinet Maker's Assistant* published in 1840 which illustrated how machinery and veneers could be used to create elegant furniture at a price the middle class could afford.

Harlequin set - An English term for similar pieces of furniture that have been assembled as a set but that did not originally start out as a set.

Heart grain - The wood grain on the centermost section of a piece of wood. Heartgrain usually looks like a series of stacked chevrons on most wood.

Hewitt, John - The inventor of the cast iron hook that replaced bed bolts and mortise-and-tenon joints which were used to hold bed frames together.

Heywood-Wakefield - One of the largest American furniture manufacturers.

High boy dresser - A chest of four drawers on top of a matching aproned dressing table. The American term for a *chest-on-stand*.

High relief carving - Decorations formed by carving away the background wood to produce deeply cut projecting forms.

Hoosier cabinet - The true name for "comprehensive kitchen cabinets". The Hoosier cabinet evolved from the simple kitchen work table and contained a work area, storage bins, flour sifters, condiment and spice jars and a variety of other additions which were supposed to make a housewife's job easier.

Hubbard, Elbert - The brother-in-law of *John D. Larkin*. He was a member of the creative staff for the Larkin Soap Manufacturing Company and was credited with the marketing idea for the Larkin Clubs and the furniture premiums they offered. He became a convert to the *Arts and Crafts Movement* and left Larkin to form *The Roycrafters*, a colony of artisans in East Aurora, New York.

Hybrid chair - A chair made from odd parts of other old chairs.

Ice box - The predecessor of today's refrigerator. A metal-lined wooden box which held a block of ice and was used to keep food cold.

"In the style of" - Furniture made in the fashion of an earlier period but made at a later time than the original period.

Inlay - Small pieces of wood or other materials set into carved recesses in wood to form a design.

Japanning - A furniture finish consisting of lacquer darkened with lampblack. Multiple layers were applied to simulate the depth and appearance of Oriental lacquerwork. Gold and vermilion powder were often used to add decorations. The term "Japanning" was also used around the end of the 1800s and beginning of the 1900s to describe enamel paint used on metal furniture.

"Jenny Lind" beds - A popular name for spool beds. The beds were named after the famous singer Jenny Lind.

Kerf marks - Marks left in wood by a saw blade.

Klismos - An ancient Greek chair form with a broad top rail and curved stiles and legs. The form was revived in the late 18th and early 19th centuries.

Lacquer - The earliest lacquer was made from undiluted natural sap from the Asiatic sumac. Colorants were added to alter the color of the sap. Lacquer as we know it today, became a popular finish after World War I and was made from synthetic resins, driers and a lacquer thinner solvent.

Lady's chair - Part of a matching set of chairs. The female version of the *"gentleman's chair"*. This chair was not as wide as the *gentleman's chair* and did not have arms.

Lannuier, Charles-Honoré - One of the first cabinetmakers to introduce the *Empire style* to Americans.

Larkin, John D. - Founder of the Larkin Soap Manufacturing Company which manufactured furniture that they offered as premiums for soap product purchases.

Liming - A method of adding a whitish-gray aged look to furniture by using lime.

Lloyd Loom - A machine invented in 1917 by Marshall Burns Lloyd which allowed furniture to be machine-made out of strands of twisted paper that resembled wicker.

Low relief carving - Decoration formed by carving away the background to produce slightly projecting forms.

Marbling - A type of *false graining* which simulatates marble, other types of stone, or tortoiseshell.

Marquetry - A decorative form of *inlay* using veneer.

Married - A term used for furniture that has been created from components from two or more pieces of furniture, usually but not always, from the same period.

Méridienne - A style of daybed. A high-backed settee with a single arm on one side.

Milk paint - A distinctive flat finished paint predominately found on *country furniture* and primitive antiques. It is made from rancid milk and colored by the addition of clay, blood, berries and other natural products.

Mission style furniture - An adaption of the *Arts and Crafts* style.

Morris, William - A furniture designer from the *Gothic Revival* period who is best remembered as being the inventor of the *Morris chair*.

Morris chair - A simple, rectangular, oak Mission-style easy chair upholstered with leather . The chair, designed by *William Morris*, had the unique ability to adjust the angle of the back for the comfort of the person sitting in it..

Muntin - A strip, usually made of wood, that divides the panes of glass in a sash.
.

Nutting, Wallace - A cabinetmaker who made *Colonial Revival* furniture based upon exact specifications from original pieces. His reproductions were so authentic that even today they can be hard to differentiate from originals.

Ox bow chest - A piece of furniture with a hollow center and a swell on each side. Oxbow fronts are found almost exclusively on Chippendale chests and

Federal chests.

Ormolu - A decorative trim using bronze or brass mixed with a thin layer of gold. It is usually used in place of *gilding* to decorate furniture.

Papier mâché - Pulped paper which was molded into small pieces of furniture which were coated with lacquer for both decoration and to increase the durability.

Parlor suite (also **parlor suit**) - A set of matching furniture usually consisting of a sofa or love seat, four side chairs, an arm chair and a chair with partial arms. A small suite would include at least a love seat and two side chairs.

Pastiches - Genuine furniture that has been rebuilt and modified into something more useful or desirable.

Patina - A mellowed aged look which is acquired over time.

Pegged furniture - Early furniture constructed by mortises and tenons held together by dowels.

Period piece - A *period piece* of furniture has design elements of a particular period and was manufactured during that era.

Pier table - A side table designed to stand in the space between two windows. Also called a *console*.

Platform rocker - A rocking chair with a rounded wooden bottom that is mounted on an elevated trestle-like base. The chair is connected to spring mechanisms which are attached to the sides of the base. This allows the rocker to rock back and forth on the platform not the floor.

Poor man's mahogany - A thin wash of red paint which was applied to some woods to make them look like mahogany.

Pot metal - An inexpensive copper and lead alloy, usually of poor quality, used to create furniture hardware. Once broken, it is impossible to repair.

Press cupboard - A simple enclosed chest used to store clothing and household linens.

Pressed back chair (or **press back chair**) - Chairs made at the end of the 1800s with "carved" backs created by forcing the design into the wood with a metal die.

Primary wood - The wood used for the main body or *carcass* of the furniture. Primary wood is almost always used for exposed areas of the furniture.

Provenance - The history and documentation of what is known about a piece of furniture.

Queen Anne style - An English furniture style with curving *Rococo* elements and fine carving that was popular in the United States from 1725 to 1750.

Railroad tracks - A popular furniture decorating technique during the *Eastlake* period which consisted of parallel lines carved into the wood.

Rattan - The stems from a species of palm trees used as a material for making furniture.

Relief carving - Decorations formed by carving away the background wood to produce projecting forms.

Récamier - A style of daybed made famous by Julliette Récamier in her 1800 portrait painted by Jacques-Louis David.

Renaissance style - An American revival style that was popular from 1850-1870 and then reappeared in the 1890s. It was noted for its use of architectural elements such as pediments, columns and balusters which were decoratively used but had no structural purpose on the furniture.

Revolving chair (or **revolver**) - A chair made by the Shakers that had a pedestal base with a mechanism which allowed the chair to turn and be raised or lowered. The predecessor of today's office chair.

Robinson, Enoch - A carpenter who invented the technique to mass-produce glass.

Rococo style - An ornate style that originated in France in the 18th century evolving from the Baroque style. A *Rococo revival* occured in the United States from 1840 to 1860.

Rococo Revival style - A furniture style introduced in the United States around 1840 and based on the European *Rococo style.*

Rolltop desk - Technically called a *tambour desk.* A desk with a moveable top made up of slats of wood attached to a canvas backing. Inside the rolltop desk was a variety of drawers and cubbyholes to hold writing accessories and supplies. Some rolltop desk tops were made in a double ripple which looks like an "S" when the lid is closed. Most rolltop lids only round out once.

Roycrafters - The name of the artisan colony formed by *Elbert Hubbard.*

Runners - Strips of wood on which drawers slide.

Rush - A grass-like marsh plant used to weave chair seats.

Ruskin, John - A social reformer and writer, who was one of the founding fathers of the American *Arts and Crafts movement.*

Saddle seat - A chair seat shaped like a saddle and carved to fit the human form. Very common on Windsor chairs.

Scotch glue - A natural glue made from animal hooves and hides.

Scrolled-splat chairs - An early term for ladder back chairs.

Secondary wood - Wood used for the unexposed parts of furniture.

Serpentine chest - A chest bowed at the center and hollowed out at each side.

Settee - A piece of furniture that was larger than a love seat, and usually twice the width of a chair, with an upholstered seat and back.

Settle - A long bench with a high back. Settles were the earliest form of chair that could accomodate two or more people and were a standard fixture in most Colonial houses.

Shagreen - The thick skin of a shark, used by early woodworkers as an abrasive to smooth wood.

Shaker chair tape - A woven fabric tape used originally by the Shakers as a seating material and now often found on Early American style furniture.

Shellac - A clear furniture finish made from a secretion created by the lac bug. The natural resin is dissolved with denatured alcohol prior to use. Shellac was the most commonly used clear furniture finish during the Victorian era. From 1800 to 1850 just about every piece of furniture with a clear finish was coated with Shellac.

Skyscraper furniture - A uniquely modern and sophisticated style of furniture that consists of blocks of various sizes fastened together in imitation of the architectural skylines which represented the mechanical age.

Somnoe - A small *commode*, also called a half commode, which contains one drawer and one cabinet and was created for smaller areas or modest budgets.

Splat - A flat section of wood inserted into the back of a chair. The central upright piece of wood on a chair back.

Spool furniture - An unpretentious style of machine-made furniture created from wood carved into rows of spools, balls or buttons strung together.

Stickley, Gustav - Stickley devised a style of furniture (based on the *Arts and Crafts style*) which combined mass-production with the look of handcraftsmanship.

Stickley, Leopold and J. George - Gustav Stickley's brothers who became his competitors in producing *Arts and Crafts style* furniture.

Stretching paint - The process of using the solvent for the paint to repair damaged areas on the painted surface.

Studio furniture style - A furniture design developed after 1945 which was handmade in small quantities in artist's studios.

Tack rag - A piece of cheesecloth or other lint-free cloth which has been impregnated with varnish to make it sticky. The cloth is used to remove dust particles from a surface before applying a coat of finish.

Tannin - One of the most common chemicals found in wood.

Tête-à-tête - A form of sofa made popular during the *Rococo Revival* period with two seats facing in opposite directions with backs forming an "S" shaped curve.

Tramp Art - A type of folk art generally considered to date from the Civil War through the 1930s. Wood was notch-carved into various geometric shapes and then layered into three dimensional stacks to create patterns. No glue was used to hold original *Tramp Art* pieces together. They were solely held together by the notching of the wood.

Treenails - Wooden pegs used in early furniture construction.

Turkeywork chairs - A nickname for chairs from the Colonial period that were upholstered in fabric with needlework patterns based on those found in Turkish carpets. Turkish carpets were commonly called "turkie carpets".

Vegetable stain - A furniture stain made from natural substances acquired from various plants, roots, nuts, berries, leaves, etc. The results are similar to water-based analine dye stains.

Victorian Revival style - A furniture style popular in the United States from 1840-1880 consisting of three revival styles: *Gothic Revival, Rococo Revival* and *Renaissance Revival.*

Vitrine - A glass-fronted cabinet with a mirrored back inside used to display knicknacks and collectibles.

Wakefield, Charles - The inventor of a process to make furniture from wicker. Founder of the Wakefield Rattan Company which later became *Heywood-Wakefield.*

Whatnot - A multi-purpose shelf unit commonly found in Victorian parlors and sitting rooms. They were originally designed to hold sheet music and books, but Victorians found many other uses for them.

William and Mary style - Named after the king and queen of England, William of Orange and his queen Mary. The William and Mary style in the United States was an interpretation of the Baroque mode popular in Europe earlier in the century.

Wing chair - An upholstered chair with protruding sides that resemble wings designed to keep drafts off of the occupant.

Wooten, William S. - The inventor of the *Wooten desk* which is probably the most compact and organized desk ever invented.

Wooten desk - A compact desk with two half-barrel-shaped sides which opened to expose a writing surface, and compartments for books, letters, book keeping supplies, and a multitude of other writing accessories. An entire office worth of supplies could be neatly stored and organized inside the desk.

Wright, Frank Lloyd - An architect/furniture designer who incorporated *Mission, Arts and Crafts* and *Art Nouveau* elements into his furniture designs.

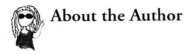 ## About the Author

Donna Morris has been involved in the restoration of furniture and antiques for more than 30 years. She is a member of the Speaker's Bureau of the Southern California Collector's Association, has guest lectured at California Polytechnic University, Pomona, and taught restoration and repairs seminars throughout the Southern California area including special seminars for the Southern California Collector's Association and College for Appraisers.

Donna is a contributing author to the I.D.G. book *Antiquing for Dummies* by Ron Zoglin and Deborah Shouse, and is the author of *More Than 100 Furniture Repairs You Can Do Yourself – A Practical Handbook for Anyone Who Buys, Sells, or Owns Furniture*, and *Furniture Repairs from A to Z – A Quick Reference Guide of Tips and Techniques*. Her next book, *The Big Book of Furniture Repairs* is scheduled for release in the Winter of 2002. Her books evolved from the most frequently asked questions from her clients and students.

She has run a successful restoration business and assisted the Santa Ana School District in restoring the Hiram Clay Kellogg house.

When she is not writing or teaching, Donna spends her free time collecting and repairing antiques and restoring her 1920s Allan Herschell carousel horse.

Index